Professor Hans Kelsen is considered the greatest living international jurist. His many works in international and constitutional law are classics in their fields. Among them are *The Law of the United Nations, Legal Techniques in International Law, Pure Theory of Law* and *Law and Peace in International Relations.* Professor Kelsen is the leader of the ' Vienna School' which represents within the realm of legal theory the quest for pure knowledge in its most uncompromising sense. In the course of his distinguished teaching career, he has taught at the Universities of Vienna, Zürich, Prague, Cambridge, Harvard, the University of California and the Naval War College.

# THE COMMUNIST THEORY OF LAW

AUSTRALIA
The Law Book Co. of Australasia Pty Ltd.
Sydney : Melbourne : Brisbane

GREAT BRITAIN
Stevens & Sons Limited
London

INDIA
N. M. Tripathi Ltd
Bombay

NEW ZEALAND
Legal Publications Ltd.
Wellington

PAKISTAN
Pakistan Law House
Karachi

U.S.A. AND CANADA
Frederick A. Praeger Inc.
New York

No. 12 of Praeger Publications in Russian History and World Communism

# THE COMMUNIST THEORY OF LAW

BY

## HANS KELSEN

*NEW YORK*
FREDERICK A. PRAEGER, Inc.
1955

## BOOKS THAT MATTER

First published in 1955
in the United States of America
by Frederick A. Praeger, Inc.
105 West 40th Street,
New York 18 New York

Published in Great Britain
by Stevens & Sons Limited
of 119 & 120 Chancery Lane
London

Printed in Great Britain
by Bradford & Dickens of
London W.C. 1

Library of Congress
Catalog Card No: 54–8511

# CONTENTS

# PREFACE

It is a paradoxical fact that so-called historic materialism, that is, the economic interpretation of social reality, inaugurated by Karl Marx, has influenced and is still influencing the social science of our time, including the anti-Marxian school, to a much greater extent than its representatives are aware. This fact manifests itself in the widespread tendency to reject any normative interpretation of social phenomena, even if they undoubtedly fall within the realm of morality or law. There exists among social scientists a certain proclivity to reduce human relations, which in ethics and jurisprudence are presented as duties, responsibilities, rights established by moral or legal norms, to factual relations of political or economic power; and to characterise value judgments concerning right and wrong, just and unjust, as propositions about facts observable by individual or social psychology, in opposition to their interpretation as judgments concerning conformity or disconformity with a norm presupposed as valid. It is an anti-normative tendency, based on the unwillingness or incapacity of recognising the specific meaning of a norm or a normative order. It justifies itself by denouncing any normative interpretation as 'unscientific'. This intellectual attitude is of particular importance in the modern science of law, which tries to replace jurisprudence by legal sociology.

The anti-normative approach to social phenomena is an essential element of the Marxian theory in general and of the Marxian theory of law in particular. The question as to whether the law is a system of norms or an aggregate of social relationships plays a decisive role in the legal theory which in the Soviet Union has been developed on the basis of orthodox Marxism. This legal theory is a characteristic part of the political system known under the name of communism.

A critical analysis of the communist theory of law seems to the author of this essay to be of value not only to scientific jurisprudence but—for the above-mentioned reasons—to social science in general.

The Soviet legal theory, to which the second part of this essay is devoted, is dominated almost exclusively by political factors.

In accordance with Marx' theory of the ideological super-structure, it was from the very beginning intended as an ideological weapon in the fight of socialism against capitalism. Soviet legal theory adapts itself submissively to every change in the policy of the Soviet government. The following examination of this theory will show the shameful decline of a social science that is not able to emancipate itself from politics.

At a time when everywhere the power of the state is steadily increasing, the fact must be taken most seriously that the degradation of science to an accomplice of power is effected in the Soviet Union under the leadership of intellectually outstanding scholars. Hence it was possible to restrict the present study of Soviet legal theory to a review of the doctrines advocated by the most prominent writers. Since the main contributions of these writers are translated into German, French and English—and only through these translations can they assume international importance—the author, who has no knowledge of the Russian language, was able to become familiar with them without apprehension of having missed any essential feature of their doctrines.[1]

Finally, the author wishes to make it as clear as possible that he is not dealing with communist law but with the general theory of law advanced by writers applying, or pretending to apply, the principles of communism; and he is dealing with the policy of the communist government of the Soviet Union only in so far as this policy influences the communist theory of law.[2]

HANS KELSEN

*September,* 1954

---

[1] An English translation of the most important contributions of Soviet writers to the theory of law has recently been published in *Soviet Legal Philosophy,* by V. I. Lenin, P. I. Stuchka, M. A. Reisner, E. B. Pashukanis, J. V. Stalin, A. Y. Vyshinsky, P. Yudin, S. A. Golunskii, M. S. Strogovich, I. P. Trainin. Translated by Hugh Babb. With an introduction by John Hazard. The Twentieth Century Legal Philosophy Series, Vol. 5, Cambridge, Mass., Harvard University Press, 1951 (London, Geoffrey Cumberlege).

[2] As to the relationship between the legal theory of Soviet writers and the economic policy of the Soviet government, cf. the study: Rudolf Schlesinger, *Soviet Legal Theory,* Its Social Background and Development, 2nd ed., London, Routledge & Kegan Paul Ltd., 1951.

## CHAPTER I

# THE MARX-ENGELS THEORY OF STATE AND LAW

## Primacy of economics over politics in the Marxian theory of the bourgeois (capitalist) state.

THE Marxian theory of law is inseparably connected with the theory of state.[1] It is based on the assumption that the economic production and the social relationships constituted by it (the *Produktionsverhaeltnisse*) determine the coming into existence as well as the disappearance of state and law. Neither phenomenon is an essential element of human society; they exist only under definite economic conditions, namely when the means of production are at the exclusive disposition of a minority of individuals who use or misuse this privilege for the purpose of exploiting the overwhelming majority. This implies the division of society into two groups of antagonistic economic interests, two 'classes', the class of the exploiting owners of the means of production and the class of the exploited workers.

This is especially the situation of a society where the economic system of capitalism prevails and society is split into the two classes of the bourgeois (capitalists) and the proletariat. The state together with its law is the coercive machinery for the maintenance of exploitation of one class by the other, an instrument of the class of exploiters which, through the state and its law, becomes the politically dominant class. The state is the power established for the purpose of keeping the conflict between the dominant and the dominated class 'within the bounds of "order"'.[2] This 'order' is the law, which—according to this view—although something different from the state, is in essential connection with the state. The state is 'normally the state of the most powerful economically ruling class, which by its means becomes also the politically ruling class, and thus acquires new

---

[1] Cf. my *Sozialismus und Staat*, 2. Aufl., Leipzig, 1923, and my *The Political Theory of Bolshevism*, University of California Press, Berkeley and Los Angeles, 1948.

[2] Friedrich Engels, *Der Ursprung der Familie, des Privateigentums und des Staates*. Internationale Bibliothek, Stuttgart, 1920, p. 177 *et seq.*

means of holding down and exploiting the oppressed class'.[3]
That means that the political power of the bourgeoisie is the
effect of its economic power, that the bourgeoisie becomes the
politically ruling class because it is the economically ruling class.
This primacy of economics over politics is quite consistent with
Marx' economic interpretation of history in general and of
present society in particular. A society split into classes, says
Engels, 'needs the state, that means an organisation of the
exploiting class for maintaining the external conditions of its
production, especially for holding down by force the exploited
class'.[4] The dominance of one class over the other, which is
the essence of the state, is identical with the exploitation of one
class by the other, the dominant class being essentially the
exploiting class.

**Reality and ideology**

The interdependence which according to this economic or
materialistic interpretation of society exists between the economic
conditions on the one hand, and state and law on the other, is of
decisive importance for the theory of state and in particular
for the theory of law. It is usually assumed that Marx describes
this interdependence in the well-known metaphor of a political
and legal 'superstructure' set up above the relationships of
production constituting the economic structure of society.
'Ideologies' form the superstructure, whereas the basis, the substructure, represents social reality. In his work *Zur Kritik der
politischen Oekonomie* (Contribution to the Critique of Political
Economy) he says:

> 'In the social production which men carry on they enter
> into definite relations that are indispensable and independent
> of their will; these relations of production correspond to a
> definite stage of development of their material powers of
> production. The sum total of these relations of production
> constitutes the economic structure of society—the real
> foundation, on which rise legal and political superstructures
> and to which correspond definite forms of social conscious-
> ness'.[5]

[3] Engels, *Der Ursprung der Familie etc.*, p. 180.
[4] Engels, *Herrn Eugen Dührings Umwälzung der Wissenschaft* (*Anti-Dühring*), Stuttgart, 1919, p. 302.
[5] Karl Marx, *Zur Kritik der politischen Oekonomie*, herausgeg. v. Karl Kautsky, Stuttgart, 1919, p. lv.

The 'superstructures' are 'forms of social consciousness', which he later characterises as 'ideological forms in which men become conscious' of social reality. It is usually assumed that Marx understands by 'legal and political superstructures' law and state. Engels, *e.g.*, interprets the Marxian formula in the statement that 'the economic structure of society forms the real basis, by which the total superstructure of legal and political institutions as well as religious, philosophical and other ideas (*Vorstellungsweisen*) of each historical period in the last analysis may be explained'.[6] If this interpretation is correct and, hence, law has the nature of an ideology, the meaning of this term is of the utmost importance for a Marxian theory of law.

In his fragmentary work *Einleitung zu einer Kritik der politischen Oekonomie* (Introduction to the Critique of Political Economy) Marx says that in the study of social science it must be borne in mind that society is given 'as in reality so in our mind'.[7] Social ideology as a form of social consciousness is society as it is given in the human mind, in contradistinction to society as it is given in reality. In *Das Kommunistische Manifest* (Communist Manifesto) Marx and Engels refer to 'the charges against communism made from a religious, a philosophical and, generally, from an ideological standpoint', thus meaning by ideology in the first place religion and philosophy. Then, they maintain that 'man's ideas, views, and conceptions, in one word, man's consciousness changes with every change in the conditions of his material existence, in his social relations and his social life'. Hence 'ideology' means the content of man's consciousness, the ideas man forms in his mind of reality, especially of social reality.

But mostly Marx uses the term 'ideology' not in this wider sense as identical with 'idea', but in a narrower and decidedly deprecatory sense. By ideology he means a false consciousness, an incorrect—in contradistinction to a scientifically correct—idea of social reality. He says, in considering social transformations :

> 'the distinction should always be made between the material transformation . . . which can be described with the precision of natural science, and the legal, political, religious,

---

[6] Friedrich Engels, *Die Entwicklung des Sozialismus von der Utopie zur Wissenschaft*, 6 Aufl., Berlin, 1911, p. 33.
[7] Marx, *Zur Kritik der politischen Oekonomie*, p. xliii.

æsthetic or philosophic—in short ideological forms in which men become conscious ' of these transformations. ' Just as our opinion of an individual is not based on what he fancies himself, so we cannot judge such a period of transformation by its own consciousness '.[8]

The ' ideological ' consciousness is false because it is determined by the social situation of the man whose mind reflects the social reality, especially by the interests of the social group, or class, to which the man belongs. Marx has the rather naïve epistemological view according to which man's consciousness reflects—like a mirror—the real objects. In his main work, *Das Kapital,* Marx says, in opposition to Hegel's view that reality is a reflex of idea :

> ' With me, on the contrary, the idea [*das Ideelle*] is nothing but the material transformed and translated in the mind of man [*das im Menschenkopf umgesetzte und uebersetzte Materielle*] '.[9]

And Engels writes in his pamphlet *Ludwig Feuerbach und der Ausgang der klassischen Philosophie* [10] : ' We conceive of ideas . . . as pictures of real things ' ; and in his *Die Entwicklung des Sozialismus von der Utopie zur Wissenschaft* [11] : ' thoughts are only more or less abstract images of the real things and events '. An ideology is a form of consciousness that reflects social reality in a distorted way, it counterfeits something that, in reality, does not exist, it veils reality or something in it instead of unveiling it, it is a deception and even self-deception and, above all, it is an illusive consciousness. Hence there is always an antagonism or conflict between the reality and the ideological consciousness man has of this reality ; and, since Marx speaks of conflicts or antagonisms as of ' contradictions ', there is always a contradiction between reality and ideology.

The epistemological doctrine which is at the basis of Marx' theory of ideology is formulated in these famous statements :

> ' The mode of production in material life determines the general character of the social, political and spiritual process of life. It is not the consciousness (*Bewusstsein*) of men that

---

8 *Loc. cit.*, p. lv–lvi.
9 Marx, *Das Kapital* (Volksausgabe, herausgeg. von Kautsky, 8. Aufl. 1928), I, p. xlvii.
10 Friedrich Engels, *Ludwig Feuerbach und der Ausgang der klassischen Philosophie*, Marxistische Bibliothek, Bd. 3, p. 51.
11 Engels, *Die Entwicklung des Sozialismuss von der Utopie etc.*, p. 31.

determines their existence (*Sein*) but, on the contrary, their social existence (*gesellschaftliches Sein*) determines their consciousness '.[12]

Although the second sentence is supposed to express the same idea as the first, the two are not quite the same. In the first sentence only the 'mode of production' is the determining factor, in the second, it is the entire 'social existence'. In the first sentence not only the 'spiritual' but also the 'social' and 'political' process of life is the determined factor; in the second, it is only the 'consciousness' which is identical with the spiritual process of life. By the 'social' and 'political' process of life law and state as social institutions may be understood; and this 'social' and 'political' process of life—as distinguished from the 'spiritual' process of life in the first sentence—may very well be conceived of as part of the 'social existence' of men referred to in the second sentence. Hence there is a strange ambiguity as to the meaning of the relationship between reality and ideology, which makes the foundation of Marx' theory of cognition highly problematical. This ambiguity plays a particular part in the theory of state and law when the question arises whether these social phenomena belong to the substructure, *i.e.*, the real basis, or to the ideological superstructure.

If Marx' sociological theory of knowledge is taken in its second version (the social existence of men determining their consciousness) the question arises whether a consciousness other than an ideological, *i.e.*, false, illusive consciousness is possible at all. Since man's consciousness is 'ideological' in this sense because it is determined by man's social existence, the answer must be in the negative. Hence there can be no true, *i.e.*, objective theory of reality in general and of social reality in particular. It is evident that Marx cannot maintain his fundamental position, for the very statement that the social existence determines the consciousness of men must claim to be a true and that means an objective theory of the human consciousness, not determined by the social existence of the one who makes this statement. There can be no doubt that Marx presents his own social theory as a non-ideological, correct description of social reality, as a 'science'.

In an above-quoted statement Marx makes a clear distinction

[12] *Zur Kritik der politischen Oekonomie*, p. lv.

between a description of reality performed 'with the precision of natural science', that is to say a 'scientific' consciousness, and 'ideological forms' in which man becomes conscious of social reality, that is to say, an ideological consciousness. As we shall see later, Marx explains the deficiency of an ideological consciousness by the deficiency of the social reality producing such an ideological consciousness. In the communist society of the future, which represents a perfect social reality, there will be no 'ideological' consciousness; but there will be a consciousness, there will certainly be science; and if science, as a content of consciousness, is to be conceived of as ideology, not in the derogatory sense of the term but as something different from its object, *i.e.,* from reality reflected in the consciousness, the term 'ideology' may be used not only in the sense of a false, illusive, but also in the sense of a scientifically correct, consciousness.

Marx was evidently aware of the fact that his doctrine of ideology endangers his own social theory. It is probably for the purpose of defending his theory against the objection to be a mere 'ideology' in the derogatory sense of the term that in *Das Kommunistische Manifest,* he asserts that at a certain stage of the class struggle 'the bourgeoisie itself supplies the proletariat with weapons for fighting the bourgeoisie', that 'a portion of the bourgeoisie goes over to the proletariat and, in particular, a portion of the bourgeois ideologists, who have raised themselves to the level of comprehending theoretically the historical movement as a whole'. Thus, these 'bourgeois ideologists' cease to produce ideologies and develop a true science of the historical movement. But how is such a metamorphosis possible, how can they escape the fundamental law that their social existence, that is their belonging to the bourgeois class, determines their social consciousness? This is—seen from the point of view of Marx' social theory—a miracle.

### State and law as reality

The typical and most characteristic ideology is religion. 'Religion', says Marx, 'is the general theory of this world'; and of religion he says that it is a 'perverted consciousness of the world',[13] the 'opium of the people', an 'illusion'.[14] It is

---

[13] Karl Marx, 'Zur Kritik der Hegelschen Rechtsphilosophie'. *Karl Marx —Friedrich Engels. Historisch-kritische Gesamtausgabe,* erste Abteilung, Bd. I–1, Frankfurt, 1927, p. 607.
[14] *Loc. cit.,* Bd. I–1, p. 608.

significant that Marx, when he denounces religion as an illusive ideology, defines it as a 'theory'. In a letter to Ruge he speaks of 'religion and science' as of the 'theoretical existence of man'[15] in contradistinction to his practical existence, that is, the 'reality' of his true existence. In this sense only a theory, a function of cognition, a form of consciousness, not the object of theory or cognition, not reality—correctly or incorrectly reflected in man's consciousness, could be characterised as ideological. Marx frequently speaks of ideology as a mere 'expression' (*Ausdruck*) of reality and denounces as an ideological fallacy to take what is a mere 'expression' of the reality for reality,[16] whereby he evidently presupposes that the expression is false, illusive. Hence, only a certain—namely a false—theory of the state or a certain —namely illusive—philosophy of law, not the state or the law, could be conceived of as an ideology. In accordance with his thesis that the social existence of man, that is, his social reality, determines man's social consciousness, Marx says that the state 'produces religion as a perverted consciousness'[17] and opposes 'the state together with the social reality connected with it' to the 'legal consciousness, the most distinguished, most universal, to the rank of science elevated expression of which is the speculative philosophy of law'.[18] Here the state is presented as social reality upon which an illusive legal philosophy as an ideological super-structure is set up.

In his *Zur Kritik der politischen Oekonomie* he identifies the relationships of production, that is, the social reality in opposition to the social ideology, with legal relations. 'At a certain stage of their development the material forces of production in society come in conflict with the existing relations of production—or what is but a legal expression for the same thing—with the property relations within which they had been at work before'.[19] Property relations, that is, legal relations, are relations of production, that is, economic relations. 'Property' or 'legal' relations is only another name for relations of production, economic relations.[20] Marx, it is true, characterises here the law, just as

---

[15] *Loc. cit.*, Bd. I–1, pp. 573–574.
[16] *Loc. cit.*, Bd. V, p. 453.
[17] *Loc. cit.*, Bd. I–1, p. 607.
[18] *Loc. cit.*, Bd. I–1, pp. 613–614.
[19] Marx, *Zur Kritik der politischen Oekonomie*, p. lv.
[20] On the basis of this identification of legal relationships with economic relationships, some Marxian writers define the law as an aggregate of economic relationships in opposition to the bourgeois definition of the law as a system of norms. Cf. *infra*, p. 62.

he characterises ideology, as an 'expression' of the relations of
production, *i.e.*, an expression of the social reality.  But the law
is not—as an ideology by its very nature must be—a false, illusive
expression, an expression which is in contradiction to the object
that it expresses.  The expression of economic reality which is
the law, is in harmony with reality, corresponds to reality.

Marx rejects the view that sovereigns make law for the
economic conditions.  'Legislation, political as well as civil, could
do no more than give expression to the will of the economic
relations'.[21]  That economic relations have a 'will' is a rather
problematical metaphor.  But the meaning of it is : that the law
corresponds to the economic conditions which it 'expresses', that
the law is a correct, and hence not an ideological, expression of
economic reality.  'Law is only the official recognition of fact'.[22]
Marx says of the forms of division of labour :  'Originally born
of the conditions of material production, it was not till much
later that they were established as laws'.[23]  The law prescribing
division of labour is in perfect harmony with division of labour
in economic reality.  That the law is an 'expression' of economic
conditions means that it is the product of economic reality, that
it is its effect.  But—according to Marx—the law is not only the
effect of economic reality; the law has itself effects on this reality.
In *Das Kapital* we read :

> 'By maturing the material conditions and the combina-
> tion on a social scale of the process of production, it [the
> law] matures the contradictions and antagonisms of the
> capitalist form of production, and thereby provides, along
> with the elements for the formation of a new society, the
> force for exploding the old one'.[24]

In his *Einleitung zu einer Kritik der politischen Oekonomie*[25]
Marx writes :

> 'Laws may perpetuate an instrument of production, *e.g.*,
> land, in certain families.  These laws assume an economic
> importance if large landed property is in harmony with
> the system of production prevailing in society, as is the case
> *e.g.*, in England'.

[21] Karl Marx, *Misère de la Philosophie*.  Gesamtausgabe, erste Abteilung,
   VI, p. 160.
[22] *Loc. cit.*, p. 163.
[23] *Loc. cit.*, p. 198.
[24] Marx, *Das Kapital*, I, p. 443.
[25] Marx, *Zur Kritik der politischen Oekonomie*, p. xxxii *et seq.*

In stressing the 'harmony' of the law with the relationships of production, Marx goes as far as to characterise the positive law as 'natural' law. He says of the English Factory Acts, they are 'just as much the necessary product of modern industry as cotton yarns, self-actors, and electric telegraph'.[26] 'They develop gradually out of the circumstances as natural laws of the modern mode of production'.[27] Marx expressly refers to 'the effect of legislation on the maintenance of a system of distribution and its resultant influence on production'. If the law is not 'in harmony' with the conditions of production, it ceases to be effective, as *e.g.*, in France, where in spite of the 'legislative attempts to perpetuate the minute subdivision of land' achieved by the revolution, 'land ownership is concentrating again'. In so far as the law—or the fact Marx has in mind when he refers to 'law'—is an effect of economic reality and has itself effects on this reality, that is to say, if the law is within the chain of cause and effect, it is within reality, and hence belongs to the substructure of the ideological superstructure.

## State and law as ideology

However, on the other hand Marx refers to the real state and the existing law, and not to a theory of the state or a philosophy of law, as to ideologies. In *Das Kommunistische Manifest* the charges against communism made from an ideological standpoint are formulated as follows : 'Undoubtedly—it will be said—religious, moral, philosophical and juridical ideas have been modified in the course of historical development. But religion, morality, philosophy, political science, and law constantly survived this change'. Here morality and law are placed as ideologies on the same plane with philosophy and science. In *Die deutsche Ideologie*,[28] which is an important source for an understanding of Marx' doctrine of ideology, Marx refers to 'morality, religion, metaphysics, and other ideologies'. Morality is an effective normative order regulating human behaviour; and if morality is an ideology on the same level as religion and metaphysics, then law, too, may be conceived of in this way. Marx says of the 'laws' as well as of 'morality' that they are the

---

[26] *Das Kapital,* I, p. 422.
[27] *Loc. cit.,* p. 231.
[28] *Gesamtausgabe,* Bd. V, p. 16 ; cf. also pp. 21, 49.

'*ideelle* expression of the conditions of the existence' of the dominant class (conditioned by the development of production) and by the '*ideelle*' expression he means an ideological expression in opposition to the economic reality thus expressed.

It is characteristic of 'ideologists', says Marx, that 'they take their ideology for the creative force and the purpose of all social relationships, although they are only their expression and symptom'.[29] 'The law', says Marx, 'is only symptom, expression of other relationships, on which the power of the state is based'. The real bases are the relationships of production.[30] It is especially the legal institution of property which is the 'legal expression' of 'certain economic conditions, which are dependent on the development of the forces of production'[31] for 'the relationships of production among the individuals must also express themselves as political and legal relationships'.[32]   In his critique of Stirner, Marx reproaches this philosopher of having taken 'the ideological-speculative expression of reality, separated from its empirical basis, for the very reality'; and as one of these ideological expressions of reality, mistaken as reality by Stirner, Marx points to the law.[33]

According to this view, the law—and not an illusive legal philosophy—is an ideological superstructure set up above the social reality, the relationships of production.   Hence one is quite justified to interpret the 'legal and political superstructures' referred to in *Zur Kritik der politischen Oekonomie* to mean the law and the state—as pointed out, Engels himself and consequently almost all interpreters of Marx do so[34]—although

---

29 *Loc. cit.*, p. 398.
30 *Loc. cit.*, p. 307; cf. also p. 321.
31 *Loc. cit.*, p. 335.
32 *Loc. cit.*, p. 342.
33 *Loc. cit.*, pp. 261, 294.
34 Cf. *e.g.* Hans Barth, *Wahrheit und Ideologie*, Zurich, 1945, who defines Marx's concept of 'ideology'—in conformity with Marx—as a specific, namely false or illusive, form of cognition (*Erkenntnis*) and, nevertheless, speaks—in conformity with Marx—of state and law as of ideologies, although he—again in conformity with Marx—deals with them also as with social realities. Cf. also M. M. Bober, *Karl Marx' Interpretation of History*, 2nd ed., Cambridge, 1948. Bober (p. 115 *et seq.*) assumes that the Marxian 'superstructure' is composed of 'institutions and ideas'. He does not stress the difference between the two elements since he is not particularly concerned with the problem of the 'ideological consciousness'. He misinterprets Marx' theory in this respect. He assumes that according to Marx 'illusionism' is to be explained by the fact that 'the generality of men are mentally sluggish'; that 'with the multitude, observation is a superficial performance, and appearances are

Marx, a few lines later, identifies the law with the relationships of production, and, in other connections, characterises the state as a specific social reality producing ideology, and not as an ideology produced by a specific social reality.

If the law is part of the ideological superstructure as something different from and opposed to its substructure, the social reality constituted by economic relationships, then the law cannot be the effect of these relationships and, especially, cannot itself have effect on them. When Marx—in the above-quoted statements—admits an interaction between law and economics, he deals with law as with a social reality. If the law is a social reality in the same sense as economic production, then the scheme of super- and sub-structure is not applicable to the relationship between the two social phenomena. But it is just of the ideological superstructure that Engels maintains that it 'influences' the substructure. In a letter to J. Bloch [35] he writes:

> 'The economic situation is the basis, but the various elements of the superstructure—political forms of the class struggle and its consequences, constitutions established by the victorious class after a successful battle, etc.—forms of law and then even the reflexes of all these actual struggles in the brains of the combatants : political, legal, philosophical theories, religious ideas and their further development into systems of dogma—also exercise their influence upon the course of the historical struggles'.

That means that the ideological superstructure, especially the law as element of this superstructure, has effects on the substructure. Hence 'ideology' is 'reality' in the same sense as the economic relationships which Marx identifies with reality;

allowed to pass undisturbed into an inactive mental medium'; that 'the ordinary person confuses cause and effect, and mistakes symptoms for causes; . . . fails to perceive that his beliefs are merely the product of class tradition. . . In brief, the "ordinary mind" exemplifies precisely what dialectical materialism repudiates. The "ordinary mind" lives in a world of illusionism' (p. 121). But, according to Marx, it is not the 'ordinary mind', the 'multitude', but the philosophers and scientists of the bourgeois class, and among them the most outstanding thinkers who produce the illusions.

Karl Mannheim, *Ideology and Utopia*, 1952, uses the term 'ideology' only for a certain type of thinking and characterises the relationship between substructure and superstructure as the relationship between differentiated social groupings and 'the corresponding differentiations in concepts, categories, and thought-models' (p. 248).

[35] Marx-Engels, *Correspondence 1846–1895*. A Selection. New York, 1935, p. 475.

and he must identify reality with economic relationships in order
to oppose these relationships as 'reality' to that which he wants
to disparage as 'ideology': above all, to religion. Since the
identification of social reality with economic relationships is the
essence of his economic interpretation of society, this interpretation breaks down as soon as 'ideologies' are recognised as
'realities'. A very characteristic application of this interpretation is Marx' statement:

> 'Society is not based upon law; this is a juridical fiction.
> On the contrary, the law must rest on society. It must be
> the expression of its common interests and needs arising
> from the actual methods of material production against the
> caprice of the single individual'.[36]

The bourgeois doctrine, rejected by Marx, that society is based
on law, means, if not intentionally misinterpreted, that the law
—or more exactly formulated, certain acts by which law is
created or applied—influences social life, without excluding that
social life influences the formation of the law. Hence the rejected
doctrine is not a juridical fiction. It is the description of social
reality within which economic and legal elements are in a relationship of interaction or interdependence, a fact which Marx
and Engels in the above-quoted statements admit.

## The confusion of law and theory of law

If it is the characteristic function of an 'ideology' to mis-
represent reality, to reflect—like a defective mirror—reality in a
distorted way, neither state nor law as real social institutions can be
ideologies. Only a theory as a function of thinking, not the law,
which is a function not of thinking but of willing, can be an
ideology.

If we examine why Marx considers the law as an ideological
expression of economic reality, we see immediately that it is not
the law but a certain theory of the law which he has in mind.
Law and morality are '*ideelle*', and that means ideological
expressions of the relationships of production as the conditions
of existence of the dominant class, because 'the ideologists' of
this class present law and morality 'as norms of life to the
individuals belonging to the dominated class', partly in order to
'palliate' these conditions, 'partly as an instrument of domina-

[36] *Karl Marx vor den Koelner Geschworenen,* Berlin, 1895, p. 15.

tion'.[37]    Law and morality are ideologies because they are *interpreted* by bourgeois ideologists as *norms*.    Hence it is the normative interpretation of the law, a special theory of the law, not the law itself, the object of a theory, that is an ideology. The law created by a legislator and applied by the courts is not the product of ideologists, not the 'ideological-speculative' doctrine of a philosopher.    It is—as the specific meaning of acts of human beings performed in space and in time—a social (not a natural) reality.    The view according to which the law is an ideology is the result of a confusion of the law with a certain theory of the law, a confusion which is quite frequent not only among Marxian but also among bourgeois legal scientists.    This confusion is at the basis of the misleading but frequently made statement:    the law presents or interprets itself as norm and hence as just.    But it is not the law; it is always some jurist who presents or interprets the law in a certain way and thus may produce—by his presentation or interpretation—an ideology.

In a letter to Conrad Schmidt,[38] Engels writes:

'The reflection of economic relations as legal principles is necessarily also a topsy turvy one: it happens without the person who is acting being conscious of it; the jurist imagines he is operating from *a priori* principles, whereas they are really only economic reflexes; so everything is upside down.    And it seems to me obvious that this inversion, which, so long as it remains unrecognised, forms what we call ideological conception, reacts in its turn upon the economic basis and may, within certain limits, modify it'.

The law is an ideology because the lawmaker 'imagines' that it is the expression of an *a priori* principle.    This imagination is an illusive theory which the lawmaker has of the law he is making.    For the law is not, as the lawmaker imagines, the expression of an *a priori* principle, such as justice, but the reflection of economic relationships.    Hence Engels characterises the lawmaker's imagination as an 'inversion'.    If Engels, in other connections, designates the law as an ideology he identifies the law with a distorting theory of the law.    But there are makers of bourgeois law and bourgeois jurists who do not believe, and

[37] *Gesamtausgabe*, V, p. 16.
[38] Marx–Engels, *Correspondence*, p. 482.

do not make others believe, that the law is the expression of *a priori* principles, since they do not believe in the existence of *a priori* principles of the law.

## The law as norm

Marx denounces the presentation of the bourgeois law as norm—or the bourgeois 'law'—as an ideology because he, like some bourgeois writers, understands by norm a moral value and consequently identifies the statement : the law is a norm, with the statement : the law is just. When Marx denounces the bourgeois law as an 'ideology', he means that the theory according to which the law is a norm and hence just, is an illusive theory distorting social reality. But it is quite possible to describe the bourgeois law by the statement that it is—according to its own immanent meaning—a norm or a normative order without being guilty of any ideological distortion of social reality : if the term 'norm' is used without any moral connotation, if by this term, or the corresponding term of 'ought' (*sollen*), not a moral but a specific logical meaning is expressed, namely the specific meaning of the connection between condition and consequence in the rules of law by which the science of law describes its object, the law is an object of cognition or the legal reality. This is just what a 'bourgeois theory of law' in its anti-ideological tendency has achieved. It is the so-called pure theory of law, advocated by the author of this study and his followers.[39]

As a norm, that is to say, as a specific meaning of human actions, the law exists as an idea in the human mind or—to use the Marxian terminology—in the consciousness of man. If for this reason the law is to be characterised as an 'ideology', it is an ideology in a sense quite different from that in which this term is used by Marx. For the law as an idea does in no way 'reflect' a corresponding reality as a mirror reflects the picture of a real thing existing outside the mirror and independent of it. The legal norms regulate human behaviour by prescribing or permitting such behaviour (including that behaviour by which the law is created and applied). If the human behaviour prescribed or permitted by the law or, what amounts to the same,

---

[39] Cf. my *General Theory of Law and State,* Harvard University Press (1945), pp. 35 *et seq.,* 45 *et seq.* ; cf. also my 'Causality and Imputation', *Ethics,* Vol. 61 (1950), p. 6 *et seq.*

if the human behaviour which forms the content of the legal norms, takes place in space and time, this real behaviour is evidently not reflected in or by the legal norms prescribing or permitting it, but, on the contrary, the legal norms are, so to speak, reflected in or by this behaviour.

If the relationship between a legal norm prescribing or permitting a certain human behaviour, and the real human behaviour corresponding to this norm is compared with the relationship between a real thing and its picture reflected in or by a mirror, the legal norm as an idea in the mind of man, or man's consciousness, does not play the part of the mirror which reflects the picture of a thing after this thing has been placed before the mirror. For, first, the legal norm must be established and only then may there be a real behaviour corresponding to this norm, that is, a real behaviour similar to that prescribed or permitted by the legal norm. Hence it is the real behaviour which, analogous to the mirror, reflects the legal norm or the behaviour which, prescribed or permitted by the legal norm, is the content of this norm. Since this 'reflection' must be in complete conformity with the content of the legal norm, there is no room for a distorted, illusive reflection, no room for an 'ideology' in the specific Marxian sense of this term.

## Legal and natural reality

In so far as the law as a norm or normative order is the specific meaning of acts of human behaviour which take place in time and space, and a legal order is considered to be valid only if the human behaviour regulated by it corresponds by and large to this normative order, we may speak of a legal reality. By this term we mean human behaviour as interpreted according to a normative legal order, in contradistinction to natural reality, that is to say, facts (including human behaviour) interpreted— not according to norms—but according to laws of causality. However, from a religious-metaphysical point of view there is no difference between a legal and a natural reality, because, according to this view, nature comes into existence in conformity with a norm issued by a transcendent authority. Thus we read in *Genesis*: 'And God said, Let there be light, and there was light'. This religious belief is the basis of Hegel's view that the real world is the reflection of the idea, that is the idea of the world spirit, of God. In so far as Marx rejects the metaphysical normative interpretation of natural reality by maintaining that the ideas man has in his mind of natural reality are only the reflection of this reality, and not the other way round, he is in principle right. But he is certainly wrong if he applies the same formula to the law, as to norms prescribing or permitting human behaviour in the relationship to the real behaviour corresponding to these norms. With respect to natural reality Hegel's dialectics stands indeed—as Marx says—'on its head', and Marx may boast of having 'turned it right side up again'.[40] But with respect to the law he has done just the contrary. For the law as an idea in man's mind is not—like the idea men have of natural reality—a reflection, a mirrored reproduction of this reality. It is just the other way. We consider the real behaviour corresponding to the law as its realisation, that is to say, we recognise in the legal reality, like in a mirror, a kind of reproduction, and in this sense the reflection, of an idea, *i.e.*, of the law as norm.

### The double bottom of reality : the ideological and the real reality ; a self-contradictory reality

The Marxian doctrine of ideology is ambiguous not only because the same object—as the law or the state—is declared one time as belonging to the ideological superstructure, the other time as element of the substructure, the real basis ; but also because the fundamental antagonism between true reality and illusive ideology is sometimes presented as immanent in reality itself. In a letter to his father [41] (1837), Marx—evidently under the influence of Hegel's philosophy—writes :

'. . . starting from the idealistic philosophy, which I, by the way, compared and nourished with that of Kant and Fichte [according to which reality and idea, as the "is" and the "ought", are to be distinguished and not to be mixed up], I arrived at the conviction that the idea must be searched in reality itself. Whereas formerly the gods dwelt above the earth, they have now become its centre'.

If the idea is immanent in and thus part of reality, reality is composed of two very heterogeneous elements ; and if the idea assumes the character of an 'ideology', as something con-

[40] Marx, *Das Kapital*, I, p. xlvii.      [41] *Gesamtausgabe*, I–2, p. 218.

tradictory to reality, then this speculation arrives at the absurd concept of a self-contradictory reality. This concept is indeed one of the most important instruments of Marx materialistic interpretation of society, which from a critique of the ideological consciousness proceeds to a critique of an ideological reality as its main object.

In *Das Kapital,* Marx formulates the relationship in question as the antagonism between the visible form in which things appear (*Erscheinungsform*), their illusive appearance or surface, and the true internal essence, hidden or disguised by the external appearance : 'The existing conformation of economic conditions, as seen in reality on the surface of things, and consequently in the conceptions which the leading human agents of these conditions form in trying to understand them, are not only different from the internal and disguised essence of these conditions, and from the conceptions corresponding to this essence, but actually opposed to them, or their reverse'.[42]   In another connection, Marx distinguishes a 'visible and external', 'merely . . . apparent' from the 'internal actual', the 'real' movement; 'it is a work of science to resolve the merely apparent (*bloss erscheinende*) movement into the internal real (*innere wirkliche*) movement'.[43]   Another formulation of the same distinction is that of 'phenomenal form' and 'hidden substratum'.   In discussing the problem of value and price of labour, Marx writes [44] :

'In respect to the phenomenal form (*Erscheinungsform*), "value and price of labour", or "wages", as contrasted with the essential relation manifested therein, *viz.*, the value and price of labour-power; the same difference holds that holds in respect to all phenomena (*Erscheinungsformen*) and their hidden substratum (*verborgenen Hintergrund*).   The former appear directly and spontaneously as current modes of thought; the latter must first be discovered by science'.

Reality has, so to speak, two layers : an external, visible, but

---

[42] Marx, *Das Kapital,* III–1, p. 170.   Bober, *loc. cit.,* p. 118, quotes this passage ; but in his quotation the words 'and consequently in the conceptions which the leading human agents of these conditions form in trying to understand them', are dropped and replaced by dots.   The passage dropped shows clearly that 'illusionism' is not a deficiency of the 'ordinary mind', as Bober interprets Marx' theory of ideology, but is produced by the 'leading human agents (*die Traeger und Agenten*)'.
[43] *Loc. cit.,* III–1, p. 265.
[44] *Loc. cit.,* I, p. 478.

2

illusive and hence ideological reality; and an internal, invisible (because hidden by the external layer), but true, 'real' reality. The ideological consciousness reflects only the external, illusive, ideological reality, it takes appearance for truth; whereas the task of science is to discover the true, the 'real' reality and thus to reveal the ideological character of its form of appearance. That a real reality is a meaningless pleonasm, and an ideological reality an absurd contradiction, is no objection to a theory which —under the guidance of Hegel's dialectic logic—transfers logical contradictions from thinking into being.[45]  With Hegel, reality was but a reflection of the idea, and hence a reality contradicting itself was to a certain extent the consequence of this view.  But Marx rejects this view.  With him, ideas are only pictures of real things, consciousness being a mirror reflecting the pictures of things.  Logical contradictions are defects of the consciousness, and defects of the mirror cannot be interpreted as defects of the things.  It is quite obvious that the absurd construction of a reality contradicting itself is the result of projecting in reality an illusive ideology contradicting reality.  What Marx calls the 'phenomenal form' of reality in contradistinction to the 'hidden substratum' of reality, is reality as seen in the perverted conception of bourgeois ideology, that is to say, the ideological reflection of reality in bourgeois consciousness; and the 'disguised essence', the 'hidden substratum' of reality, the 'internal' and 'real' reality, is but the reality as seen in the conception of another, the socialist ideology, a picture of reality corresponding to his ideal of justice.  The contradiction he has in mind is not the self-contradiction of reality, it is the contradiction of two opposite ideologies.

In the above-quoted letter to Ruge, Marx writes : 'Reason has always existed, but not always in reasonable form'.[46]  In this paradoxical statement Marx evidently tries to maintain Hegel's thesis that the Reasonable is real and the Real reasonable. He, like Hegel, identifies reason with justice.  But, on the other hand, his whole philosophy aims at demonstrating that the existing social reality is unreasonable; and that means unjust. In order to reconcile Hegel's identification of reality and reason with his critique of social reality, Marx distinguishes between a reasonable content and an unreasonable form of reality.  It is

---

[45] Cf. *infra*, p. 49.          [46] *Gesamtausgabe*, I–I, p. 574.

the same distinction as the one referred to above : between the external ideological form and the internal true essence of reality. In the letter to Ruge, Marx asserts that it is possible 'to develop out of the specific forms of the existing reality the true reality as its ought (*Sollen*) and its final end'. It is quite interesting to note that the 'true reality', the inner essence of reality in contradistinction to its external illusive form, its mere appearance, is here openly declared to be a *norm,* an ought. It is Hegel's idea, the absolute value, immanent in reality. But this idea is with Marx his ideal of socialism. This becomes quite evident when he applies the just-quoted distinction to the state :

> 'As to real life, it is just the political state which, even where it does not yet fulfil consciously the requirements of socialism, contains in all its modern forms the postulate of reason [meaning justice]. And it does not stop at it. It pretends (*unterstellt*) everywhere to realise reason. Thus there is everywhere a contradiction between its ideal destination and its real conditions. Out of this conflict of the political state with itself everywhere the social truth can be developed'.[47]

That means : the existing reality of the state is unjust, but the state pretends to be just, *i.e.,* the realisation of justice, which is its *Sollen,* the norm of its existence and hence its true reality, covered by its existing reality. Hence the total reality of the state contradicts itself. It is the contradiction between what it really is and what it ought to be. But this contradiction is hidden by the fact that the state pretends to be what it ought to be. The contradiction is hidden by the ideological character of its 'existing reality'. The state in its existing reality is an ideology, and this ideological reality contradicts its true, its real reality, which is the norm of its existence. It stands to reason that it is not the state but an apologetic theory of the state which pretends that the state is the realisation of reason, and that this theory of the state, not the real state, is an ideology; and that what Marx here calls the 'true reality', in opposition to the 'existing reality' of the state, is his ideal, namely socialism. Consequently there is no self-contradiction within the reality represented by the state, but a contradiction between two ideologies, the capitalist and the socialist ideology.

[47] *Loc. cit.,* I–1, p. 574.

Whereas according to one version of the doctrine of ideology, the decisive contradiction exists in the relation between the ideological superstructure and the social reality as its basis, according to the second version of the doctrine, the contradiction exists within the social reality itself and consequently has the character of a self-contradiction. Whereas according to the first version, the law is an ideology because it is presented by an ideological theory as norm, according to the second version the ' true reality ' is a norm (*Sollen*) or the true picture of reality corresponds to a norm, *i.e.*, to the Marxian ideal of justice, and the character of ideology is attributed to the ' existing ' reality, hiding the ' true ' reality.

## Marx' interpretation of society as a natural-law doctrine

When Marx applies the distinction between the existing, merely external reality and the true, hidden reality as the *Sollen*, the ideal destination of reality, to the state, he adopts exactly the same scheme of interpretation as the natural-law doctrine. This doctrine presupposes that justice—or, what amounts to the same, reason—is immanent in reality presented as ' nature ', nature of things or nature of man, just as Marx assumes that his ideal is hidden in the existing reality. And just as the natural-law doctrine asserts—as a consequence of its presupposition—that it is possible to deduce from nature the just, *i.e.*, the natural law and attributes to science, the science of law, the task of discovering this natural law somehow hidden in nature, so Marx affirms that out of social reality the justice of socialism as ' the social truth can be developed '. Just as the natural-law doctrine can deduce from nature only what it has previously projected into it—its pretended deduction from nature is in truth an unavowed presupposition of the interpreter of nature, and the desired justice is hidden not in nature but in the jurist's consciousness—the social truth which Marx pretends to develop out of social reality is his own socialist ideology projected into it. His reality, like the top-hat of a magician, has a double bottom, out of which anything you want can be produced by magic.

What Marx says of the state, exactly the same could be said of the law : that even where it does not fulfil the requirements of socialism it contains in its modern form the postulate of reason, *i.e.*, justice, and that it pretends to realise reason, that is to say, to be just. Hence, out of this conflict between the positive, that is, the existing law as the external form of the total legal reality, and the right, *i.e.*, ideal law as its internal essence and ideal destination, the social truth, the natural law—justice, socialism— can be developed. The task of 'scientific' socialism, says Engels, is not only 'to examine the historic economic development from which the classes of the bourgeoisie and the proletariat and their conflict have arisen with necessity' but also 'to discover in the economic situation created by this development the means for the solution of the conflict'.[48] The means for the solution of the conflict are the revolutionary establishment of a communist, classless society. The means for the solution of the conflict, says Engels, 'are not by chance to be invented in the head [*i.e.*, produced by man's imagination] but by means of the head to be discovered in the existing natural facts of production'.[49] The means for the solution of the class conflict : the just social order of communist society, is immanent in the social reality of production and, hence, can be discovered by an examination of this reality. This is genuine natural-law doctrine.

Since according to the natural-law doctrine reason or justice is immanent in nature as a creation of God, and especially in the nature of man (as the image of God), man is by his very nature good, that is, just ; and, since justice means freedom, man is by his very nature free. In this respect, Locke is the most consistent representative of the natural-law doctrine. If man's actions are actually unjust and man is in reality not free, this cannot be attributed to man's nature. The evil, the existence of which cannot be denied, has its seat outside of man, like its symbol, the serpent, in the garden of Eden. Marx' position is exactly the same. He maintains that 'the defects of human existence' in capitalist society, and that means the injustice man suffers and, above all, the fact that he is not free but a slave in the process of production, have their origin 'not in the nature of man' (*im Wesen des Menschen*), but 'in circumstances outside of his life'.[50] These circumstances can be only the relationships of production of which Marx speaks as of relations

---

[48] Engels, *Die Entwicklung des Sozialismus von der Utopie zur Wissenschaft,* p. 33.
[49] *Loc. cit.,* p. 35.
[50] *Gesamtausgabe,* III, p. 15.

that are 'indispensable and independent of man's will',[51] 'a blind force' which dominates man instead of being dominated by him.[52] And just as the natural-law doctrine, in order to reconcile man's freedom, deduced from his nature, with his actual situation which is more or less contrary to natural freedom, distinguishes two natures : a nature before the fall of man and a nature after the fall of man, a pre- and a post-lapsarian nature,[53] Marx distinguishes between the nature of man before and the nature of man after the division of society into classes. Like the reality of society, the reality of man has, so to speak, two layers. An external, the existing reality, and an internal, the true reality, the essence of man, his idea.

During the epoch of capitalism, when man is a slave of the economic relationships, there is a conflict between the external reality of man and his essence, his internal, true reality, his freedom, a conflict between what man is and what he ought to be, a self-alienation of man. But in the primitive, classless society of early man there was complete harmony between the two, man really was what he ought to be : free. And so will man again be free when the capitalist society will be replaced by a society of perfect communism, which will be the realm of freedom, in contradistinction to capitalist society, the realm of necessity. Then man will 'return to himself', the existing reality of man will coincide with his true existence, man will again be what he ought to be. Communism 'is the dissolution of the conflict between existence and essence (*Wesen*)', between 'necessity and freedom'.[54] Only 'within a communist society' is the 'original and free development of the individual not a mere phrase',[55] that means, not an ideological pretence. Freedom, the justice of socialism, which is the essence, the internal substratum of society, hidden by the existing reality of capitalist society, will again become also the external reality.[56] That means that the state of nature, which according to the natural-law doctrine existed prior to the coming into existence of the political

---

[51] Marx, *Zur Kritik der politischen Oekonomie*, p. lv.
[52] Marx, *Das Kapital*, III–2, p. 355 ; *Gesamtausgabe*, V, pp. 537, 22.
[53] Cf. my article 'The Natural-Law Doctrine before the Tribunal of Science ', *The Western Political Quarterly*, Vol. 2 (1949), p. 481 *et seq.*
[54] *Gesamtausgabe*, III, p. 124.
[55] *Loc. cit.*, V, p. 270.
[56] Marx' interpretation of history as the loss and reconquest (restoration) of man, is very well presented by Barth, *loc. cit.*, p. 112 *et seq.* The above-quoted passages of the writings of Marx are quoted by Barth.

state, a status of perfect freedom and justice, where no private but only collective property existed, will be re-established. Marx' social philosophy is in its essential points a natural-law doctrine.

### Self-contradictory reality and ideological consciousness

Marx tries to establish a certain relation between the two contradictions, the contradiction between reality and ideological consciousness or superstructure on the one hand, and the contradiction within reality on the other, by the doctrine that only a social reality which is contradictory in itself produces an ideological consciousness and hence a contradiction between itself and its superstructure. He says of religion, as the most characteristic ideological superstructure set up above social reality as its basis :

> ' This state, this society produce religion, a perverted consciousness of the world, because this world itself is perverted (*verkehrt*)'.[57]

And :

> ' The fact that the worldly basis stands out against itself and an independent realm establishes itself in the skies, can be explained only by the fact that the worldly basis itself is split and contradictory in itself'.[58]

But the self-contradiction of reality, which is the essential condition of the coming into existence of an ideological, that is, illusive consciousness, or an ideological superstructure, is not always presented as the contradiction between the existing reality and its immanent idea, but as the contradiction between the ' forces of production' and the ' relationships of production'. In *Zur Kritik der politischen Oekonomie*, Marx says :

> ' At a certain stage of their development the material forces of production in society come in conflict [the German term is *Widerspruch,* meaning contradiction] with the existing relations of production or—what is but a legal expression for the same thing—with the property relations within which they had been at work before. From forms of development of the forces of production these relations turn into their fetters. Then comes the period of social revolution'.[59]

---

[57] *Gesamtausgabe,* I–1, p. 607.     [58] *Loc. cit.,* I–1, p. 534.
[59] Marx, *Zur Kritik der politischen Oekonomie,* p. lv.

Later, he refers to the 'ideological forms in which men become conscious of this conflict', that is, the ideological consciousness. We cannot judge the social reality 'by its own consciousness' which is a false, illusive consciousness.

> 'On the contrary, this consciousness must rather be explained from the contradictions of material life, from the existing conflict between the social forces of production and the relations of production. . . . The bourgeois relations of production are the last antagonistic form of the social process of production'.

But 'at the same time the productive forces developing in the womb of bourgeois society create the material conditions for the solution of that antagonism'. The solution is communism, the communist relations of production, which are in complete harmony with the forces of production. Since communist reality will not be self-contradictory, this social reality will not have an ideological—that is to say, a false, illusive—consciousness, will have no ideological superstructure.

### The non-ideological reality of the socialist state

However, in the description of the communist society of the future it is not the ideological superstructure, the consciousness of this society, the reflection of this society in the mind of its members, its religion or lack of religion, its philosophy or science, that plays the decisive part, but the structure of the society itself, the social reality. And the most important feature of this reality is that there will be no state in communist society. The famous 'withering away' of the state is not presented as a gradual change of consciousness, its transformation from a false into a true consciousness, but as a fundamental change of the social reality. In his critique of the Gotha Programme of the German Social-Democratic Party,[60] Marx formulates the question concerning the future of the state as follows : 'What are the changes which the state will undergo in the communist society? What are the social functions analogous to the functions of the existing state, which will be left there?' He does not refer to changes in the consciousness but to changes in social reality, although these changes may be—according to his opinion—accompanied by

---

[60] 'Zur Kritik des sozialdemokratischen Parteiprogramms'. Aus dem Nachlass von Karl Marx. *Neue Zeit*, IX-1, 1890–1891, p. 561 *et seq.*

changes of the social consciousness. And when Engels answers this question—to which Marx himself has never given a clear answer—he, too, speaks only of social reality and not of its ideological superstructure, only of the real state, and not of an illusive theory of the state. 'The state', he says, 'is the product of society at a particular stage of evolution'; and this stage of evolution is characterised by the fact that society 'has involved itself in insoluble self-contradictions and is cleft into irreconcilable antagonisms'. These antagonisms are those of 'classes with conflicting economic interests'. The state is the power— a real power—established for the purpose to keep this conflict between the dominant class, the bourgeoisie, and the dominated class, the proletariat, within the bound of order.[61] As soon as the proletariat has seized state power and by nationalisation of the means of production has abolished the antagonism of classes, that is to say, as soon as the split of society into classes, and hence the contradiction within society constituted by this class conflict is abolished, the state as a real institution of society withers away.[62] The contradiction within society, which is the condition of the existence of the state, is here the contradiction between two classes, not the contradiction between the forces of production and the relationships of production. The two contradictions are not identical, although the one may somehow be connected with the other. And the state as part of social reality is not necessarily an ideological layer of reality, a reality pretending to be something that it is not. For the state must exist during the transition period of the dictatorship of the proletariat, and the proletarian state makes no pretence whatsoever. The Soviet state presents itself—or, to avoid this misleading formula: the Soviet writers present the Soviet state— just as that which it in truth and reality is, as the dictatorship of one group over the other. There is no contradiction between the 'visible, merely apparent' and the 'inner, real movement' of this reality. The proletarian state cannot be an ideology and does not produce an illusive consciousness, a false philosophy of itself. It is no ideology in either of the two meanings of this ambiguous term.

---

[61] Engels, *Der Ursprung der Familie etc.*, p. 178.
[62] Engels, *Herrn Eugen Dührings Umwälzung der Wissenschaft (Anti-Dühring)*, p. 302.

**Primacy of politics over economics in the Marxian theory of the proletarian (socialist) state.**

This is not the only inconsistency which the concept of a proletarian state implies. According to its original definition as an instrument for the maintenance of exploitation of one class by another, the state can exist only in a society divided into two classes, and the division into two classes is essentially connected with the fact of exploitation, exploitation being the inevitable consequence of the fact that the means of production are in the exclusive possession of a minority. However, in open contradiction to the definition of the state as an instrument for the maintenance of exploitation, the dictatorship of the proletariat (the establishment of which is the goal of the proletarian revolution, the purpose of which is to expropriate the minority of capitalists, to transfer the ownership in the means of production to the entire society and thus to abolish exploitation) is recognised by Marx and Engels as a state. In *Das Kommunistische Manifest* we read :

> 'The immediate purpose of the communists is . . . the overthrow of the dominance of the bourgeoisie, the conquest of the political power by the proletariat. . . . The prole-tariat will use its political dominance to tear away from the bourgeoisie step by step all capital, to concentrate all means of production in the hands of the state, that is to say, of the proletariat organised as dominant class . . .'.

And Engels says in his *Anti-Dühring* : 'The proletariat seizes state power and then transforms the means of production into state property'.[63]   During this period the proletariat is the politi-cally ruling class.   But the political power of the proletariat is not the effect of its economic power; on the contrary, its economic power is the effect of its political power, which the proletariat acquires by means of revolution, a specifically political means; and it is through its political power that the proletariat tears away from the bourgeoisie the means of production in order to concentrate them in the hands of the state.   But this means the primacy of politics over economics; which is hardly compatible with an economic interpretation of society.   And the dominance of the proletariat over the bourgeoisie does not at all consist in the exploitation by the one of the other but, on

[63] Engels, *Anti-Dühring*, pp. 301–302.

the contrary, in putting an end to exploitation. Thus the state of the proletarian dictatorship is in every respect the contrary or—as Marx says in *Der Buergerkrieg in Frankreich*—the 'antithesis' of the bourgeois state, which, according to the original definition, is 'the' state *par excellence*. What remains of this definition is nothing but the dominance of one group over the other. It does not contain any reference to the economic basis of the domination exercised by one group over the other, and cannot contain such a reference if it is supposed to comprise a bourgeois as well as a proletarian dictatorship. But such a definition of the state is hardly compatible with the economic interpretation of society. Even the class element cannot be maintained in this definition. For neither the dominant nor the dominated group within a state that is a proletarian dictatorship can be characterised as a 'class'.

Strange as it may seem, there is in Marx' writings no clear definition of this concept, which plays such a decisive part in his theory. The last chapter of his unfinished *Kapital* is devoted to this problem, but does not present more than some introductory remarks. There can be no doubt that the concept of 'class', or more exactly, of 'classes'—the concept being a *plurale tantum* —as used by Marx in his economic interpretation of society, is essentially connected with the concept of exploitation and class struggle. Where there is no exploitation there are no classes. It is the exploitation of one group by another which makes the two groups in their mutual relation 'classes'. This relation is by its very nature that of a conflict of interests, which manifests itself as a struggle between the groups, the class struggle, which inevitably leads to the use of force by the exploited group against the exploiting group, that is to say, to revolution. In a letter to Weydemeyer,[64] Marx writes :

'As touching myself, neither the service of discovering the existence of classes in modern society, nor the discovery of their struggle *inter se* is a service the merit of which belongs to me. Bourgeois historians—long before me—described the historical development of the struggle of the classes, and bourgeois economists—long before me—set out the economic anatomy of the classes. My service is that I showed : (1) that the existence of classes is bound up with

64 *Neue Zeit*, XXV-2, p. 164.

definite historical stages of the struggle in the sphere of production; (2) that the struggle of the classes inevitably leads to the dictatorship of the proletariat; and (3) that this dictatorship is itself only a transition to the abolition of all classes and to a society without classes'.

Within the classless society of perfect communism there will be no revolutions : 'the social evolutions will cease to be political revolutions'.[65] If one group dominates over another group without exploiting it, neither the one nor the other is a 'class' in the original sense of the term; and if there is a conflict at all, it has not the character of class struggle leading to revolution. A domination, the purpose of which is to abolish exploitation, has the immanent tendency to put an end to all class antagonisms.

'If the proletariat', say Marx and Engels in *Das Kom-munistische Manifest,* 'by means of a revolution makes itself the dominant class and as such sweeps away by force the old conditions of production, then it will, along with these conditions, have swept away the condition for the existence of class antagonisms, and of classes generally, and will thereby have abolished its own dominance as a class'.

During the period of its dictatorship the proletariat will abolish not its dominance as such, but only its dominance 'as a class', *i.e.,* the class character of its dominance. And only after the dictatorship of the proletariat has achieved its purpose, the dominance as such will disappear, because only then there will be 'an association in which the free development of each is the condition for the free development of all'. There will be no longer any dominance whatsoever. There will be freedom. Engels says in his *Anti-Dühring*[66] : 'The proletariat seizes state power and then transforms the means of production into state property. But in doing this, it puts an end to itself as the proletariat . . .' That means that as soon as the proletariat has seized the government and has nationalised the means of production—which necessarily implies the abolishment of economic exploitation of the ruled group by the ruling group— the ruling group ceases to be what it was before : a proletariat, and this means a class. If it is assumed that there still exists during the period of the dictatorship of the proletariat some

65 Marx, *Misère de la Philosophie,* p. 228.
66 Engels, *Anti-Dühring,* p. 302.

exploitation, it can only be exploitation of the proletariat by the still existing bourgeoisie; this may be possible since the old economic system can only gradually be abolished. Only for this reason classes may continue to exist in the dictatorship of the proletariat. But, then, the politically ruling class is, at least to a certain extent, exploited by the politically ruled class, and the proletariat is the politically, the bourgeoisie, at least to a certain extent, the economically ruling class. This means the complete abandonment of the economic interpretation of society.

Nevertheless, the assumption which leads to such paradoxical results is at the very basis of the Marx–Engels theory of the proletarian dictatorship. In *Das Kommunistische Manifest* they say: 'When in the course of evolution the class differences have disappeared and all production has been concentrated in the hands of the associated individuals the public power will lose its political character'. That means that the socialisation of the means of production, the abolition of exploitation and class differences take place in the course of an evolution which begins at the moment when the proletariat has seized the political power. Engels describes the situation during the dictatorship of the proletariat as follows: 'the interference of state power in social relations becomes superfluous in one sphere after another and then becomes dormant of itself'.[67] The interference of state power in social relationships can take place only for the purpose of eliminating the remnants of the capitalist system, of completing the socialisation of the means of production. Here, too, the process is characterised as a *gradual* one.

## The contradiction in the Marxian theory of the state : a coercive machinery for the maintenance and for the abolition of exploitation

The contradiction which consists in defining the state as a coercive machinery for the maintenance of exploitation and, at the same time, declaring a coercive machinery for the abolishment of exploitation—namely the dictatorship of the proletariat, a state—becomes manifest when Engels, in his *Anti-Dühring*, writes: 'Former society, moving in class antagonism, had need of the state, that is, an organisation of the exploiting class at each period for the maintenance of its external conditions of produc-

[67] Engels, *Anti-Dühring*, p. 301 *et seq.*

tion'. Even when Engels speaks of the dictatorship of the
proletariat, the purpose of which is to abolish exploitation, he
maintains the definition of the state as 'organisation of the
exploiting class'. Nevertheless, he presupposes that this dictatorship of the proletariat is a state; this is implied in his statement 'that the proletariat seizes state power'. It is probable
that Engels was aware of this contradiction, for he shows a certain
tendency to weaken somehow this statement that the dictatorship
of the proletariat is a state. In a letter he wrote in 1875 to
August Bebel,[68] he said with respect to the use of the term 'state'
by the German Social-Democratic Party:

> 'It would be well to throw overboard all this chatter
> about the state, especially after the Commune, which was no
> longer a state in the proper sense of the word. The
> Anarchists have too long thrown this "People's state" into
> our teeth, although already in Marx' work against
> Proudhon, and then in *Das Kommunistische Manifest,* it
> was stated definitely that, with the introduction of the
> socialist order of society, the state will dissolve of itself (*sich
> aufloesen*) and disappear. As the state is only a tran-
> sitional phenomenon which must be made use of in struggle,
> in the revolution, in order forcibly to crush our antagonists,
> it is pure absurdity to speak of a "people's free state". As
> long as the proletariat still *needs* the state, it needs it, not in
> the interests of freedom, but for the purpose of crushing its
> antagonists; and as soon as it becomes possible to speak of
> freedom, then the state, as such, ceases to exist. We would,
> therefore, suggest that everywhere the word "state" be
> replaced by "community" (*Gemeinwesen*), a fine old
> German word, which corresponds to the French word
> "commune"'.

Thus the dictatorship of the proletariat is a state, but at the same
time it is no state.

### The contradiction in the Marxian theory of the form of govern-ment of the proletarian state : democracy and dictatorship

If the organisation of society during the transition period
of the proletarian dictatorship is a state, the question arises, which
form of government this state shall or will have according to

[68] Marx–Engels, *Correspondence*, p. 336.

Marx and Engels. Their answer to this question is highly ambiguous. They frequently declare that the state established by the proletarian revolution will be a democracy because it will be the domination of the overwhelming majority, that is, the proletariat, over a minority, that is, the bourgeoisie or former bourgeoisie. In *Das Kommunistische Manifest* they say that the proletarian movement which leads to the proletarian revolution is a movement of the 'enormous majority in the interest of the enormous majority', and that the first step in the revolution of the workers is 'the raising of the proletariat to the dominant class, the forcible establishment (*Erkaempfung*) of democracy'. There can be no doubt that the term democracy is used in the meaning of dominance of the majority over the minority, with political rights of all citizens. In his *Buergerkrieg in Frankreich* [69] Marx expressly declares that the Commune of 1871, which he considers as the model of a revolutionary organisation of the proletariat, was a 'democratic state' and that the 'universal suffrage'—that is the right to vote of all citizens, whether they belong to the majority or the minority—was an essential element of the constitution of that proletarian state. But, at the same time, Marx and Engels call the proletarian state preferably a 'dictatorship', the dictatorship of the proletariat. This term has been interpreted by many of their followers to designate something totally different from a mere majority rule, the formalistic concept of democracy maintained by the bourgeois writers.

The dictatorship of the proletariat is understood to be the realisation of true democracy, that is a government in the interest of the entire people, which is identical with socialism; and the realisation of socialism is possible only in a dictatorial way, that is to say, by the forcible oppression of the bourgeois class. The decisive difference between the old, the bourgeois-capitalist concept of democracy and the new proletarian-socialist concept of democracy consists in that according to the former the minority has a right to exist and to participate in the formation of the will of the state, whereas according to the latter the minority has no such right, but, on the contrary, is to be abolished by all means of forcible oppression. The new 'democracy' is indeed

---

[69] Karl Marx, *Der Buergerkrieg in Frankreich*. Adresse des Generalraths der Internationalen Arbeiter-Assoziation an alle Mitglieder in Europa und den Vereinigten Staaten. Separatabdruck aus dem *Volksstaat*. Leipzig, Verlag der Expedition des *Volksstaat*, 1871, p. 46 *et seq*.

a dictatorship. Just as the concept of state is transformed from the dominance of an exploiting class over an exploited class into the dominance of one group over another, the concept of democracy is transformed from the government of the majority over the minority into a government in the interest of all to be realised through the oppression of the minority by the majority. If this interpretation of the dictatorship of the proletariat is correct, then there are within the political theory of Marxism two contradictory concepts of democracy, just as there are two contradictory concepts of the state.

## The doctrine of the ' withering away ' of the state

About the duration of the dictatorship of the proletariat neither Marx nor Engels has made a definite statement. But they have left no doubt about the fact that the dictatorship will be only a state of transition and that during this period the state will gradually disappear. It is the already mentioned doctrine of the 'withering away' of the state. In *Das Kommunistische Manifest* we find hardly more than a hint in the statement quoted above. It is in the writings of Engels that the disappearance of the state is dealt with in more detail. In addition to the quoted statements, we refer to the famous passage in his *Ursprung der Familie, etc.*, where he expressly declares that together with the ' classes '—and that means in this connection the bourgeoisie and the proletariat—' the state will inevitably fall. The society which organises production anew on the basis of free and equal association of the producers will put the whole state machinery where it will then belong—into the museum of antiquities, next to the spinning wheel and the bronze ax'.[70] And in his *Anti-Dühring* he says, after stressing that during the transition period of the dictatorship of the proletariat the interference of state power in social relations becomes superfluous in one sphere after another and becomes dormant of itself :

> ' Government over persons is replaced by the administration of things and the direction of processes of production. The state is not "abolished" [as the anarchists demand], it withers away'.[71]

It is important to note that the stage of a stateless society may be reached, according to this prediction, within a single community as a final result of the proletarian revolution carried out

70 Engels, *Der Ursprung der Familie etc.*, p. 182.
71 Engels, *Anti-Dühring*, p. 302.

successfully in one state. The prediction is made without any regard to the possible international situation in which the proletarian state, as an effect of the socialisation of the means of production, withers away. It may be that if Marx and Engels had taken into consideration the international aspect, they would have modified somehow their prediction. But, as a matter of fact, they ignored this problem; and that may be explained by the fact that they, in particular Marx, were not very much concerned with a situation that according to their opinion would develop in a rather remote future. They were much more interested in a criticism of capitalism and in a political propaganda for a revolutionary overthrow of the capitalist state as the proximate task of the socialist movement.

## The future of the law

As to the future of the law, there are only very few statements in the writings of Marx and Engels. They were probably of the opinion that what they said about the state applied also to the law, which they considered to be a coercive order issued by the state. It is obviously the law that Engels has in mind when he, in the above-quoted statement, refers to an 'order' within the bounds of which the class conflict is kept by the state as an organisation of the ruling class. Neither Marx nor Engels had a clear idea of the relationships between state and law. That state and law are essentially connected with one another, they probably considered as self-evident; but they were more interested in the state aspect of society than in its law aspect. It may be assumed that according to the Marx-Engels doctrine of the state, the law as a coercive order and specific instrument of the state exists only in a society divided into two classes, a dominant exploiting and a dominated exploited class. In one of his most frequently quoted statements, Marx says that in the phase of transition from the proletarian revolution to the establishment of perfect communism, that is to say, during the period of the dictatorship of the proletariat, there will be still a law, but that this law, in spite of its progress as compared with the bourgeois law, will still be 'infected with a bourgeois barrier (*mit einer buergerlichen Schranke behaftet*)'.[72] By this not very

---

[72] This statement is made in a letter Marx wrote on May 5, 1875, to Bracke, concerning the draft of the Gotha Programme of the German Social-Democratic Party. The letter is published: *Neue Zeit*, IX-1, 1890–1891, p. 561 *et seq.*

fortunate metaphor he expresses the idea that the law of the socialist state will still have a certain bourgeois character, because there will still be a ruling class and a ruled class and hence a class antagonism; and that only 'in the highest phase of communist society', that is, that phase where the socialisation of the means of production is completely achieved and all class antagonisms radically abolished, 'can the narrow horizon of bourgeois law be completely overcome, and only then will society inscribe on its banner: from each according to his capacities and to each according to his needs'. This may be interpreted to mean that in this phase of the development of communism there will be no law, because the law is by its very nature bourgeois law, and that means class law. It must, however, be admitted that the statement is ambiguous and that it may also be interpreted to mean that even in the perfect communist society there will be law, but not bourgeois law, meaning a coercive order guaranteeing the exploitation of one class by another, presented by an ideological doctrine to be the realisation of justice. Communist society will have law, but no 'legal superstructure' because no ideological superstructure at all (provided that by legal superstructure not the real law but an illusive, apologetic doctrine of the law) is to be understood. There will be no reason to pretend that communist law is just, because communist law will really be just, legal reality will not be self-contradictory, its external form will be in complete harmony with its internal essence, its ideal destination, the idea of justice. Hence law may be conceived of as a normative order, and such a concept of the law will have no ideological character in the derogatory sense of the term. Since even the perfectly just reality of communist society will have a consciousness—there will be science, although no religion —the reflection of the real law in the consciousness of communist society, that is to say, the description of the law as a normative order, as a *Sollen,* will not be in conflict with its immanent idea, for the law will really be identical with justice, and justice means *Sollen,* norm.

The concept of 'norm' or *Sollen* is not in itself an ideological fraud. It assumes this character only if applied to something which, from the point of view of the interpreter, does not deserve to be interpreted as norm. From the point of view of the Marxian critique, bourgeois law only pretends to be a norm—

and is therefore an illusive ideology because it is not just—and only justice is a true norm, only a just law a true *Sollen*, a genuine 'norm'. That there will be justice, and hence a true norm, in communist society cannot be denied. The norm of communist justice becomes evident in the principle inscribed on the banner of communist society : 'From each according to his capacities, to each according to his needs', which is nothing else but the principle of communist justice, the principle of true equality, in opposition to capitalist injustice, only pretending to be justice. Bourgeois law, according to Marx, pretends to be an equal law for all, but in truth it is the contrary, a law of inequality; and this applies also to the law in the transition stage. The workers will get for an equal quantity of labour an equal quantity of products. But in view of the fact that the individual workers are not equal—the one is stronger and more intelligent than the other, works more and consequently gets more than the other—'this equal law is unequal for unequal work'. 'It is, therefore, as far as its content is concerned, a law of inequality as all law'. This is evidently the meaning of his figure of speech 'the bourgeois barrier' of the law in the transition stage.

Marx does not say that the law during the transition period of the dictatorship of the proletariat will be bourgeois law. He says only that the law of the socialist state will be infected with an evil of bourgeois society : inequality. He seems not to exclude the possibility of a law that is not infected with this evil, a law of true equality. But he adds to the words 'a law of inequality' the words 'as all law'. Here, as mentioned before, the words 'all law' may, in conformity with the preceding words, mean bourgeois law as well as the law of the socialist state; the law of the communist society guaranteeing true equality is not included, because supposed to be justice. In this connection Marx says :

'These defects [the inequality of the law] are inevitable in the first phase of communist society, when, after long travail, it first emerges from capitalist society. The law can never be on a higher level than the economic structure of society and the evolution of civilisation conditioned by this structure'.

This could be interpreted to mean : in the second phase of communist society, the economic structure of which will represent the highest possible degree of civilisation, the law, too, will reach the highest possible level. However, the words 'as all law' may also mean what they say : all law whatsoever, so that there is no law even where the principle of true equality prevails.

It is important to note that the same ambiguity which characterises the view presented by Marx in his *Gotha Programme* concerning the future of the law in communist society is implied in the statements he makes in the same essay concerning the future of the state. Criticising the Programme's postulate of a 'free state' he says :

> 'It is not at all the purpose of the workers . . . to make the state "free". In the German Reich the "state" is almost as "free" as in Russia. Freedom consists in transforming the state, which is not an organ superior to society, into an organ subordinated to society . . . '.[73]

Marx does not say that freedom consists in eliminating the state from society, but that it consists in organising the state in a way that it will become an instrument of society. As pointed out, he formulates the question of the future of the state as follows : 'What are the changes which the state will undergo in the communist society?' He does not ask : Under what conditions will the state disappear? And he objects to the Gotha Programme that it does not deal with the revolutionary dictatorship of the proletariat, nor 'with the future state of the communist society'.[74] This statement may be interpreted to mean that there will be in the future communist society a state, although not a state which dominates society but a state dominated by society, a state which is an instrument of this society[75]; just as there will be—according to the above presented interpretation of Marx' statements about the future of the law—a just law in this society.

This interpretation of Marx' statements concerning the future of the law may be summarised as follows : There will be in communist society no law of inequality, hence no ideological, *i.e.*, illusive, legal theory, and no law pretending to be just; con-

---

[73] *Loc. cit.*, p. 572.
[74] *Loc. cit.*, p. 573.
[75] The German text corresponding to the words 'with the future state of the communist society' runs as follows : '*mit dem zukuenftigen Staatswesen der kommunistischen Gesellschaft*'. The term *Staatswesen* means by and large the same as *Staat,* that is, state. But it is significant that Marx does not use the more precise term *Staat*.

sequently there will be no law as an 'ideology' in the derogatory sense of the term, but a real law of true equality, a law which will be the realisation of justice. If this law is conceived of as norm or normative order, it is an ideology in a non-derogatory sense—in the same sense as science will be an ideology of communist society. This view is confirmed by some statements he made in his *Einleitung zu einer Kritik der politischen Oekonomie.* There he says that 'there can be no society where there is no property in some form', although it would be a mistake to assume that it must be private or individual property. Since property presupposes a legal order, the statement that there is no society without some form of property implies the view that where there is society there is law, expressed in the famous formula of Roman jurisprudence *ubi societas ibi jus.* He also says 'that every form of production creates its own legal relations . . .', from which follows that also in a communist society there must be law. As a matter of fact, he asserts in this connection :

> 'All production is appropriation of nature by the individual and through a definite form of society. In that sense it is a tautology to say that property (appropriation) is a condition of production. But it becomes ridiculous when from that one jumps at once to a definite form of property, *e.g.,* private property (which implies, besides, as a prerequisite the existence of an opposite form, *viz.,* absence of property). History points rather to common property (*e.g.,* among the Hindoes, Slavs, ancient Celts, etc.) as the primitive form, which still plays an important part at a much later period as communal property'.[76]

If the nationalisation of the means of production achieved during the transition period of the dictatorship of the proletariat is to be maintained within the society of perfect communism, if here the means of production must remain at the exclusive disposition of the organs of the community and private property in these goods excluded, in order to maintain true equality, that is to say, if collective property of the community in the means of production has to be an institution of the future society, then there must be a law guaranteeing this status. However, it must be admitted that the other interpretation, according to which in the perfectly

---

[76] Marx, *Zur Kritik der politischen Oekonomie,* p. xix.; cf. also *supra,* p. 7.

communist society of the future there will be no state and consequently no law, and that means that the social order will have no coercive, even no normative character, is not only not excluded but in conformity with the anarchistic tendency prevailing in the writings of Marx and especially of Engels.

**The utopia of a stateless and lawless society of perfect communism**

The prediction of the coming into existence of such a social order is based on two assumptions : first, that the socialisation of the means of production will increase production to such an extent that all economic needs can be completely satisfied, or, as Marx formulates it, that 'the production forces and all the springs of social wealth will pour forth a full flow'; and, secondly, that disturbances of the social order are caused only by economic circumstances and that if a social order guarantees the complete satisfaction of the economic needs of all members of the community, no coercive measures as reaction against violations of this order are necessary. Neither the one nor the other assumption has a basis in our social experience. As far as the effect of socialisation is concerned, it certainly implies a tendency toward increasing production, but also an opposite tendency; and the results of socialisation, in so far as they could be observed until now, do not confirm the optimistic prediction of Marx. The extraordinary increase of production in the future communist society is all the more unlikely as according to Marx the division of labour, one of the most effective means of a qualitative as well as quantitative raising of production, will be abolished. As far as the second assumption is concerned, criminal psychology shows that economic circumstances are not the only causes of disturbances of a social order, that sex and ambition play at least as great a part and may play an even greater part when the economic causes are eliminated. The prediction of a stateless and lawless society of perfect justice is a utopian prophecy like the Messianic Kingdom of God, the paradise of the future.

**Engels' description of primitive society as a stateless and lawless community**

It was evidently to meet this objection that Engels in his *Ursprung der Familie, etc.,* tries to show that such a stateless and lawless society has already existed. On the basis of Morgan's *Ancient Society* and Bachofen's *Mutterrecht,* Engels maintains that the society of primitive men, the society of the *gentes,* was a classless and hence stateless society. As to the law of this society, he is not very consistent, since he speaks frequently of rights which exist in that society. Thus he admits the possibility of a certain 'appropriation' and also the fact that the husband as well as the wife 'are owners of the tools which have been prepared and are being used by them'.[77] He speaks of the blood revenge prevailing within this society as of a sanction analogous to the capital punishment of modern society.[78] All this presupposes the existence of a social order which has a coercive character, that is to say, the existence of law. Nevertheless, Engels describes the condition of the people in this society as ideal. 'It is a wonderful constitution, this constitution of the *gentes*'. It is the paradise of the past, the lost paradise of mankind, but a paradise that will come again in the future with the stateless society of perfect communism.

Engels' description of primitive society cannot stand a scientific criticism. His main sources, the works of Morgan and Bachofen, were, even at the time of their publication, considered as highly problematical, and are to-day completely outdated by the results of modern ethnology. There can be not the slightest doubt that the societies to which Engels refers have lived under a strict coercive order characterised by legal institutions, such as blood revenge and expulsion from the community, collective property in land and more or less individual property in movable things. That there was no state organisation is true in so far as the coercive, and that means the legal, order of these societies did not institute special organs for the creation and application of the law, that there were no legislative and judicial organs and, in particular, no special organs for the execution of the sanctions provided for by the legal order. The principle of self-help prevailed, but this principle was a legal principle. There was a clear distinction between a murderer and an avenger who enforced the law against the murderer and the members of his family, in conformity with the perfectly legal principle of collective responsibility.

Engels' description of primitive society as an ideal status of mankind is a highly significant symptom of the above-mentioned similarity between the Marxian philosophy and the natural-

---

[77] Engels, *Der Ursprung der Familie etc.*, p. 164.
[78] *Loc. cit.*, pp. 79, 90, 164.

law doctrine which also assumes an original state of nature as a social state of happiness. This assumption is not based on facts but deduced from the presupposed postulate that men shall be free and treated equally. This postulate is usually presented in the disguise of the statement that men are by their very nature free and equal. It is on this postulate, and not on historical facts, that the doctrine is based that state and law have their origin in a contract. For if men shall be free and be treated on an equal level, they can be bound only by their own will.

### The anarchistic character of the Marx-Engels social theory

This postulate is also at the basis of the doctrine of state and law developed by Marx and Engels. Since they did not intend —as did the followers of the natural-law doctrine—to justify the existing state, they did not accept the assumption of a social contract. Consequently they considered the existing state as incompatible with the freedom and the equality of men. Since the state restricts individual freedom and establishes inequality among men, it is an evil, although in the transition period of the proletarian dictatorship a necessary evil, but even in that period an evil of which society should get rid as soon as possible. In the Preface to Marx' *Buergerkrieg in Frankreich*, Engels wrote :

'. . . the State is nothing more than a machine for the oppression of one class by another, and indeed in the democratic republic no less than in the monarchy ; and at best [is] an evil inherited by the proletariat after its victorious struggle for class supremacy whose worst sides the proletariat, just like the Commune, will have at the earliest possible moment to lop off, until such time as a new generation, reared under new and free social conditions, will be able to throw on the scrap-heap all the useless lumber of the State '.

The Marx-Engels doctrine has a thoroughly anarchistic character. The difference between the anarchistic theory of Marx and Engels and other anarchistic theories, as for instance the doctrine of Bakunin, the great rival of Marx, is that non-Marxian anarchism postulates the immediate abolishment of the state machinery by a revolution of the proletariat, whereas Marxian anarchism declares as the immediate purpose of the proletarian revolution the socialisation of the means of production, the final and inevitable effect of which will be the automatic disappearance of the state.  The basically anarchistic attitude of Marxism manifests itself not only in the doctrine of the withering away of the state but also in the contemptuous way Marx and Engels speak of the 'state' as such, and not only the capitalist state. In his *Buergerkrieg in Frankreich* Marx says, 'the constitution of the Commune would have returned to the social body all the forces which until now the parasite "state" (*Schmarotzerauswuchs Staat*) consumes, which lives on the society and hinders its free movement'.  And Engels, in his Preface, argues against the 'superstitious belief in the state', which prevailed in Germany.  Although he was forced to admit that the dictatorship of the proletariat is a state, he emphatically rejected also in his *Anti-Dühring* the phrase frequently used by the members of the German Social-Democratic Party: 'the people's free state', and said, referring to the 'withering away' of the state, that from this standpoint one must appraise this phrase, 'both its justification at times for agitational purposes and its ultimate scientific inadequacy'.

## The contradiction between moralism and amoralism in the Marx-Engels theory of state and law

The rejection of state and bourgeois law, the anarchical tendency in Marx' social philosophy, is an essential element of his critique of society.  This critique has a thoroughly moral character; it is based on a moral evaluation of social reality and culminates in a moral postulate, the realisation of freedom and equality.  The moral character of Marx' critique of the existing social reality manifests itself in the highly emotional indignation with which he condemns capitalist exploitation as slavery, and bourgeois ideology in its attempt to justify it.  In *Zur Kritik der Hegelschen Rechtsphilosophie*, Marx speaks of the proletariat as of

'a class in radical chains, a class of bourgeois society which is no class of bourgeois society, an estate (*Stand*) which is the dissolution of all estates, a group which has a universal character because of its universal suffering, and which does not claim a particular justice (*Recht*) because no particular injustice (*Unrecht*) but the injustice *par excellence* has been imposed upon it'.[79]

[79] *Gesamtausgabe*, I–1, p. 619.

He says of the historical school of jurisprudence that
> 'it legitimises the meanness of to-day by the meanness of
> yesterday, it declares each cry of the serf against the knout
> as rebellious if the knout is an aged, hereditary, a historical
> knout . . .'.

And of the critique of society he postulates, he says : in the
fight against the actual conditions
> 'the critique is not a passion of the head, it is the head of
> the passion.  Its object is its enemy, whom it does not
> intend to refute but to destroy . . . Its essential pathos is
> the indignation, its essential function the denunciation'.[80]

The moral condemnation of capitalist society is in complete harmony with the enthusiastic appraisal of the anarchic society of the
past and its counterpart, the communistic society of the future,
especially in the writings of Engels.  But, although Marxian
anarchism is, in the last analysis, the consequence of a moral
attitude toward the problem of society, and the core of Marx'
social philosophy, communism, is the expression of a social ideal,
the result of a definite idea of justice, morality is rejected—
together with religion and law—as bourgeois ideology.  In *Das
Kommunistische Manifest* we read : 'Law, morality, religion
are for the proletariat nothing but bourgeois prejudices behind
which as many bourgeois interests are hidden'.  Well known
and frequently quoted is Marx' statement in his *Buergerkrieg in
Frankreich* : 'The worker class has no ideals to realise'.[81]  In
*Die Deutsche Ideologie,* Marx writes : 'Communism is for us
not a condition which ought to be realised, an ideal to which
reality is to be conformed.  We call communism the real movement which abolishes the actual conditions'.[82]  In opposition
to other socialist writers, as for instance Proudhon who 'demands
that society shall be transformed not in accordance with its own
law of evolution but in accordance with the *pre*scriptions of
justice',[83] Marxian socialism pretends to be a morally indifferent

---

[80] *Loc. cit.,* I–1, p. 609.
[81] *Der Buergerkrieg in Frankreich,* p. 27.  But in the following sentence,
Marx speaks of the 'heroic decision' of the worker class 'to act in a way
worthy of its historic mission', thus recognising the moral ideal of
heroism.
[82] *Gesamtausgabe,* V, p. 25.
[83] Engels, *Zur Wohnungsfrage. Sozialdemokratische Bibliothek,* XIII, p. 61.
Although Engels here rejects a moral approach to the problem of
socialism, he says in his *Ursprung der Familie, etc.,* after having described
the situation in the capitalist society by the statement that each progress
in the process of production is an advantage for the capitalists but a

*de*scription of a necessary evolution from a primitive stage of freedom and equality through a stage of slavery to a final state of perfect freedom and equality.

## ' Scientific ' socialism

Marx and Engels are not the only writers who use a so-called law of evolution as a disguise for a moral-political postulate. Hegel's philosophy of history and Comte's positivism are of the same type. Marx' critique of society and his prediction of communism as the necessary outcome of an evolution determined by causal law are based on a subjective value judgment. But Marx and Engels present it as a science, that is to say, as an objective truth. They are proud of having promoted socialism from a 'utopia to science', hence they call their doctrine 'scientific' socialism. The task of scientific socialism, says Engels,[84] is not

> 'to manufacture a system of society as perfect as possible, but to examine the historic economic development from which the classes of the bourgeoisie and of the proletariat and their conflict have arisen, and to discover in the economic situation created by this development the means for the solution of the conflict'.

To find the means of realising a presupposed end is certainly a scientific task, since the relationship between means and end is a relationship between cause and effect, and the cognition of this relationship is a specific function of science. But in order to find the means for the realisation of an end, first a definite end must be determined, and the determination of an end which is not itself a means to an end is not a scientific function. It is not and cannot be the function of objective science, for it is based on a value judgment which, in the last analysis, has a subjective character. It is determined by man's wishes or fears, and cannot be verified by man's experience. The determination of the end for the realisation of which the means are to be discovered is the decisive, the essential function of the Marxian socialism. The means to be chosen depend on the end pre-

---

disadvantage, an evil for the workers: 'But this shall not be so! What is good for the ruling class shall be good for the entire society'; this is evidently a moral postulate.
[84] Engels, *Die Entwicklung des Sozialismus von der Utopie zur Wissenschaft*, p. 33.

supposed. The bourgeoisie may be not interested at all in a 'solution' of the conflict, but in a social situation in which the conflict does not involve any danger to the existence of the dominant class, an ideal situation in which the proletariat is kept in perfect submission to the bourgeoisie and unable to offer any resistance. This is the end the bourgeoisie may wish to realise, the value presupposed by this class.

The end that Engels presupposes and which he calls 'the solution of the conflict' is quite different. It is a situation which the proletariat wants to be established, a situation in which there is no conflict between the two classes, because a classless society is established in which the economic needs of all members are perfectly satisfied, so that no conflict of interests can arise. It is just that 'system of society as perfect as possible', of which Engels pretends that it is not to be 'manufactured' by scientific socialism, but to be 'discovered' by it in economic reality. But this scientific discovery is possible only because the allegedly discovered value has previously been projected into reality, the Marxian reality with a double bottom.

In presenting their socialism as 'science', Marx and Engels produce exactly the same kind of illusive ideology as the bourgeois social theory denounced by them as ideological. By pretending to be a morally indifferent, objective science, Marxian socialism tries to veil the highly subjective character of the value judgment which is at its basis. Bourgeois ideologists use religion as a means to invest the bourgeois state and the bourgeois law with a divine authority, which these social institutions in truth do not have. Marx in his critique of ideology has completely destroyed the authority of religion, but he does not renounce, for his own enterprise, the assistance of an effective authority. The only authority that his critique has left untouched is science. Hence his socialism pretends to be science and crowns with the halo of this authority its product : the communist society of the future.

### The confusion of science and politics in Marx' interpretation of society

That 'scientific socialism', *i.e.*, the social science developed by Marx and Engels is by its very nature an 'ideology', is the inevitable consequence of their opinion concerning the essential function of social science. Social science is for Marx in the first place a critique of the ideological consciousness of bourgeois society, that is, of the religion and social theory of the bourgeoisie; and its purpose is to unveil the contradiction between this consciousness and the social reality distortedly reflected by it. But, since a social reality produces an ideology, a perverted consciousness only because it is itself perverted, and that means contradictory in itself, the critique of social ideology turns into a critique of social reality. And the critique of social reality aims at a total change of this reality, at social revolution. Thus the science is from the very beginning mixed with politics. It is consciously intended to be an instrument of politics. In *Zur Kritik der Hegelschen Rechtsphilosophie,* Marx says: 'Critique of religion is the presupposition of all critique'. 'The critique of religion is *in nuce* the critique of this vale of tears the halo of which is religion'. The aim of the critique of religion is the 'abolishment of religion, as the illusory happiness of the people'; it is

> 'the postulate of its real happiness, the postulate to abandon the illusion about its condition, the postulate to abandon a condition that needs illusions . . . The critique of religion results in the doctrine that man is the supreme being for man, in the categorical imperative to overthrow all relationships in which man exists as a humiliated, enslaved, lost, despised being'.[85] 'It is the task of history [that means, the science of history as a critique of ideology], after the truth of the other world has disappeared, to establish the truth of this world . . . The critique of the heaven turns into the critique of the earth, the critique of theology into the critique of politics'.[86]

As far as the social conditions of Germany are concerned this critique means: 'War against the real conditions of Germany'. And these conditions are the object of critique just as 'the criminal is the object of the executioner'; 'the object of this critique is the enemy'. This critique 'presents itself no longer as an end in itself, but only as a means'—a means of politics, an instrument in the fight of the proletariat against capitalism. The very function of the scientific critique or critical science of

[85] *Gesamtausgabe,* I–1, p. 615.
[86] *Loc. cit.,* I–1, pp. 607–608.

Marx is to bring about a social revolution. He says : Just as at the time of the religious revolution in Germany, the Reformation, it was Luther, a monk, it is now the philosopher—that is the social scientist, the scientific critic—' in whose brain the revolution starts'.[87] Marx refers here to a social revolution in Germany, which means 'the emancipation of the German'. But, he says, 'the emancipation of the German is the emancipation of man. The head of this emancipation is philosophy, its heart the proletariat. Philosophy cannot be realised without the abolishment of the proletariat, the proletariat cannot be abolished without the realisation of philosophy'.[88] By 'philosophy' he means his scientific socialism, the critical science of society.

It is quite interesting to note that this conscious confusion of science with politics is noticeable already in his doctor thesis (1841). There he writes : 'It is a psychological law that the theoretical consciousness, when liberated, becomes practical energy, steps forth as will out of the realm of shadows, and turns against the earthly reality which exists independently of it'. There is a change from theory to practice. 'But the practice of philosophy is itself theoretical. It is the critique which judges the individual existence by comparing it with its essence, the particular reality by comparing it with its idea'. It is highly significant that with Marx the theory transformed into practice, 'philosophy as will', is, by its very nature, directed 'against' the existing reality, and that the standard by which social reality is measured, and that means evaluated, is its immanent essence or idea : a value. Marx' 'scientific socialism' is a social science the only and exclusive purpose of which is not to conceive of and to describe social reality as it actually is, without evaluating it, but on the contrary, to judge it according to a value which is presupposed by this science but delusively projected into the social reality, with the openly admitted purpose to conform it to the presupposed value. By its confusion of theory and practice, science and politics, it fulfils all the requirements of an 'ideology' in the derogatory sense of this term as used by Marx and Engels. It veils the immanent contradiction between moralism and amoralism.

---

[87] *Loc. cit.*, I–1, p. 615.
[88] *Loc. cit.*, I–1, p. 621.

**' Science ' and revolution**

This 'scientific socialism' is neither more nor less 'science' than those bourgeois doctrines which Marx denounced as ideologies. And, strange as it may seem, Marx, who is so intent on presenting his doctrine of socialism as a science and for this purpose excludes science from the law according to which man's social existence determines man's social consciousness, which thus can be only a false illusive consciousness, nevertheless criticises Proudhon's socialist doctrine by disparaging it as a 'mere' science :

'Just as the economists are the scientific representatives of the bourgeois class, so the Socialists and the Communists are the theoreticians of the proletarian class. So long as the proletariat is not yet sufficiently developed to constitute itself as a class, and consequently so long as the struggle itself of the proletariat with the bourgeoisie has not yet assumed a political character, and the productive forces are not yet sufficiently developed in the bosom of the bourgeosie itself to enable us to catch a glimpse of the material conditions necessary for the emancipation of the proletariat and for the formation of a new society, these theoreticians are merely utopians who, to meet the wants of the oppressed classes, improvise systems and go in search of a regenerating science. But in the measure that history moves forward, and with it the struggle of the proletariat assumes clearer outlines, they no longer need to seek science in their minds; they have only to take note of what is happening before their eyes and to become the mouthpiece of this. So long as they look for science and merely make systems, so long as they are at the beginning of the struggle, they see in poverty nothing but poverty, without seeing in it the revolutionary, subversive side which will overthrow the old society. From this moment, science, produced by the historical movement and associating itself with it in full recognition of its cause, has ceased to be doctrinaire and has become revolutionary'.[89]

That means that there is no such thing as an objective science established beyond the conflict of the classes, that science is either a bourgeois or a proletarian ideology; that as soon as the class struggle assumes a political character there is no longer need of a

[89] *Gesamtausgabe*, VI, p. 191.

'doctrinaire' science—which means a scientific science that sees in poverty nothing but poverty, without evaluating this phenomenon. Now, science sees poverty as a revolting defect of society, and consequently becomes the mouthpiece of the revolutionary struggle of the proletariat against the bourgeoisie; thus it ceases to be doctrinaire, that is to say, 'merely' science, and becomes revolutionary, that means politics. For Proudhon —Marx says—'science reduces itself to the slender proportions of a scientific formula'.[90] Proudhon—Marx says in his letter to Annenkov[91]—is a 'doctrinaire'. 'He wants to soar as a scientist above the bourgeois and the proletarians', that is to say, he wants to be objective. But, according to Marx, 'he is merely the petty bourgeois, continually tossed back and forth between capital and labour, political economy and communism',[92] instead—as Marx with his 'scientific' socialism— abandoning doctrinaire science and siding with the proletarians against the bourgeois, with communism against capitalism. Thus Marxian socialism is science, but is opposed to Proudhon's socialism, because the latter is merely science, 'doctrinaire' science.

### The contradiction between political anarchism and economic authoritarianism

It is a no less striking contradiction in the system of 'scientific' socialism that the political status of the communist society of the future is supposed to be that of an individualistic anarchy, whereas the economic status is to consist in the replacement of the 'anarchy of capitalist production' by a highly organised production on the basis of collective property in the means of production, necessarily concentrated in the hands of a central authority. The authoritarian character of a centralised organisation, as is the organisation of the communist society of the future, has not been denied, neither by Marx nor by Engels. Engels even expressly admitted that the economic organisation of the future will not be possible without authority, although he added that such authority will be established only to the extent as required by the relationships of production.[93] In his *Anti-*

90 *Loc. cit.*, p. 192.
91 Marx-Engels, *Correspondence*, p. 15.
92 *Gesamtausgabe*, VI, p. 192.
93 Cf. *Neue Zeit*, XXXII. Jahrg., 1. Bd., 1913–1914, p. 40. Cf. also my *Sozialismus und Staat*, p. 87 *et seq.*

*Dühring,* where he predicted that the state will not be 'abolished' but will simply 'wither away', he said of the communist society of the future: 'Government over persons is replaced by the administration of things and the direction of the processes of production'.[94] But since things are administered and processes of production are directed by persons, the administration of things and the direction of processes of production are not possible without a government over persons; and there can be little doubt that the centralisation of the entire process of economic production will require a high degree of authority. Since, just from the viewpoint of an economic interpretation of society, it is impossible to separate the economic from the political aspect of social organisation, it is an open contradiction to deny the need for any kind of authority in the political field, but to admit the necessity of authority in the economic field.

## The admissibility of contradictions according to the logic of dialectics

However, the fact that a theory is involved in logical contradictions is no objection from the point of view of the new logic, the dynamic logic of dialectics, which Marx and Engels have taken over from Hegel's philosophy of history. For the main function of this logic is to eliminate the principle according to which contradictions are inadmissible.[95] An essential element of this dialectics is the view that contradictions are inherent in reality, especially in social reality, a view according to which opposite forces in nature or society are interpreted as logical contradictions. If logical contradictions are inherent in reality, then contradictions in thinking are, as Hegel in his *Logic* expressly affirms, not a logical defect. Since in his idealistic philosophy thinking and being are identified, the idea of logical contradictions inherent in reality is, as a consequence of this identification, to a certain extent understandable. But within the framework of the materialistic philosophy of Marx and Engels, who reject this identification, it is absurd to interpret antagonistic forces or conflicting interests in society as logical contradictions.

[94] Cf. *supra*, p. 32.
[95] Cf. the critical analysis of Hegel's dialectical method in my *Political Theory of Bolshevism*, p. 14 *et seq.*

4

Hegel's dialectics has the effect, intended by its author, to open the way for irrational metaphysical speculations. Marx and Engels, it is true, were opposed to Hegel's metaphysics; but they made abundant use of the new logic of dialectics, which permitted them to say that the state is by its very nature an instrument for the maintenance of exploitation and at the same time that the state, as the proletarian state, is the specific instrument for the abolition of exploitation; that the proletarian state is a dictatorship and at the same time that it is a democracy; that communism is the realisation of individual freedom and at the same time the organisation of collective authority; to present the theory of socialism as a morally indifferent science and at the same time to proclaim in the name of science the true justice of freedom and equality; to assert that there cannot be such a thing as objective science and at the same time to boast of having promoted socialism from a utopian wish to the rank of an objective science. Indeed, 'dialectics is the soul of Marxism', as Stalin declared.[96] But nothing is more significant of the true function of this dialectics than the following statement of Stalin in the Political Report of the Central (Party) Committee to the Sixteenth Congress, 1930[97]:

'It may be said that such a formulation of the problem is "contradictory". But surely we have a "contradiction" of the same kind with the problem of the state? We are for the withering away of the state, while at the same time we stand for strengthening the dictatorship of the proletariat which represents the most potent and mighty authority of all the state authorities that have existed down to this time. The highest development of state authority to the end of making ready the conditions *for* the withering away of state authority: there you have the Marxist formula. Is this "contradictory"? Yes, it is "contradictory". But it is a living, vital contradiction and it completely reflects Marxist dialectics'.

---

[96] Stalin, The Right Deviation in the Communist Party of Bolsheviks. *Soviet Legal Philosophy,* p. 228.
[97] *Soviet Legal Philosophy,* p. 235.

## CHAPTER 2

# LENIN'S THEORY OF STATE AND LAW

## The proletarian state a 'semi-state' withering away by its very nature

THE first and basic work of the Soviet theory of the state (essentially connected with the Soviet theory of law) is V. I. Lenin, *State and Revolution,* published 1917.[1] The main purpose of this work is to 'resuscitate the real teachings of Marx on the state', which—as Lenin maintains—have been obliterated and distorted by the opportunists within the labour movement, especially in Germany.[2] Lenin lays stress on the revolutionary tendency of Marx' theory of the state, that is to say, on the fact that according to Marx and Engels the bourgeois state can be replaced by a socialist state, the dictatorship of the proletariat, only by revolution and not by evolution. He emphasises that only the socialist state will 'wither away' and he insists on the dictatorial character of the proletarian state in the transition period. In respect of this transition period he underlines the necessity of the 'strictest discipline', the 'strictest control by society and by the state of the quantity of labour and the quantity of consumption'.[3] He says of the dictatorship of the proletariat :

'The dictatorship of the proletariat produces a series of restrictions of liberty in the case of the oppressors, the exploiters, the capitalists. We must crush them in order to free humanity from wage slavery; their resistance must be broken by force; it is clear that where there is suppression there is also violence, there is no liberty, no democracy'.[4]

In another connection he says of the period of transition from capitalism to communism, the 'period of overthrowing and completely abolishing the bourgeoisie' :

'this period inevitably becomes a period of unusually violent

[1] Lenin, *Collected Works,* Vol. XXI–2, New York, 1932, p. 149 *et seq.*
[2] *Loc. cit.,* p. 153.
[3] *Loc. cit.,* p. 226.
[4] *Loc. cit.,* p. 219.

class struggles in their sharpest possible forms and, therefore, the state during this period inevitably must be a state
that is democratic in a new way (for the proletariat and
the poor in general) and dictatorial in a new way (against
the bourgeoisie) '.[5]

Thus, the proletarian state is a democracy and at the same time
no democracy. Although Lenin, on the one hand, emphasises the
authoritarian character of the socialist state during the period
of transition, he, on the other hand, following the Marx-Engels
doctrine, maintains that this state is from the very beginning of
its existence withering away. He says that,

'in the first place, the proletariat, according to Marx, needs
only a state which is withering away, *i.e.*, a state which is
so constituted that it begins to wither away immediately,
and cannot but wither away'.[6]

He speaks of the proletarian state as of 'the transitional form
of its disappearance (the transition from the political state to
no state)'.[7] Consequently he characterises the proletarian state
as a 'semi-state'; and explains the difference between the
capitalist state and the proletarian state as follows :

'Under capitalism we have a state in the proper sense
of the word, that is, special machinery for the suppression
of one class by another. . . . During the transition from
capitalism to communism suppression is still necessary; but
it is the suppression of the minority of exploiters by the
majority of exploited. A special apparatus, special
machinery for suppression, the "state" is still necessary,
but this is now a transitional state, no longer a state in the
usual sense . . . '.[8]

Thus, the dictatorship of the proletariat is a state and at the same
time it is no state. In complete conformity with Marx and
Engels, Lenin maintains that the coercive power of the proletarian state is to be exercised only against the former
bourgeoisie, and that as soon as the bourgeoisie is completely
abolished the coercive machinery of the state will disappear.
'The state is withering away in so far as there are no longer
any capitalists, any classes and, consequently, no class can be

⁵ *Loc. cit.*, p. 177.
⁶ *Loc. cit.*, p. 168.
⁷ *Loc. cit.*, p. 194.
⁸ *Loc. cit.*, p. 220.

suppressed '.[9]  There are no 'classes' because there are no
'capitalists' and that implies, no proletarians.  Lenin presupposes as self-evident that the concept of class is essentially
connected with the exploitation of the proletariat by the
capitalists.  In a speech delivered in 1920 he said :

> 'What are classes in general?  Classes are that which
> permits one section of society to appropriate the labour of
> another section.  If one section of society appropriates all
> the land, we have a landlord class and a peasant class.  If
> one section of society possesses the factories and works, has
> shares and capital, and the other section works in these
> factories, we have a capitalist class and a proletarian
> class '.[10]

To 'appropriate the labour of one section of society' means to
exploit this section of society.

## The coercive character of the proletarian state and the gradual disappearance of classes

The tendency to stress the coercive character of the proletarian state is still more manifest in N. Boukharin's *Programme
of the Communists,* which, in this respect, was certainly in conformity with Lenin's theory.  In this pamphlet we read :

> 'The proletarian state . . . is an organisation of the
> dominating class (the dominating class here is the working
> class) and an organisation of violence over the bourgeoisie,
> as a means of getting rid of the bourgeoisie and of putting
> an end to it.  He who is afraid of this kind of violence is
> not a revolutionist '.[11]

The meaning which the Soviet theory in the first period attributed
to the term 'dictatorship' appears clearly in the *Programme of
the Communist International,*[12] adopted by the Sixth World
Congress, September 1, 1928, in Moscow : 'The characteristic
feature of the transition period as a whole is the ruthless suppression of the resistance of the exploiters, the organisation of
socialist construction, the mass training of men and women in

[9] *Loc. cit.,* p. 224.
[10] Lenin, *Selected Works,* International Publishers, New York, 1934, Vol. 9,
p. 476.
[11] N. Boukharin, *Programme of the Communists (Bolsheviks),* published by
the Group of English speaking Communists in Russia, 1919, p. 17.
[12] In *Blueprint for World Conquest, as outlined by the Communist International,* Washington and Chicago, 1946, p. 149 *et seq.*

the spirit of socialism and the gradual disappearance of classes'. Here, too, the disappearance of classes coincides with the abolishment of exploitation.

### First attempt of modifying the doctrine of the withering away of the state

In a lecture on 'The State' delivered in Sverdlov University in 1919, Lenin maintains the Marx-Engels doctrine of the origin of the state. He refers to Engels' *Ursprung der Familie etc.,* of which he says : 'You may rely upon every phrase in it as written upon the basis of enormous historical and political material'.[13] He repeats Engels' thesis that the state appears 'when the division into classes—when exploiters and exploited— appears'.[14] But he does not repeat Engels' definition of the state as a machinery for the exploitation of one class by another. Although he emphasises that 'there was no state when there were no classes—no exploiters, no exploited',[15] exploitation does not appear in his definition of the state, which evidently is formulated for the purpose of covering the socialist state of the proletarian dictatorship and not only the capitalist state. 'The state is a machine for the oppression of one class by another—for holding the other subordinated classes obedient to the one class'.[16] As to the conditions under which the state will cease to exist, Lenin says in this lecture :

> 'The machine called the state . . . the proletariat casts away, averring it a bourgeois lie. We have taken this machine from the capitalists—taken it for ourselves. With it—or with a cudgel—we shall smash exploitation of every kind and—when there shall be no more the possibility of exploitation in the world, when there shall be no more possessors of land or of factories, when there shall be no more surfeiting of some while others are starving—only then, when these possibilities shall exist no more, will we turn this machine over to be broken up. There will then be neither state nor exploitation'.[17]

In his *State and Revolution,* Lenin still upheld the view of Marx

[13] Lenin, The State, *Soviet Legal Philosophy,* p. 3.
[14] *Loc. cit.,* p. 4.
[15] *Loc. cit.,* p. 7.
[16] *Loc. cit.,* p. 9.
[17] *Loc. cit.,* p. 15.

and Engels that the disappearance of the state will be the result of the evolution of socialism in a single socialist community. But in his lecture on the state he seems to have changed his opinion. There is a hint—no more than a hint—to the effect that exploitation must disappear everywhere and not only in one country, before 'we'—that can only be the government of the socialist state—will 'turn over this machine to be broken up', which is not quite the same as the gradual and automatic withering away of the state during the period of the proletarian dictatorship.

### The possibility of a stateless society based on the force of habit

As to the doctrine of the withering away of the state, Lenin tries to explain the possibility of a stateless society of perfect communism. In his *State and Revolution* he declares expressly that 'the fundamental social cause of excesses which consist in violating the rules of social life is the exploitation of the masses, their want and their poverty. With the removal of this chief cause excesses will inevitably begin to "wither away"'.[18] Then he refers to the decisive effect that habit has on the behaviour of men. The state will wither away for the 'simple' reason that

'freed from capitalist slavery, from the untold horrors, savagery, absurdities and infamies of capitalist exploitation, people will gradually become accustomed to the observation of the elementary rules of social life that have been known for centuries and repeated for thousands of years in all school books; they will become accustomed to observing them without force, without compulsion, without subordination, without the special apparatus for compulsion which is called the state'.[19]

This is an unmistakably ethical approach to the problem of communism based on a highly moral indignation toward capitalist exploitation, hardly compatible with morally indifferent 'scientific' socialism. The rules to which Lenin refers are nothing else but the norms of traditional morality of capitalist society and, according to Marx' economic interpretation of history, an ideological superstructure essentially determined by the economic circumstances which exist in capitalist society and, hence, have no place in communist society. These rules can

---

[18] Lenin, *State and Revolution*, p. 221.
[19] *Loc. cit.*, p. 220.

hardly be identical with the rules of social co-operation in the stateless community of the future, under the most complex order of a centralised organisation of collective production. And this is just the problem : whether such a social order can be maintained without coercion. This problem is not solved by Lenin's appeal to the force of habit.

## The confusion of the theoretical with the political approach

Lenin's theory of the state shows clearly two characteristic features of Soviet theory. First of all its political tendency. The question as to 'what is the essence of the state' is placed on the same level as the question 'what is the attitude of our party— struggling to overthrow capitalism—the party of the communists : what is its attitude toward the state?' And the meaning of the latter question is expressly indicated as : 'What should be the basic attitude toward the state taken by the worker-class party— struggling for the complete overthrow of capitalism—the party of communists?'[20] There is no separation of the theoretical from the political question. On the contrary, there is a conscious and intentional confusion of the two. The problem of this 'theory' is not to find out what the state really is from the point of view of objective cognition, but to formulate a definition of the state which may be effectively used in the fight of the communist party against capitalism. This 'theory' justifies itself quite openly as an appropriate instrument of politics; it is just the opposite of 'pure science'. But, on the other hand, Lenin recognises the postulate of a pure science, for he rejects the 'bourgeois' theory of the state because it does not supply us 'with the viewpoint of pure science'; it lacks 'impartiality'.[21] The 'bourgeois' scholars and writers have only 'confused'[22] the matter; their doctrine of the state serves only 'to justify social privileges and the existence of exploitation and capitalism'.[23] That means that the bourgeois theory of the state is not reliable because it is nothing but a political instrument. It is evidently only to the bourgeois theory of the state that his statement refers : in this theory 'the conflict of the different classes among themselves' finds 'expression in conflicting views of the state—in the

[20] Lenin, The State, *Soviet Legal Philosophy*, p. 2.
[21] *Loc. cit.*, p. 3.
[22] *Loc. cit.*, p. 1.
[23] *Loc. cit.*, p. 3.

appraisal of its role and its significance'[24]; for in the next passage he characterises the Marx-Engels doctrine of the state as 'the most scientific approach to the problem', although according to his own statements this approach is just the same as that of the bourgeois science, which he, on account of this approach, refuses to recognise as a true science.

Lenin's criticism of certain bourgeois theories of the state, as for instance the one according to which the state is of divine origin and consequently a divine institution, is certainly correct. But in the Marx-Engels doctrine of the state God is only replaced by the devil, called exploitation; and from the point of view of science there is no difference between a doctrine the purpose of which is to justify the state and a doctrine the purpose of which is to condemn the state. It is strange that a follower of the economic interpretation of history is so blind in this respect. But it is perhaps understandable that he takes no notice of the fact, which he conceals from his readers, that scholars who according to his view are bourgeois writers because they are not communists, have long before him severely criticised as political ideologies the theories of the state which he rejects, and have developed a theory which in no way can be used to defend the interests of a ruling class. For this is a fact which cannot be explained by an economic interpretation of history.

## The law within the proletarian socialist state : bourgeois law without the bourgeoisie

Lenin's theory of the law is, just as that of Marx and Engels, hardly more than casual remarks interspersed in his theory of the state; and nothing else but an interpretation of the words of his masters. As a result of this interpretation Lenin states that in the first phase of communist society, that is during the period of the proletarian dictatorship, there is still law, but this law is still to a certain extent 'bourgeois' law. In his *State and Revolution* he says :

> 'In the first phase of communist society (generally called socialism) "bourgeois law" is not abolished in its entirety, but only in part, only in proportion to the economic trans- formation so far attained, *i.e.*, only in respect of the means of production. "Bourgeois law" recognises them as the

[24] *Loc. cit.*, p. 3.

private property of separate individuals.  Socialism con-
verts them into common property.  To that extent, and to
that extent alone, does "bourgeois law" disappear'.[25]
To the extent the bourgeois law disappears, the law assumes the
character of socialist law.  Hence the law during the transition
period is at the same time bourgeois and socialist law.  That it is
—to a certain extent—still bourgeois law,

> 'is a "defect", says Marx, but it is unavoidable during the
> first phase of communism; for, if we are not to fall into
> utopianism, we cannot imagine that, having overthrown
> capitalism, people will at once learn to work for society
> without any standards of law; indeed, the abolition of
> capitalism does not immediately lay the economic founda-
> tions for such a change—and there is no other standard yet
> than that of "bourgeois law".  To this extent, therefore,
> a form of state is still necessary'.[26]

That means that in the first phase of communism, during the
transition period of the dictatorship of the proletariat, there will
be a law, for then a 'standard of law' will still be necessary to
induce people to work for society.  A 'standard' of law means
exactly the same as a normative order, a system of norms.  In
the German edition of Lenin's work the Russian term translated
into English by 'standard of law' is probably more correctly
translated by *Rechtsnormen*.  Lenin says later :

> 'In its first phase or first stage communism cannot as yet
> be economically ripe and entirely free of all tradition and
> of all taint of capitalism.  Hence the interesting phenomenon
> of communism retaining, in its first phase, "the narrow
> horizon of bourgeois law".  Bourgeois law, with respect to
> distribution of articles of consumption, inevitably presup-
> poses, of course, the existence of the bourgeois state, for the
> law is nothing without an apparatus capable of enforcing
> the observance of the law'.

The law, the observance of which is to be enforced by the state,
can be only a system of norms, because only norms can be
observed.  Lenin considers the law of the Soviet state as normative order and does not at all disparage it as a mere ideology.
He, as most of the Soviet writers, uses the term ideology to

[25] Lenin, *State and Revolution,* p. 224.
[26] *Loc. cit.,* p. 224.

designate any system of ideas.[27] He defines Marxism as 'ideology of the proletariat',[28] without implying any derogatory meaning.[29] Lenin speaks of the law as of a social reality and justifies its existence as a necessary means to induce men to work for society. And his theory of the law is by no means an illusive or perverted reflection of social reality in the head of an ideologist. He continues : 'Consequently, for a certain time not only bourgeois law but even the bourgeois state remains under communism, without the bourgeoisie!'[30] A 'bourgeois state' and a 'bourgeois law' without bourgeoisie is a self-contradictory concept, for the bourgeois state is a coercive machinery, and the bourgeois law a coercive order, both for the purpose of maintaining the exploitation of the proletariat by the bourgeoisie. If there is no bourgeoisie, that is to say, no class exploiting another class, how

---

[27] Cf. Max Eastman, *Marxism, is it Science?* 1940, p. 101.

[28] Lenin, *One Step Forward, Two Steps Back.* Selected Works, Moscow, 1950, Vol. 1, p. 618.

[29] In a recently published pamphlet : F. V. Konstantinov, *The Role of Socialist Consciousness in the Development of Soviet Society* (a translation of an essay published in the symposium *Soviet Socialist Society* prepared by the Institute of Philosophy of the Academy of Sciences of the U.S.S.R. and published by the Gospolitizdat, Moscow, 1949) Moscow, 1950, the Marxian theory of ideology is formulated as follows : 'the ideology of the bourgeoisie presents a perverted, distorted picture of capitalist society. Marxism-Leninism [which is the Soviet socialist ideology] is the only scientific, accurate and adequate reflection of the needs of development of the material life of society in our epoch. It is the only theory that arms us with scientific knowledge of the laws of social development' (p. 24 *et seq.*). Socialist ideology, that is, the social consciousness of socialist society under the leadership of the communist party—in contradistinction to bourgeois-capitalist consciousness—is the manifestation of 'human reason', and human reason is identical with 'the reason of the Communist Party'. 'Against this gloomy background of bourgeois society, with its corrupt and decaying culture, its mysticism, marasmus, human degradation and the spurning of reason, there shines like the sun the Land of Socialism, where human reason, the reason of the Communist Party, armed with the most profound scientific knowledge of social laws, directs the activities of millions who are consciously moulding their present and their future' (p. 9). 'Soviet, socialist ideology is fundamentally hostile to bourgeois ideology, the ideology of the exploiting classes. . . . Within the integral socialist consciousness, the integral socialist ideology, one must discern the following component forms : (a) Soviet science, (b) Soviet political, law consciousness, (c) Soviet morality, (d) Soviet art, including literature. The forms of socialist consciousness, the forms of Soviet ideology, differ ; but in character and content, Soviet, socialist ideology is one. The theory of Marxism-Leninism is the highest form of socialist consciousness. All other forms of socialist consciousness develop on the ideological basis of Marxism-Leninism as the prevailing scientific world outlook, the prevailing ideology' (pp. 78, 79).
*Loc. cit.,* p. 228.

could there be a coercive machinery or a coercive order for the purpose of maintaining exploitation?

### Justice, not law, prevailing in the communist society of the future

According to the foregoing statements, the difference between the first and second phases of communism will be this, that in the first phase the 'bourgeois law' will disappear only to a certain extent, whereas in the second phase it will disappear completely. In the first phase the law is to a certain extent already socialist law. Will it in the second phase be completely socialist law? Lenin says that in the first phase of communism the state does not altogether wither away, 'since there still remains the protection of "bourgeois law" which sanctifies actual inequality. For the complete extinction of the state, complete communism is necessary'. Lenin does not refer to a complete extinction of the law! Lenin's interpretation of Marx' doctrine does not remove this ambiguity with respect to the future of the law. That there will be justice, Lenin does not say expressly, but this idea is implied in his description of the transition period. Following Marx, Lenin declares bourgeois law as a law of inequality, although it pretends to be a law of equality and 'is really a violation of equality and an injustice'. This implies that Lenin considers equality—true equality, not only pretended equality— as justice. 'Injustice' is—according to Lenin—the meaning of Marx' formula of the 'narrow horizon of bourgeois law' which still is characteristic of the law in the first phase of communism. This 'narrow horizon of bourgeois law' 'compels one to calculate, with the hard-heartedness of a Shylock, whether a man has not worked half an hour more than another, whether he is not getting less pay than another—this narrow horizon will then [in the second phase of communism] be left behind'. That means that in the second phase of communism there will be justice. The 'hard-heartedness of a Shylock' is a value judgment full of moral indignation. Lenin says: 'The first phase of communism, therefore, still cannot produce justice and equality; differences, and unjust differences in wealth will still exist'[31]; this statement evidently implies that the second phase of communism will produce 'justice and equality'. Lenin says

[31] *Loc. cit.*, p. 233.

further : in the first phase of communist society the principle prevails : 'He who does not work shall not eat', and adds, 'this socialist principle is already realised'.[32] And also the other principle prevails : 'For an equal quantity of labour an equal quantity of products'. This principle, too, is, according to Lenin, a socialist principle, but not yet communism; and 'bourgeois law'—which gives to unequal individuals in return for an unequal amount of work an equal quantity of products— is not yet abolished. The two 'socialist' principles represent already a certain degree of justice, but not yet the highest degree, which will be reached in the second phase of communism. In the first phase there will still be a state, and 'while the state exists, there is no freedom. When there is freedom, there will be no state'.[33] In the second phase of communism there will be no state, and hence there will be freedom. In this phase of communism 'the antagonism between mental and physical labour disappears, that is to say . . . one of the principal sources of modern social inequality disappears'.[34] Hence there will be equality. That means, the second phase of communism will be the realisation of the ideals of freedom and equality, and that means the realisation of justice.

[32] *Loc. cit.*, p. 224.
[33] *Loc. cit.*, p. 225.
[34] *Loc. cit.*, p. 225.

## CHAPTER 3

# STUCHKA'S THEORY OF LAW

**The law as a system of social relationships**

THE first important attempt to develop a specifically Soviet theory of law—not as a mere by-product of a theory of the state—was P. L. Stuchka's *The Revolutionary Part Played by Law and the State: A General Doctrine of Law*,[1] published in 1921. Stuchka in 1918 became Commissar of Justice and, in 1919, the Commissariat of Justice edited certain guiding principles of criminal law formulating the 'Soviet' understanding of law; among them the following definition of the law: 'Law is a system (or order) of social relationships which corresponds to the interests of the dominant class and is safeguarded by the organised force of this class'.[2] Stuchka's theory of law, as presented in the above-mentioned work, is nothing more than a paraphrase of this formula. He specifies the statement that law is a system of 'social relationships' by emphasising that these relationships are only relationships of production and distribution.

> 'By the word society, Marx thus understands primarily the aggregate of production relationships, and then the aggregate of distribution relationships as well. "The individual relationships of production—and of exchange, it may be added—in each society, constitute a single whole", as Marx says; from which it follows that our definition of law—with its allusion to "a system of social relationships" as a single whole, or a social order—is in complete accord with the view of Marx'.[3]

That means that the law is identified with society and society with economy. Hence, there cannot be such a thing as law different from economy. This, of course, is no objection from the point of view of an economic interpretation of society, which has the tendency to reduce all social phenomena to economic phenomena. But, if such economic interpretation of society is

[1] *Soviet Legal Philosophy*, p. 17 *et seq.*
[2] *Loc. cit.*, p. 20.
[3] *Loc. cit.*, p. 31.

consistent, it must come to the conclusion that law as something different from economics—whether it be capitalist or socialist law—does not really exist, that a theory pretending the existence of law is nothing but an ideology, because a theory of law different from an economic theory is impossible. And, indeed, it seems as if Stuchka had the intention of rejecting all jurisprudence as incompatible with socialism. He attacks the socialist 'jurist' 'betraying the revolution at every step under the mask of Marxism', and asserts :

> 'There is no place for revolution in the present under-
> standing of law; and as the German revolutionary peasants
> sent their doctors of laws packing, and the Spaniards cursed
> their jurists (*togados*), so must the proletarian revolution
> also be on guard against its jurists'.[4]

That seems to mean that under the dictatorship of the proletariat there is no room for 'jurists', since there is no law as something different from economic relationships. But, on the other hand, Stuchka deals with law as the real object of a science which he does not, or not expressly, identify with the science of economics. He denies the existence of law only in a communist society of the future, and affirms that there is such a thing as law in the transitional period of the dictatorship of the proletariat.

### The law as a system of norms

The definition of the law as a system of social relationships is apparently not quite in harmony with another statement contained in the 'principles' edited by the Commissariat of Justice :

> 'Criminal law is composed of legal norms and other legal
> measures with which the system of social relationships of a
> given class society protects itself from violations (crimes) by
> means of repression (punishment)'.[5]

According to this statement the law is not a system of social relationships but—at least partly—an aggregate of legal norms issued for the purpose of guaranteeing or protecting certain social relationships. It might seem that Stuchka, in defining the law as an 'order', refers to these norms. But this is not so, for in his explanation of the term 'social relationships' he interprets the term 'order' to mean a system as a single whole. Stuchka

---

[4] *Loc. cit.*, p. 21.
[5] *Loc. cit.*, p. xxiv.

expressly rejects the view which conceives of the law under the category of norm as prevailing among bourgeois writers.

> 'Although the vast majority of these also start from the concept of a juridic relationship, yet law in the objective sense, they see—almost every one of them—only in the totality of norms—that is to say, in a code of statutes or of volitional imperatives . . . '.[6]

To justify his rejection of the definition of law as a system of norms, he refers to the statement of the Roman jurist Paulus : '*non ex regula jus sumatur, sed ex jure, quod est, regula fiat*', which he interprets to mean 'that the law is not taken from the rule : the rule comes into being out of the existent law'. But the statement of Paulus has nothing to do with the question as to whether the law is or is not norm. It only means that the individual law, the concrete right or judicial decision cannot be derived from a general rule, that the general rule can be established only—as an abstraction—on the basis of the law as it exists in its individual or concrete manifestations. The meaning of Paulus' statement could very well be determined in terms of norm : the individual legal norm cannot be derived from a general legal norm since the general legal norm can be formulated only as an abstraction from the individual norms. For by *regula* Paulus means a general rule or norm, and by *jus* an individual right or judicial decision which is an individual norm. But Stuchka misunderstands the statement by interpreting *regula* as 'norm' and *jus, quod est* as the existing social relationships. However, Stuchka is right when he refers to a modern school of jurisprudence, the so-called sociological school, as supporting his definition of the law as social relationships. He says :

> 'In reality, it would seem that since the time of the appearance of the sociological trend in legal science, one thing at least has been firmly established : that it is specifically social relationships themselves which are law'.[7]

The statement in the *Small Soviet Encyclopædia* (1931) that Stuchka's contribution to Soviet legal theory

> 'was to contrast law as a system of social relationships corresponding to the interests of the dominant class and protected by the force of that class with traditional and contemporary bourgeois theories of law as norms, or as an emotion or as justice',[8]

[6] *Loc. cit.*, p. 22.          [7] *Loc. cit.*, p. 22.          [8] *Loc. cit.*, p. xxiv.

is therefore not quite correct. There is no real 'contrast' between Stuchka's definition of the law and that of the contemporary bourgeois theory of sociological jurisprudence.

## The law as a social reality, not a mere ideological superstructure

In defining the law as an aggregate of social relationships and not as a system of norms, Stuchka claims to be 'in complete accord with the view of Marx'.[9] But at the same time he rejects Marx' formula of the 'legal superstructure', which he interprets to refer to the law as to a mere ideology.

'He who has assimilated the form of thinking of Marx and Engels concerning capital, money, and so forth as social relationships will at once understand also what we are saying as to the system of social relationships. This will be a more difficult matter for a jurist to whom law is a purely technical and artificial superstructure, dominant—however strangely—over its foundation. To this understanding even Marx paid tribute in a small way when and in so far as he speaks of law as an ideological superstructure : for Marx was, of course, nurtured in Roman law and—in general— in the legal concepts of the thirties which saw in law an expression of the general will (*Volkswillen*) and was habituated to its terminology'.[10]

This is, to be sure, a misinterpretation of Marx' doctrine of the ideological superstructure, which is neither 'technical' nor 'artificial' and certainly not 'dominant' over its foundation. And although Marx, indeed, studied Roman law at the University of Bonn, he never accepted the bourgeois theory of law and from the very beginning denounced the definition of the law as expression of the general will as an illusive

[9] *Loc. cit.*, p. 31. In an article 'Notes on the Class Theory of Law' (*Sovetskoye Pravo* [*Soviet Law*], 1922, No. 3, p. 10, quoted in Vyshinsky, *The Law of the Soviet State*, New York, 1948, p. 15), Stuchka refers to the above-quoted passage in Marx, *Zur Kritik der politischen Oekonomie*, where 'property relations' are characterised as 'legal expression of the existing relations of production'. Cf. *supra*, p. 7. Stuchka quite correctly interprets this passage to mean that legal relations are relations of production. Hence his definition of the law as an aggregate of economic relations may indeed be based on a view of Marx. Vyshinsky tries in vain to reject this interpretation of the statement in Marx, *Zur Kritik der politischen Oekonomie* by the assertion that Stuchka has used an incorrect translation or has himself translated it incorrectly from the German.

[10] *Soviet Legal Philosophy*, p. 27.

ideology.  Stuchka is right when he assumes that according
to Marx—or at least according to some of his statements—
the law belongs to the ideological superstructure, and not
to the substructure of social relationships.  But he is right, too,
when he asserts that his rejection of this view, and his definition
of the law as social relationships, are, likewise, in conformity
with Marx' view.  Here the ambiguity of Marx' doctrine of
ideology becomes quite manifest.  But Stuchka is certainly
wrong when he supposes—as he seems to do—that the definition
of the law as a normative order is incompatible with an economic
or materialistic interpretation of society.  As pointed out, the
concept of norm is not in itself an illusive ideology and may be
applied in a perfectly 'scientific' description of the law, even if
the term 'norm' has the connotation of 'justice'.  For, then,
to present the law as norm is an illusive ideology only if the law
is in truth not just; if the law is just—and the answer to this
question depends on the definition of justice—it is correctly
presented as something that ought to be.  An interpretation of
society which culminates in the prediction of communism as a
perfect state of mankind does not only not exclude the idea of
justice and hence the concept of norm in a moral sense of the
term, but essentially implies it.  Stuchka, it is true, rejects the
concept of justice.  He says :
> 'the eternal and indistinct concepts of truth and justice
> universal among mankind, held by the bourgeoisie, are
> perishing and purely class concepts are taking their place
> among us.  But when we speak of law and justice in the
> class sense, we have in mind the revolutionary watchwords
> of a purely class content . . . .'.[11]

Thus not only the bourgeois ideologists, also the communists
speak of 'law and justice'; but their law and justice are only
class-law and class-justice.  But what about a classless society,
the existence of which in the past Stuchka emphatically asserts
and the existence of which in the future he certainly does not
deny.  Of such a classless society he says only that 'there is no
law in such a society'[12]; he does not say that there is no justice,
and certainly not that there is no truth in a classless society.  And
if there is justice and truth in the communist society of the

[11] *Loc. cit.*, p. 27.
[12] *Loc. cit.*, p. 33.

future, it cannot be class-truth and class-justice for there will be no classes in this society. But the idea of truth as well as the idea of justice implies the concept of norm.

### The law by definition class law

It is evident that Stuchka's definition of the law as an aggregate of relationships of production and distribution is not complete. Otherwise, there would be law—as something identical with these relationships—not only in the capitalist but also in the communist society, in the communist society of the past as well as in the communist society of the future. But just this consequence Stuchka tries to avoid, and thinks that he must avoid it, in order not to be in conflict with the Marx-Engels doctrine of law. For he interprets this doctrine to mean that law can exist only in a society split into opposite classes. Hence he adds 'the class point of view'. That this point of view is not present in bourgeois jurisprudence, is his main objection against it. 'Only the class understanding of law introduces the essential definiteness without which jurisprudence is verbal technic and nothing more'.[13] The 'class point of view' is expressed in the statement that the law is an order, and that means a system of social relationships 'corresponding to the interests (or rather assuring the interests) of the dominant class'; 'wherever and in whatever form a division of mankind into classes and the dominance of one class over another are present, we find law or something analogous thereto'.[14] Stuchka quite correctly lays stress on the connection which exists between the concept of classes and that of revolutionary class struggle.[15] The class character of the law necessarily leads to coercion or constraint as an essential element of the law. The social relationships established in the interest of the dominant class are 'safeguarded by the organised force of that class', or, what amounts to the same, 'the domination of the class of oppressors over the oppressed' is safeguarded by 'organised authority'.[16] By this term Stuchka has in mind the state.[17]

As to the relationship between law and state, Stuchka does not go a step farther than his masters. 'However we look at the

[13] *Loc. cit.*, p. 24.
[14] *Loc. cit.*, p. 25.
[15] *Loc. cit.* p. 42 *et seq.*
[16] *Loc. cit.*, pp. 20, 52.
[17] *Loc. cit.*, p. 52.

part played by the state in the problem of law, the close bond between the concepts of law and state is beyond any doubt. Naturally the question of their mutual relationship arises. Which was first—law or the state? Which defines which? Does the law define the state or does the state define law?' [18] But Stuchka does not answer these questions. He has nothing else to say but that there is a close relationship between the two concepts. It seems that he accepts the view of bourgeois writers who see the relationship first of all in the fact that the state creates the law. For he says : ' In general and as a whole, the state is a monopolist acting the part of safeguarding the regulation of law '.[19]

Stuchka accepts Engels' description of the primitive society of the *gentes* as a classless communist community. He says :

> ' In this *gens*-union there is a certain plan of economy —although it be a weakly organised plan—and there is also a sort of division of labour : *but there is no law.* . . . In their mutual relationships, the kinsfolk are guided by *mores* (habits) and by customs. But these customs are essentially only the technical modes which are suggested by experience and instinct. . . . Our only knowledge of primordial man is specifically in such a closely-knit—and yet more or less broad—life together. There was no statute. There was no law. Yet there was an extremely stable and closely-knit society, whose sole regulation (if any) was by the laws of nature '.[20]

If the members of this society are ' guided ' by *mores* and customs, they consider their mutual behaviour as regulated by norms. These norms are perhaps not law as defined by Stuchka ; but he himself admits that they are ' law ' in another sense, that the ' regulation ' of the ' closely-knit society '—and it could be closely knit only by such regulation—' was by the laws of nature '. This is just the way in which many followers of the natural-law doctrine characterise the social order of primitive mankind.

### The law not necessarily exploiter law : the Soviet law

Although Stuchka emphasises the class viewpoint in his definition of the law and insists upon the essential connection

[18] *Loc. cit.*, p. 56.
[19] *Loc. cit.*, p. 65.
[20] *Loc. cit.*, p. 33.

between the concept of classes and the concept of revolutionary class struggle, although he characterises the relationship between the opposite classes as oppression—he speaks of 'the domination of the class of oppressors over the oppressed, of the haves over the have-nots' [21]—and thus refers to exploitation as an essential element of the oppression, the element of exploitation is not inserted into his concept of the law. For this definition must cover not only the capitalist but also the socialist law of the socialist state established by the October Revolution. Of this revolution Stuchka says :

> 'Applying its real force, it first of all overthrows the power of the bourgeois and the bourgeoisie's means of appropriation : annulling private property in the means of production (or, more accurately, in the means of another's production). But if even this work of destruction appears a protracted process, the process of reorganising the new production—and that in the conditions of the ruin caused by war—is then an extremely lengthy work. Before us is the period of a time of transition, in which we—taking into account the social material at hand—must consciously apply the laws of the development of capitalist society—laws which we have acquired or are still only in the process of acquiring—to the end of changing our social relationships. And this work must furnish a synthesis of primordial communism and all the subsequent development of private property in scientific communism'.[22]

'The laws of the development of capitalist society' can only mean 'the law' of the capitalist society as a normative order, not the causal laws of nature determining social evolution. These laws cannot be 'applied' because they work independently of man's will. Thus the law of the socialist state is still capitalist law. Stuchka continues :

> 'Naturally this epoch of transition is likewise an epoch of the dominance of a class—but that is the class of the heretofore enslaved majority. The transitional epoch, however, puts all relationships on their feet and makes them comprehensible and manifest to all. In place of the former artificial complication, the transitional epoch introduces a

[21] *Loc. cit.*, p. 52.
[22] *Loc. cit.*, p. 40.

natural simplification. But having its form of state, the soviet social order, the transition period possesses also its own characteristic social order as well as its soviet law'.

### Soviet law : a coercive but natural order, a capitalist and at the same time socialist law

As to the coercive character of this law, Stuchka does not allow any doubt. Referring to a statement of Engels, 'the great prophet', Stuchka declares that it is necessary for the 'coercive support of law' in the proletarian class state 'to employ terror'.[23] This in spite of the just-quoted assertion that the law of the transition period 'puts all relationships on their feet' and 'introduces a natural simplification'. This can only mean that this law regulates the social relationships in an adequate, *i.e.*, just, way, which corresponds to their nature and hence would make the employment of force superfluous. Besides, the idea of a law which corresponds to the nature of the relationships regulated by it is typical natural-law doctrine. As to the qualification of this law, Stuchka's doctrine is no less contradictory. The law applied by the proletarian class state, although still capitalist law, is nevertheless the socialist state's 'own characteristic social order', 'its soviet law'. It is socialist law but at the same time capitalist law. This contradiction is the inevitable consequence of a doctrine which maintains that law—as an essential element of the state—exists only in capitalist society, *i.e.*, a society where the means of production are in the hands of a small minority exploiting the vast majority, but which is forced to admit that law, together with the state, exists also in a socialist society where the means of production are nationalised, that is to say, concentrated in the hands of the whole people in order to abolish exploitation.

It is highly characteristic that this striking difference between the capitalist and the socialist law is not mentioned at all. It is another difference which Stuchka emphasises :

'The class of exploiters can never aspire to destroy or to exterminate the class which they exploit. In cases when it has not been true to this principle, it has itself perished together with the exploited class. From this flows the adaptability, the conciliatory attitude of the class of

[23] *Loc. cit.*, pp. 67–69.

oppressors, and its compliance (which sometimes it can itself hardly understand) as regards the class of the exploited. The entire development inevitably leads to the dictatorship of the proletariat—but the proletariat, as the oppressed class, cannot but desire to destroy the class of its oppressors'.[24]

That the proletariat, as the 'oppressed' class, can 'destroy the class of its oppressors', is a contradiction in terms. For in destroying the other class, the oppressed class is the oppressor class and the oppressor class the oppressed class. This is not merely inaccurate language which could easily be corrected by speaking of the *formerly* oppressed and the *formerly* oppressor class; this is the contradiction which is implied in the concept of the 'dictatorship of the proletariat', one of the fundamental concepts of the Marxian theory. A class has the character of proletariat only because and in so far as it is oppressed by another class for the purpose of its exploitation. As soon as it becomes an oppressor class, it ceases to be a proletariat. And a class has the character of a bourgeois class only because and in so far as it oppresses another class for the purpose of exploiting it. As soon as it becomes the oppressed class it ceases to be a bourgeoisie. But to admit this change means to admit that within the state called 'the dictatorship of the proletariat' there is neither a proletariat nor a bourgeoisie because there is no exploitation; and that means to admit that neither the state nor the law is a specific instrument of capitalist society.

## The scientific character of jurisprudence and the recognition of the class character of the law

Just as Lenin opposed his Marxian doctrine of the state as a true science to the pseudo-science of the state developed by bourgeois writers, Stuchka opposes his Marxian doctrine of the law as a true scientific doctrine to the bourgeois doctrine of the law, to which he denies any scientific character. Bourgeois jurisprudence, he says,

'is still revolving, even at the present time, around wretched formulæ and is itself actually dubious as to whether or not it is, in general, a science. We will answer frankly in the negative—hitherto it neither was nor could it be a science'.[25]

[24] *Loc. cit.*, p. 51.                    [25] *Loc. cit.*, p. 20.

The 'most fundamental merit' of his definition of the law is
'that for the first time it puts upon firm scientific ground
the problem of law in general : it renounces the purely
formal view of law [which is the view of bourgeois juris-
prudence] and sees in law a changing social phenomenon
rather than an eternal category [as does bourgeois juris-
prudence]. It renounces the attempt of bourgeois science
to reconcile the irreconcilable, while on the contrary it finds
a measure applicable to the most irreconcilable species of
law since it rests on the viewpoint of the class struggle and
class contradictions '.[26]
Bourgeois jurisprudence is 'hushing up and shading out the
class character of its [the law's] authority'.[27]  Bourgeois jurists
are 'dreaming of an eternal and immutable type of phenomena',
whereas Soviet jurists 'discern in a juristic institution only a
historically changing of social relationships'.[28]  This criticism
of bourgeois jurisprudence is contradictory in itself and is directed
against an imaginary opponent.  A legal theory cannot be
formalistic and at the same time define law as an eternal category.
That school of bourgeois jurisprudence which tries to describe
law as an eternal category, namely the natural-law doctrine, is
just the opposite of a formalistic jurisprudence and is consciously
directed against formalism in jurisprudence.  Besides, Stuchka,
who rejects the natural-law doctrine,—as shown above—comes
very close to it sometimes himself, whereas the majority of the
bourgeois writers at the time Stuchka published his Marxian
doctrine of the law were certainly not followers of the natural-
law doctrine and certainly did not consider the law as an eternal
category.  They insisted and still insist, in opposition to the
natural-law doctrine, upon the historical and changing character
of the law ; and the sociological school of jurisprudence—certainly a bourgeois school—lays stress on the essential relationships
which exist between law and economic circumstances.

If the bourgeois jurisprudence which is opposed to the
natural-law doctrine shows in its definition of the law more or
less a formalistic tendency, it is just because it tries to make the
concept of law 'applicable to the most irreconcilable species of

[26] *Loc. cit.*, p. 20.
[27] *Loc. cit.*, p. 68.
[28] *Loc. cit.*, p. 42.

law', which, according to Stuchka, is the most fundamental merit of his own definition, because, as he says, it establishes 'the concept of law of every sort in general and not of Soviet law alone'[29]—a merit which his definition can have only because it is 'formal' enough to cover two legal orders as different as capitalist and socialist law. No serious bourgeois writer who is not a follower of the natural-law doctrine excludes from his definition of the law a social order which is in the interest of a dominant class, and most of the bourgeois writers will certainly not deny that the existing law is more in the interest of one class than in the interest of the other. Even Stuchka admits in one of his above-quoted statements that the bourgeois law protects to a certain extent also the interests of the 'oppressed class'. It is just because bourgeois jurisprudence wants to attain the merit of having its concept of law 'applicable to the most irreconcilable species of law' that it does not put into the definition the element of class domination, so that not only a social order which protects solely the interests of one class against those of another, but also the social order of a classless society, that is, of a primitive society or a future society of perfect communism, can be conceived of as law. If the scientific character of a doctrine lies in its objectivity, that is to say, in its independence of the subjective value judgments of the scientist, then bourgeois jurisprudence is certainly more scientific than Soviet jurisprudence. For the former is willing to conceive a socialist and even a communist social order under the same concept as a capitalist social order, although the bourgeois writers may prefer capitalism to socialism and communism; whereas Soviet jurists refuse to conceive the communist social order under the same concept as a capitalist social order only and exclusively for the reason that they prefer communism and hate capitalism.

However, Stuchka, who boasts of having put the problem of law 'upon firm scientific ground', has a different idea of science. He says that jurisprudence

> 'can become a science only if it takes its stand upon the class point of view. It makes no difference whether it is upon the worker class point of view or upon that of the class hostile to the worker class: but it must be upon a class point of view'.[30]

[29] *Loc. cit.*, p. 20.          [30] *Loc. cit.*, p. 20.

That means that there are two class points of view, one 'hostile' to the other; and this is possible only if these viewpoints are the viewpoints of two opposite value systems. Marxian 'science' in general, and Marxian science of law in particular, is indeed characterised by the fact that it takes its stand upon the point of view of the worker class, hostile to the class of capitalists, for it is consciously and intentionally built up as an instrument in the fight of the worker class against the capitalist class. Does Stuchka really think that bourgeois jurisprudence is no science because it does not describe the law from the viewpoint of a person who prefers capitalism to communism, that is to say, from a point of view of the class hostile to the worker class? Is not just the contrary true, that he denies to bourgeois jurisprudence a scientific character because it stands upon a viewpoint of the class hostile to the worker class, because it is prejudiced by capitalist interests and hence is 'hushing up and shading out the class character of the law'? If so, then Soviet jurisprudence, too, is no science, for it certainly views the law from the standpoint of the worker class hostile to the class of capitalists and just for this reason stresses the class character of capitalist society. He says that bourgeois jurisprudence cannot be upon a class point of view

> 'for if jurisprudence introduced the revolutionary (class) viewpoint into the concept of law, jurisprudence would be "vindicating"—it would be legalising—the proletarian revolution as well'.[31]

Now, the phrase 'upon a class point of view' has changed its meaning. Now, it does not mean that jurisprudence in order to be a science must take its stand upon the viewpoint of the capitalist or of the worker class, that is, upon one or the other of two points of view hostile to each other, but only that jurisprudence must introduce the class viewpoint into the concept of law; that is to say, that only the definition of law as a coercive order imposed by one class upon another is scientific. This is not true, because such a definition covers only a particular type of law; and in this restricted sense it can be accepted by a science which itself does not at all take its stand upon the point of one of two hostile views. But Stuchka misrepresents bourgeois jurisprudence by stating that it does not accept the definition of the

[31] *Loc. cit.,* p. 20 *et seq.*

law as a coercive order imposed by one class upon another, and hence cannot claim to be a science because, otherwise, it would justify the proletarian revolution : bourgeois jurisprudence is not scientific because it refuses to justify the proletarian revolution. If bourgeois jurisprudence does not introduce the class element into the concept of law, that is to say, if it does not restrict— as Soviet jurisprudence does—the concept of law to a social order which corresponds only to the interests of the dominant class, it does so not because it ignores the class character of society. Marx himself admitted expressly that bourgeois science, long before him, has revealed the class character of capitalist society.[32] Bourgeois jurisprudence does not restrict the concept of law to a class law because it wants to comprise in its description of the phenomenon called law not only capitalist law but any possible kind of law, even the law of a communist society ; but because it wishes to understand and to explain not only the social order of a capitalist but of any other society, without justifying the one or the other. What the Soviet writers call 'bourgeois' science does not consider the vin- dication, legalisation, justification of any social phenomenon described by it as its legitimate function ; in contradistinction to Marxian 'science' it recognises the postulate of an objective science, and that means of a science independent of political value judgments. Of course, there are bourgeois writers who do not comply with this postulate and who attempt some kind of 'scientific' justification of the capitalist system. But there are also bourgeois writers who energetically reject any such attempt. However, there is no Soviet writer who would reject the vindica- tion of the proletarian revolution. It is this very vindication that constitutes the 'scientific' character of Soviet jurisprudence. It is by such a vindication that Stuchka thinks he has put the problem of law 'upon firm scientific ground'.

### The political tendencies of Stuchka's theory of law

The political tendencies of his legal theory manifest them- selves in many respects, for instance in the way the theory of Marx, the absolute authority of Soviet writers, is viewed : 'The theory of Marx was not a mere theory in a book : it was a living theory. Personified by the proletarian masses, it was knocking

[32] Cf. the passage in his letter to Weydemeyer, quoted *supra*, p. 27.

at the doors of the bourgeoisie'.[33]    That this theory is 'personified by the proletarian masses' is a bombastic phrase, the simple meaning of which is that this theory was developed for the benefit of the proletariat, that it is a proletarian, in contradistinction to a bourgeois theory; and that this theory 'was knocking at the doors of the bourgeoisie' means that it is used in the political fight of the proletariat against the bourgeoisie, that it is an instrument in the class struggle.    But it is just the argument that the bourgeois theory is such an instrument and not, as it pretends, a pure theory, that plays the decisive role in Stuchka's criticism of that theory.

Since the very function of the Soviet doctrine of law is not to describe and explain social and especially legal reality in an objective way, but to form this reality by destroying an existing social order and replacing it by another, considered to be better, it is not astonishing that this doctrine of law considers itself competent to prescribe certain actions, to determine the tasks of the proletarian class.    In his book, which he presents as a 'general doctrine of law', Stuchka writes:

'Our task, however, is to avoid the excrescences (which are artificial but essential in our society) since our strength must consist in sincerity and openness (and not in the hypocrisy and insincerity characteristic of bourgeois society). We have conquered the class of landowners and the big bourgeoisie; and our task is to admit neither the one nor the other to dominance in any new form whatsoever'.[34]

It is in the name of science, the Soviet science of law, that Stuchka proclaims this political programme.

[33] Stuchka, *loc. cit.*, p. 31.
[34] *Loc. cit.*, p. 41.

## CHAPTER 4

# REISNER'S THEORY OF LAW

## A normative interpretation of Marxian socialism

THE ambiguity of Marx' social theory in general and his theory of law in particular shows itself quite openly in the fact that on its basis M. A. Reisner [1] developed a doctrine very different from and even opposed to that of Stuchka, his contemporary. Reisner was very much impressed by Petrazhitskii's psychological approach to the problem of law and he tried to combine with it the principles of an economic interpretation of society. In opposition to the traditional jurisprudence of his time, Petrazhitskii understood by law certain normative ideas existing as psychological reality in the mind of men, not identical with the law of the state and sometimes even directed against it. These normative ideas—the so-called 'intuitive law'—are different according to the group within which they develop, so that there exists an 'intuitive law'

'of the separate family, of a little group, of a particular circle, of society, of a class, and the like. And to the extent that it embraces ever broader and broader circles intuitive law becomes *pro tanto* both powerful and dominant in a given milieu'.[2] 'It needs no force in order that it may exist . . . the norms of intuitive law . . . are an exalted standard and criterion for the appraisal of positive norms [which means the law of the state] and for disapproving them if their content is incongruous'.[3]

The intuitive laws of Petrazhitskii are evidently ideas of justice arising within definite groups; his theory is a kind of pluralistic natural-law doctrine. The Marxist Reisner was probably attracted by this doctrine because he, from the very beginning, accepted a normative interpretation of Marxian socialism. He, as many other Marxists, spoke immediately after the October

---

[1] M. A. Reisner, *The Theory of Petrazhitskii: Marxism and Social Ideology* (1908), *Soviet Legal Philosophy*, p. 71 *et seq.*; and *Law, Our Law, Foreign Law, General Law* (1925), *loc. cit.*, p. 83 *et seq.*
[2] *Soviet Legal Philosophy*, pp. 82, 84.
[3] *Loc. cit.*, p. 85.

Revolution of a 'revolutionary legal consciousness of the proletariat' and hence thought it possible to conceive of the justice required by or for the proletarian class as the intuitive law of this class. Long before the October Revolution, he wrote:

> 'When the production forces outgrow a particular means of production, and when the latter turns into a brake pressing upon them and fetters confining them, then intuitive law is born under the veil of the existing traditional law. Sometimes it grows for a long time in the unconscious stillness. Finally—as a real law existing and operative, defining the psyche of a given class—it collides with positive law (and in particular with official law) and on this basis of the struggle of two laws the tragedy of insurrection and suppression, of revolution and a turn backward, is played. Each class takes its stand under the banner of its own law: the oppressing class clings to the authority of traditional symbols, ideas and state practice; while the insurgent class relies on the demands of a "justice" whose foundation is in philosophy and morality and history, and not on considerations of historical necessity or on the laws of sociology'.[4]

In the work published in 1925, he says:

> 'I refashioned Petrazhitskii's doctrine concerning intuitive law in the sense that I put it upon a Marxist foundation, and thereby obtained not intuitive law in general (which could here and there furnish individual forms adapted to certain social conditions) but the most genuine class law which was worked out in the form of intuitive law (in the ranks of the oppressed and exploited mass) independently of any official framework whatsoever; and it is for this reason alone that we were able subsequently to utilise "the revolutionary legal consciousness of the proletariat" as the foundation of the activity of our revolutionary justice, which at the beginning was without any positive norms whatsoever'.[5]

As a consequence of the doctrine of intuitive law, Reisner had to reject the identification of law with capitalist or exploiter law, and hence the doctrine that there will be no law within

4 Quoted by himself, *loc. cit.*, p. 86.
5 *Loc. cit.*, p. 85 *et seq.*

the communist society of the future. In 1908 he wrote of the 'lawless ideal of those Marxists who acknowledge it, notwithstanding the true meaning and spirit of Marxist doctrine', that it 'entails extraordinary practical disadvantages'.

> 'The claims of the proletariat, asserted as the basis of new social conditions, are thus bereft of all the vigour of legal demands and sink to the position of economic and political importunities. They lose all the force of an ideal robed in legal vestments and all the authority of a categorical legal demand admitting of no objections. They are positively weakened by reason of the unsteady ideology of economic expediency, even though it be founded on the inevitability of the social process. . . . Only when the worker class shall be conscious of its fundamental demands in law, when the legal ideology shall become a part of the social ideal of that class and when law shall have been transferred as an organised element by that class into its future society freed from constraint of every sort—only then will the mighty struggle for economic freedom attain its culmination, and only then will the new law triumphantly take the place of the official constraint of the present time'.[6]

## The law not necessarily exploiter law

There can be no doubt that Reisner was right in maintaining that his normative interpretation of Marxian socialism was in conformity with the true meaning and spirit of this doctrine, hidden by its pretence to be a morally indifferent science. But in 1925, Reisner could maintain his original view only with certain reservations. He did not deny that he formerly 'protested with all his strength' against the identification of law with exploiter law, for—so he explained—he 'considered that the revolutionary masses have their own class intuitive law which must lie at the foundation of its future dominance'. But he added :

> 'In my eagerness to give a new revolutionary and organisational means into the hands of the proletariat it is possible that I went rather far in 1908 and, according to the law : action is equal to counteraction, exaggerated the significance of the legal element'.[7]

[6] *Loc. cit.*, p. 72 *et seq.*          [7] *Loc. cit.*, p. 89 *et seq.*

Defending himself against those who accused him of being guilty
of an idealistic, and that means bourgeois, theory of law, he
continues :

> '. . . the idealistic composition of the legal superstructure
> became clear to me at a pretty early time, and this compelled
> me then and there to examine all the dangerous aspects of
> being carried away overmuch by the legal principle . . .'.

In order to show that he applies in his theory of law the genuine
principles of an economic interpretation of society, he writes :

> '. . . history constantly binds together economy and law,
> whether it is a matter of the relationships between *gentes*
> or of the relationships between classes.  Where there is no
> economy, there is no law; and in the society of the *gentes*
> law is formed only in so far as the economic competition
> of separate *gentes* there gives us corresponding collisions
> between them.  That the basis of law in class society is
> economic is beyond any doubt; for each class here builds
> its law on the basis of its position in production and
> exchange, and the general legal order reflects in itself the
> features of that form of production which in its turn defines
> the class order.  We must make the same observation also
> with regard to the future communist society whereof the
> modern Soviet and socialist order is the precursor :  law is
> here built in conformity with its collective economy and with
> the part played by the proletariat in production.  The
> association between law and economy thus provides us with
> the first point of our definition :  law is the result of economic
> relationships—and in particular of production relationships.
> Every one knows that Marxist theory of law is sustained in
> this regard by a series of thinkers even from the camp of the
> bourgeoisie'.[8]

The view that the law is the result of—not identical with—
economic relationships is quite compatible with a specific science
of law different from a theory of economics, and with a definition
of law as a system of norms or a normative order.

> 'For some reason or other certain Marxists entertain a
> strange doubt as to one point alone, that is to say :  one
> must read as if law—being solely a category of class relation-
> ships—did not exist prior to the appearance of class society

[8] *Loc. cit.,* p. 97 *et seq.*

and was consequently unknown so long as the *gens* manner of life continued. This hypothesis merely reveals the fact that our Marxists are not sufficiently familiar with the genuine theory of Marx and Engels'.[8]

Thus, Reisner tries to demonstrate that the identification of law with the law of a capitalist society is not the necessary consequence of an economic interpretation of society, that from a strictly Marxian point of view the existence of law in a noncapitalist society, as the society of the *gentes* and even the future society of perfect communism, may be admitted. Reisner quotes certain passages in Marx' *Zur Kritik der politischen Oekonomie*, especially the statement that 'each form of production brings into being its own characteristic legal relationships', which indeed confirm Reisner's view concerning the existence of law in the future society of perfect communism; and he shows that Engels in his description of the primitive communism of the *gentes* society cannot help speaking of 'rights', which presupposes the existence of a law stipulating these rights.[9] This, of course, was in open contradiction to the interpretation of the Marx-Engels doctrine predominant at this time in the Soviet Union.

**Renewal of Marx' doctrine of the ideological character of the law**

With a view to meeting attacks against his doctrine, he proceeds to a counter-attack by accusing the Soviet jurists of having completely ignored or perverted one of the most important points of the Marxian theory of law : the ideological character of the law. With respect to the juridic literature following Stuchka's work he says : 'the fundamental teaching of Marxism concerning law—its teaching as to the ideological character of law—is, with negligible exceptions, either ignored or perverted'.[10] At the same time he denounces this literature as being ideological itself :

'The most typical feature of these pamphlets and booklets is a sharply expressed ideological character. The overwhelming mass of them is constructed upon the model of a commentary—sometimes an extremely risky commentary—on the detached propositions of law which are scattered about more or less at random in the productions of Marx

[9] *Loc. cit.*, p. 98 *et seq.* ; cf. *supra*, p. 38.
[10] *Loc. cit.*, p. 95.

6

and Engels, and not after the manner of a scientific
investigation. . . . The object of these works is, however,
at once made clear : the aspiration to invest the dictatorship
of the proletariat and the republic of the Soviets with the
decent garment of bourgeois-like law at whatever cost'.[11]

In this statement Reisner opposes the ideological character
of the juridic literature to a scientific investigation, that is to say,
he uses the term 'ideology' to characterise a certain kind of
thinking, a certain type of theory, namely, a perverted thinking,
an illusive theory, which invests a real object with a 'garment'
in order to hide its true nature. The real object is in this statement the Soviet state. But thereby a little incorrectness slips in.
The Soviet state cannot be ideologically invested with the garment
of a law because it really has a law ; and Reisner is the last to
deny it. If there is an ideological element in the legal theory
rejected by Reisner, it is the presentation of Soviet law as something 'decent' in spite of its bourgeois character. That the
Soviet law is bourgeois-like is a fact which Reisner himself
emphasises. He says 'the socialist legal order or Soviet law'
contains elements of bourgeois law.

> 'The influence of the bourgeois legal order may vary
> greatly, and the socialist legal order may take on certain
> features of the bourgeois legal order, as is shown by the
> example of Soviet Russia and this was predicted by Marx
> and Lenin'.[12]

It is evidently the law as a social reality, and not the law as a
mere ideology, to which Reisner here refers. But he says the
Soviet writers are ideologists because they invest the Soviet state
with the garment of a bourgeois-like law, instead of saying that
they are ideologists because they describe the Soviet law as a
decent garment ; for, if he would use the latter formula, he would
present the law as a social reality, and only a wrong theory of
this law as an ideology. But his main objection against the
writers on Soviet law was that they did not conceive of this law
as an ideology. In order to avoid—at least in his language—
this contradiction, he substituted for the Soviet law the Soviet
state, although according to the Marxian formula on which he
bases his thesis of the ideological character of the law, the formula

11 *Loc. cit.*, p. 94 *et seq.*
12 *Loc. cit.*, p. 97.

of the 'legal and political superstructure', the state is an ideology in the same sense as the law. The contradiction Reisner tried, in vain, to avoid is implied in the doctrine which is his theoretical foundation. It is the identification of a certain theory, interpretation or evaluation of a real object with this object, a theory of the state with the state, a theory of the law with the law. Reisner emphasises that the law must be defined 'as one of the ideological forms'.[13] But if we analyse the statement in which he specifies this definition we see that he refers not to the law itself but to a certain interpretation or evaluation of the law, to a doctrine which pretends that the law is just, because it is the realisation of the principle of equality. Thus, *e.g.*, he says :

> 'if, as early as 1912, I defined law as ideology which "rests, in our consciousness over and above all else on the concept of truth, justice and equality in the distribution and equalisation as between people and things", I had nevertheless noted the basic features of law with its loftier criterion of "justice"'.[14]

That means the law is an ideology in so far as it rests 'in our consciousness' on the concept of justice, *i.e.*, equality ; and that means that men in their consciousness interpret the law as a just order regulating human relationships according to the principle of equality. But in reality the law is not just, and not a regulation of human relationships according to the principle of equality. It is not an equal law. Thus, what is 'ideological', that is to say, 'illusive', is not the law but this interpretation or evaluation of it. Later, Reisner, in order to show how he considered the law as an ideology, speaks of the

> 'immeasurably elastic and ambiguous ideology which . . . appears to be in the condition of sanctifying by the principle of justice the most contradictory class interests—and with the aid of a perfectly "just" justice'.[15]

But the real law does nothing else but to stipulate that a thief shall be punished, that a civil execution shall be directed against the property of a man who does not pay his debt. These legal norms do not pretend to be just. It is a certain interpretation of these norms that uses the immeasurably elastic and ambiguous

[13] *Loc. cit.*, p. 102.
[14] *Loc. cit.*, p. 89.
[15] *Loc. cit.*, p. 90.

ideology of justice. Reisner quite characteristically says that 'the features of the ideological form are inherent in law equally as they are inherent in a whole series of other similar forms'.[16] But religion, *e.g., is* an ideology; ideology is not 'inherent' in religion. Only if a social reality, a real institution is called an ideology, the ideology or ideological form is inherent in it, because an ideological interpretation of it has been projected into it. As a reality a social institution, the state or the law, cannot be something illusive, pretending, distorting; only the reflection of this reality in man's mind could have such an 'ideological' character. Besides, Reisner does not always identify a social institution, as the law or the state, with its ideological reflection in man's consciousness. In his work published in 1908 he said with reference to the dictatorship of the proletariat:

'The proletariat conquers the state only for the purpose of depriving it of any possibility of further existence. Such, according to the teaching of Marxism, is the course of social revolution, ending with the victory of the proletariat and the organisation of a new means of production. Manifestly a prominent part in this entire process is assigned to the state, whilst at the same time every sort of ideology—and therefore political ideology, too—is rejected. In the latter case it is possible, of course, to differentiate two types of ideological structures: the concern may here be with the old ideology of the bourgeois state, or with the creation of a new ideology of proletarian, state dominance—the so-called dictatorship of temporary dominance of the proletarians. Obviously when we deny the old state we must at the same time renounce its ideology in its entirety. As to the new principles of the proletarian dictatorship, Marxism has here no desire to see in them ideologies but rather something which corresponds to the demands of a scientific theory of socialism'.[17]

Here, Reisner distinguishes between the state and its ideology as between two different things. And he evidently thinks that only the capitalist state has an ideology in the bad sense of the term, whereas the proletarian state's ideology will be a true science of the state. But even in this statement there is a certain ambiguity,

16 *Loc. cit.,* p. 103.
17 *Loc. cit.,* p. 80 *et seq.*

in so far as Reisner says that Marxism will not see 'in' the proletarian dictatorship 'ideologies'.

In order to confirm his statement concerning 'the ideological form inherent in law', Reisner says :

> 'When Marx and Engels enumerate these forms, they always mention law on the same level with morality, religion, and art, as well as with political and philosophical form. The question arises, however, as to what is the distinction between law and the remaining forms'.[18]

His answer to this question is that it is 'the indicium of " justice "'; this indicium is in its turn associated with concepts of equality and inequality . . .' But these 'concepts' are products of thinking and evaluating, and play their role as ideology in the theory of law, not in the law. Explaining the concept of ideology, Reisner says :

> 'the character of legal ideology—as an ideology reflecting reality through equality and inequality and a justice built on this foundation—changes nothing by reason of the fact that legal ideology is dependent upon an economic basis, but only demonstrates to us the direction of the distortion and the refraction of the legal reflection. This, in the language of the science of optics, is the same as studying the angles of reflection of this object or that in mirrors of different forms. Law from such a point of view is nothing but one of such mirrors in which, however, the reflection is accomplished, not by means of any curved line, but by the angle of a direct equality which equalises at one time and distributes at another and which in its turn provides us with a formula for this justice or that. Thus we speak of legal form as one of the modes of portrayal which plays a part in the social process in the same way as various other modes of portrayal are manifested therein and exert influence thereon'.[19]

At the basis of Reisner's doctrine of ideology—which in this respect is indeed identical with the doctrine of Marx—is the view that man's consciousness is a mirror reflecting a portrait of reality. To say, as Reisner does, that the law is a mirror—and he must say so in order to maintain his thesis that the law is an

[18] *Loc. cit.*, p. 103.
[19] *Loc. cit.*, p. 103 *et seq.*

ideology—is possible only if one identifies the consciousness, the thinking, interpreting, evaluating of man, with the object reflected in this thinking, interpreting, evaluating.

## No law or no ideological theory of law in the communist society of the future ?

The just-quoted rather obscure and bombastic passage is understandable only in connection with the statement Marx made about the future of law in his critique of the Gotha Programme.[20] Reisner interprets this statement as follows :

> 'Marx takes his stand wholly upon the point of view of comparing equality and inequality, on the one hand, and law on the other. From this point of view, law of every sort turns out to be the law of inequality, notwithstanding its pretension to be equal law'.[21]

The law is an 'ideology' because it 'pretends' to be an equal law, that is, justice, although in reality it is an unequal law, that is, injustice. Reisner quotes also the statement of Lenin according to which the bourgeois law is a violation of equality and therefore an 'injustice'.[22] It is, of course, not the bourgeois law but an ideological bourgeois theory of law which pretends that this law is just. Then, Reisner proceeds to the problem of the law in the future society of perfect communism.

> 'For the solution of the problem of law as an ideological form based on the equality of the unequal, enormous importance attaches to the organisation of communist society in its highest stage. With regard to this we have very frequently encountered the assumption that no law of any kind will any longer exist there'.[23]

The phrase 'law as an ideological form based on the equality of the unequal' has no other function than to obscure the fact that it is not the law which is based on the equality of the unequal, but that there is a theory of the law which presents it as a law of equality, although it is a law of inequality. The interpretation of Marx' theory according to which no law of any kind will exist in the communist society of the future, has been expressly and unambiguously rejected by Reisner in a pas-

[20] Cf. *supra*, p. 33.
[21] *Loc. cit.*, p. 106.
[22] Cf. *supra*, p. 60.
[23] *Loc. cit.*, p. 107.

sage quoted above.[24] Now, referring to Marx' statement concerning 'the narrow horizon of bourgeois law' which will be
completely overcome in the communist society of the future,
Reisner asks : 'Does this mean that when the narrow horizon
of bourgeois law is abandoned every sort of law will disappear
as well?' His answer is :

> 'This problem is not so simply decided, inasmuch as
> the excerpt taken from Marx contains a proposition which
> —pointing out the contrast between factual inequality and
> juridic equality—says that "in order to eliminate all these
> evils, law must be unequal, instead of being equal". From
> this it may be supposed that law can continue to exist in
> communist society in the form of a juridic ideology which,
> however, will inscribe on its banner the formula of the
> higher justice to be found only in communist society—that
> is to say, the law which says : "From each according to his
> capacities, to each according to his needs"'.[25]

This answer means : There will be a law in the communist
society of the future, 'the law which says : "From each according
to his capacities, to each according to his needs"'. It is, of
course, not the law which says so, it is a theory which describes
the essence, the fundamental principle in accordance to which
this law has been formed. And it is not the law which exists
as an ideology, but it is the theory of the law, and this theory is
an ideology not in the derogatory sense of the term, not an
illusive doctrine of the law. The theory characterising the law
in the second stage of communism as the realisation of the
principle of equality, is a true, scientific reflection thereof in the
consciousness of man. The statement that there will be law in
the communist society is in conformity with the above quoted
statement of Marx, that each form of production brings into
being its own characteristic legal relationships.[26]

However, Reisner does not maintain this view. He asks,
'Will such law'—the law which says : from each according to
his capacities, to each according to his needs—'be law?' And
his answer is, in open contradiction to his previous statements,
in the negative. And this negative answer he manufactures with

[24] Cf. *supra*, p. 79.
[25] *Loc. cit.*, p. 107 *et seq.*
[26] Cf. *supra*, p. 37.

the aid of his—or, better, of Marx'—ambiguous doctrine of
ideology.

> '. . . law and legal ideology are by no means a merely
> objective (we would say, a merely technical) formulation
> of existing production relationships.  Then it would cease
> to be an ideology and would become merely a scientific and
> technical expression of the given relationships without the
> slightest addition of any subjectivism, refraction, or per-
> version of any character whatsoever.  It must not be for-
> gotten that law is an "ideological form", and so always
> bears within itself the seed of a similar perversion and is
> capable (with the aid of the formal method of presentation)
> of being isolated from reckoning with reality.  For it is only
> an adequate theory which is capable of expressing reality
> with precision—this can by no means be achieved through
> formal thinking with its æsthetic deviations'.[27]

In these statements law is not identified with legal ideology.
Reisner speaks of law *and* legal ideology, and legal ideology is
conceived of as false theory; if it is correct, it is not an ideological, it is a scientific, expression of reality; and such scientific
expression cannot be achieved through 'formal thinking'—the
thinking of the bourgeois ideological theory of law.  Thus
Reisner arrives at the conclusion, 'Law, manifestly, will there
die out forever—side by side with a whole series of other forms
of ideological thinking'.[28]  But law is not a function of thinking
but of willing, is not a theory as a product of cognition, but a
social institution established by acts of will.  Law as a form
of thinking is a theory of the law; and if the law only as a form
of thinking, of ideological, perverted thinking, will die out for
ever, the law as a real institution, the truly just law, will—as
Reisner maintained before—exist.  But this legal reality will not
need an ideological theory.  Jurisprudence in communist society
will have the character of exact science.  But at the time Reisner
published his book it was already too dangerous to express this
idea in a clear unambiguous way.  For a statement to the effect
that in communist society only the ideological theory of the law,
not the law, will die out for ever was in open conflict with the
official interpretation of the Marx-Engels theory of law.

[27] *Loc. cit.*, p. 108.
[28] *Loc. cit.*, p. 108 *et seq.*

CHAPTER 5

# PASHUKANIS' THEORY OF LAW

**An anti-normative doctrine**

THE most prominent representative of Soviet legal theory during the first period of its development [1] is E. B. Pashukanis. In his main work, *The General Theory of Law and Marxism*,[2] he tries to develop a 100 per cent. Marxian doctrine of law in opposition to bourgeois legal theory, which he accuses of hiding the social reality in an 'ideological fog'. It is the normative theory of law, the one that defines the law as a system of norms and especially the so-called pure theory of law against which Pashukanis directs his criticism from the point of view of an orthodox Marxist, although it is just the pure theory of law which, long before Pashukanis, tried to purify the traditional science of law of its ideological elements. The paradoxical result of Pashukanis' attempt is that he takes over some really ideological elements of the bourgeois *theory* in order to disparage the bourgeois *law*, which he—as usual—confuses with an ideological theory of this law. And, finally, following strictly a line of Marx and Engels, he declares the bourgeois law, the law of the despised capitalist society, as the only possible law in the true sense of this term.

In order to inject into the theory of law the strongest possible dose of Marxism, Pashukanis imitates Marx' economic interpretation of political phenomena by reducing, in the field of jurisprudence, legal phenomena to economic phenomena in general, and in particular to economic phenomena which can exist only within a capitalist system of economy based on the

[1] According to Professor Hazard, *Soviet Legal Philosophy*, p. xix, some experts distinguish three, others only two periods in the development of Soviet legal philosophy. The three periods are defined either as '(1) The Early Period, (2) The Climax of Marxian Theory, and (3) The Retreat to Bourgeois Positions' or '(1) The Early Period (1918–1928), (2) The Middle Period (1929–1937), and (3) The Period of Cleansing and Establishment of a New Base (1938 to date)'. The two periods are characterised as follows: '(1) when law and socialism were still treated as incompatible, and (2) after the idea of incompatibility had been openly abandoned, namely in 1936–1937'. The author agrees in principle with the division into two periods.

[2] *Soviet Legal Philosophy*, p. 111 *et seq.* The first edition was published in 1924.

principle of private property in the means of production.  He rejects the definition of law as a system of norms as 'ideological' and tries to grasp the law as a piece of social reality.  He says:
> 'A norm as such—that is to say, the logical content of a norm—is either a direct inference from relationships already existing, or (if it is promulgated as a state statute) is nothing more than a symptom from which a judgment may, with a certain degree of probability, be formed as to the emergence of corresponding relationships in the immediate future.  Knowledge of the normative content of law does not, however, justify the assertion that law exists objectively—there must further be knowledge as to whether or not that normative content is put into actual practice—that is to say, in social relationships'.[3]

He refers to the fact that even the normative theory must admit that a system of norms is considered as valid only if it is by and large effective.  But this does not justify—as the pure theory of law has shown—identifying the validity of the norm with its effectiveness, the legal norms with the human relationships effectively regulated by these norms, the law with the human behaviour which is in conformity with the law.  But it is just this erroneous identification which is at the basis of Pashukanis' theory, according to which 'the cornerstone' of the law is not the 'norms as such', but 'the objective regulating forces operative in society'.[4]  Consequently he conceives of the law—as already Stuchka did—as a system of social relationships.

## The law : the social relationships of a goods-producing society

Pashukanis formulates the problem of a theory of law as follows : 'Can law as a social relationship be understood in the same sense as that in which Marx called capital a social relationship?'[5]  Since law is evidently not identical with society, but is only one social phenomenon beside many others, such as morals, religion, art, and so on, the question arises, which social relationships are legal relationships in contradistinction to those which are not; in other terms, what is the criterion by which we can distinguish the one from the others.  Pashukanis criticises

[3] *Loc. cit.*, p. 141 *et seq.*
[4] *Loc. cit.*, p. 143.
[5] *Loc. cit.*, p. 131.

Stuchka's definition of law as a system of social relationships (which answers to the interests of the dominant class) quite correctly by saying, Stuchka does not answer the question 'How do social relationships become juridic institutions? How is law converted into itself?'[6] Having rejected the only possible answer, that legal relationships are those which are determined or constituted by a specific normative order, Pashukanis must try to find a criterion immanent in the social relationships, not outside of them (as is a normative order). His answer is : legal relationships are 'the relationships of possessors of goods',[7] 'the social relationships of a goods-producing society'.[8] But only capitalist society is a goods-producing society :

> 'First and foremost, capitalist society is a society of goods-possessors. This means that in the process of production the social relationships of human beings here take material form in the products of labour and are related to each other as values. The term "goods" signifies an object in which the concrete multiformity of useful attributes becomes merely a simple material wrapper of the abstract attribute of value which is manifested as the capacity to be exchanged into other goods in a definite ratio'.[9]

He says :

> 'we find that the juridic relationship is generated by the material production relationships of human beings immediately at hand—from which it follows that an analysis of the legal relationship in its simplest form need not start from the concept of a norm as an external authoritative imperative. It is sufficient to take for a basis a juridic relationship "whose content has been provided by the economic relationship itself" (in the words of Marx) and to investigate the "legal" form of this juridic relationship as one of the particular cases'.[10]

Following a specific bourgeois theory, Pashukanis writes :

> 'Every sort of juridic relationship is a relationship

[6] *Loc. cit.*, p. 139.
[7] *Loc. cit.*, p. 138.
[8] *Loc. cit.*, p. 149. Rudolf Schlesinger, 'Philosophy of Soviet Law', *The American Journal of Comparative Law*, Vol. 1 (1952), p. 155, suggests we translate 'commodity' producing instead of 'goods' producing.
[9] *Soviet Legal Philosophy*, p. 162.
[10] *Loc. cit.*, p. 149.

between subjects.  A subject is the atom of the juridic
theory : the simplest element, incapable of being resolved
further '.[11]

But the subject is in reality nothing but the goods-possessor, the
object is the goods :

> ' The market association discloses the antithesis of subject
> and object in the special legal sense—the object is goods ;
> the subject is the goods-possessor who disposes of goods in
> acts of acquisition and alienation.  It is specifically in the
> barter arrangement that the subject is manifested for the
> first time in all the fullness of his definitions '.[12]

> ' The juridic subject is, therefore, the abstract goods-
> possessor elevated to the heavens.  His will—understood in
> the juridic sense—has its real basis in the wish to alienate
> as it acquires, and to acquire as it alienates.  In order for
> this wish to be realised, it is essential that the wishes of
> goods-producers go out to meet each other.  This relation-
> ship is expressed juridically as a contract or accord of
> independent wills, and contract is therefore one of the
> central concepts in the law.  In more grandiloquent phrase-
> ology, it becomes a constituent part of the idea of law '.[13]

> ' When a thing is functioning as an exchange value, it
> becomes an impersonal thing—a pure object of the law—
> and he who is disposing it becomes a subject—a pure juridic
> subject '.[14]

> ' Thus it is only the development of the market that in the
> first instance creates the possibility and the necessity of turn-
> ing man who is appropriating things by way of labour (or
> plunder) into a juridic owner '.[15]

It is evident that in the law of a capitalist society—which
Pashukanis takes as the law *par excellence*—not only the relationships of possessors of goods have the character of legal relationships as, *e.g.*, the relationship of husband and wife, or parents
and children, which may exist also in a communist society.  But
even if we accept this artificial narrowing of the concept of law
and assume that only the relationships of possessors of goods are

[11] *Loc. cit.*, p. 160.
[12] *Loc. cit.*, p. 166.
[13] *Loc. cit.*, p. 169 *et seq.*
[14] *Loc. cit.*, p. 171.
[15] *Loc. cit.*, p. 172.

legal relationships or, as Pashukanis formulates it, assume the 'form' of legal relationships 'reflect' the 'form of law', the question arises, what is this 'form of law'? It cannot be identical with the specific economic relationship which 'reflects' it. But to this question, which is the essential question of a theory of law different from a theory of economics, Pashukanis does not answer and cannot answer, for the economic interpretation of society forces him to identify the legal relationships with specific economic relationships. The fact that an individual actually possesses something does not mean that he is its legal owner. Pashukanis cannot ignore this completely. He says : 'Goods-possessors were, of course, owners before they "acknowledged" each other as such'. However, since as a jurist he has to admit the difference between actual possession and ownership, he adds, 'but they were owners in another organic and extra-juridic sense'.[16] 'Ownership' in an 'extra-juridic sense' is a contradiction in terms. Pashukanis must inevitably fall into this contradiction because he describes the legal relationship of ownership without recurring to the legal norms constituting this relationship.

**All the law private law**

In order to identify law with specific economic relationships, Pashukanis declares that only private law—as a relationship between isolated individuals, subjects of egoistic interest—is law in the true sense of the term. The so-called public law as a relationship between the state and private individuals cannot be law in the true sense because the state is a meta-legal phenomenon, inconceivable as a subject of law. 'The state', Pashukanis expressly says, 'neither requires—nor essentially admits of—legal interpretation. These are domains where the so-called *raison d'état*—that is to say, the principle of bare expediency—holds sway'.[17] In his 'quest of relationships which constitute the real foundation of that form' we call law, Pashukanis comes to the result 'that the relationships which are termed public-law relationships are not the foundation we seek'. He approves of the statement of the Marxian writer Gumplowicz that only private law is the province of jurisprudence and he states :

'It is in the concrete personality of the egoistic managing

16 *Loc. cit.,* p. 170.
17 *Loc. cit.,* p. 183.

subject—the property owner, the bearer of private interests
—that a juridic subject such as "persona" finds complete
and adequate embodiment. It is specifically in private
law that juridic thinking moves with the greatest freedom
and confidence and that its conceptions take on the most
complete and symmetrical form. . . . Human conduct can
be regulated by the most complex rules, but the juridic
element in such regulation begins where the isolation and
antithesis of interests begins. "A controversy is a basic
element of everything juridic", in the words of Gumplowicz'.[18]

It is certainly true that the existence of conflicting interests
is the *raison d'être* of the law. But it is no less true that where
there exist human interests there always exist also conflicts of
interests. Besides, in the field of so-called private law there are
not only conflicts between individual, *i.e.,* private, interests but
also conflicts between collective, *i.e.,* public, interests and
individual-private interests. If the state takes an enforcement
action against the property of a debtor who does not pay his
debt to the creditor, it is not only in order to protect the individual
interest of the latter, but also because there exists—in the background—a collective, *i.e.,* public, interest in protecting the
individual-private interests of all possible creditors. In the field
of so-called public law, the conflict between the collective-public
and the individual-private interest is in the foreground, whereas
in the field of so-called private law the conflict between
individual-private interests is in the foreground. Hence, the
fact that the law is a social order for the adjustment of conflicts
of interests is no sufficient reason for identifying law with private
law, and that means, for denying any legal character to that part
of the law which is usually called public law. Those who refuse
to consider so-called public law as true 'law' base this view not
on the impossible assumption that there are no conflicting interests
within the realm of public law, but on the assumption that the
state by its very nature is beyond and above the law, that is to
say, on the dogma of the sovereignty of the state. This dogma,
however, is scientifically untenable.

[18] *Loc. cit.*, pp. 136, 137.

### Pashukanis' view of public law an ideological doctrine of bourgeois jurists

The doctrine that only private law, not public law, is true law, because the state as a meta-legal fact cannot be conceived of as subjected to the law and hence not as a legal subject, is by no means a specifically Marxian doctrine. Many 'bourgeois' writers and especially German jurists of a highly conservative attitude have advocated this doctrine, at the basis of which is the dualism of private and public law, closely connected with the dualism of law and state, subjective law (right) and objective law. And these dualisms are a characteristic element of certain legal theories developed by bourgeois writers.

But other bourgeois writers, especially the representatives of the pure theory of law—which, according to Pashukanis and other Soviet legal scientists is the most pronounced 'bourgeois' theory of law—have shown that these dualisms and, in particular, the dualism of private and public law, have a purely ideological character and have no foundation in legal reality, that a scientifically correct description of the existing law—the bourgeois law, the law of the capitalist society—is possible only if it emancipates itself from these dualisms. It has been proved, especially by the normative, the pure theory of law, that the dualism of private and public law, implying the view that public law is no true law because the state as a meta-legal fact cannot be bound by the law, is the result of an inadmissible hypostatisation of the concept of state; that the state presented as an acting person is nothing but the personification of a legal order; that acts of state are acts of human beings determined in a specific way by that legal order; that imputing these acts to the state means nothing but referring them to the legal order, the unit of which is personified in the metaphor: that the state is acting through these individuals as its organs; that these acts as acts of state are determined as the obligations or rights of the acting individuals; that, consequently, the state as an acting person is subjected to the law just as any other subject of legal obligations or legal rights; and that, if the state had no legal obligations, there could be no rights of private individuals; that there is no legal relationship to which the state is not—directly or indirectly—a party, so that all the law is by its very nature public law, and the so-called private law only a part of it, provided that a distinction between private and public law is maintained at all. And it cannot be maintained as a distinction between norms which are and norms which are not law, or between norms of a higher degree and norms of a lower degree of law; but only as a technical difference between two kinds of norms which both are law in the true sense of this term; and that means that so-called public law is in the same sense and to the same degree law as is any norm usually called private law. It has been proved by the 'bourgeois' pure theory of law that the doctrine according to which only private, but not public, law is law in the true sense of the term is maintained for the political purpose of justifying acts of the government, if the government for political reasons does not apply the existing law which imposes certain obligations on it but creates new law freeing it from these obligations.

It has been shown, again by the pure theory of law, rejected by the Soviet writers, that from the point of view of an objective, and that means a scientific description of the law, the state as a social order is by its very nature not a meta-legal, but a legal, *the* legal fact *par excellence,* since it is a coercive order of human behaviour and as such a legal order, which by definition is nothing but a coercive order. But Pashukanis accepts the dualism of law and state because the prophets of his religion, Marx and Engels, took over this dualism from the bourgeois philosopher Hegel and the bourgeois jurists of their time, although the way they speak of the bourgeois state and the bourgeois law shows clearly that they speak of one and the same thing, calling it the one time state, the other time law. Only the fact that the state is a specific, namely a relatively centralised legal order explains the—otherwise ununderstandable—fact that according to the doctrine of Marx and Engels the state comes into existence and disappears together with its 'law'. By his statement that only the relationships of private, and not the relationships of public, law are legal relationships, Pashukanis does not describe either the law in general or the law of a capitalist society. He reproduces a wrong, because ideological, bourgeois doctrine of law.

### The ideological dualism of subjective and objective law

The anti-bourgeois because allegedly anti-ideological theory of Pashukanis does not only take over from a certain bourgeois doctrine the ideological dualism of private and public law, but also the no less ideological dualism of subjective and objective law, which in English language is expressed as the dualism of 'right' and 'law'. Pashukanis says that

'there are, strictly speaking, two species of law : subjective law and objective law (*jus agendi* and *norma agendi*). Moreover, the possibility of such cleavage is absolutely unanticipated in the definition itself ; and one is therefore driven either to deny one of the species (declaring it to be a fiction, a phantasm, or the like) or to establish a purely external association between the general concept of law and its two species. In the meantime, this dual nature of law—this dichotomy of law into norm and legal power—has a significance no less essential than the dichotomy of goods into value and consumer value '.[19]

Following the doctrine of some bourgeois writers, Pashukanis maintains that the right, the subjective law, has primacy over the obligation

'because in the last analysis it rests on material interest which exists independently of external—that is to say, the conscious—regulation of social life '.[20]

The right, he says, is not a possible reflection of an obligation; on the contrary.

'Obligation is not even an independent element of that content [the content of the legal form]. Obligation always comes out as a reflection or correlate of a corresponding right '.[21]

But it has been proved, specially by the normative, that is, the pure theory of law, that the dualism of subjective and objective law has a political-ideological tendency, similar to that of private and public law. It implies the view that the subjective law, the right, is logically and historically prior to the objective law, the legal order, and that it has precedence in relation to duty (obligation); that is to say, that first rights come into existence and then the state guarantees these rights by establishing an objective legal order, imposing the corresponding obligations. A scientific, that is, politically unbiased theory shows that just the contrary is true, that there can be no right without an obligation, although there may be obligations without correspond-

[19] *Loc. cit.*, p. 119.     [20] *Loc. cit.*, p. 152.     [21] *Loc. cit.*, p. 152.

7

ing rights; that right as well as obligation (duty) is nothing different from the legal order as the objective law, that both are only this law in its relation to definite individuals; that the only purpose of this dualistic interpretation of the law is to guarantee the existing rights, that is to say, to safeguard certain provisions of the existing law stipulating these rights, especially the property rights, against abolition by a change of the legal order and, in particular, to prevent expropriation without compensation in case of a reform of the existing law, by maintaining that such a reform would be contrary to the nature of the law. It has been shown, especially by the normative, that is, the pure theory of law, that the dualism of subjective and objective law, just as the dualism of law and state, inevitably leads to insurmountable contradictions. But, strange as it seems, it is just because of these contradictions that the Marxist Pashukanis accepts the dualistic doctrine of bourgeois jurisprudence. For, as a follower of Marx and of the bourgeois philosopher Hegel, he believes that these contradictions—which, in truth, are only in the incorrect ideological thinking of some bourgeois jurists—are inherent in legal reality, and to describe this reality as being by its very nature 'contradictory' is the true Marxist way to do it. Pashukanis writes : Law—and that means for him the law of the capitalist society—'exists only in antitheses—objective law as contrasted with subjective law, public law as contrasted with private law, and so forth'. He is glad to ascertain :

> 'Only bourgeois-capitalist society creates all the conditions essential to the attainment of complete definiteness by the juridic element in social relationships' [22];

which means that only capitalist society creates these contradictions or antitheses by which certain social relationships assume the character of legal relationships. But in truth these contradictions are not inherent in capitalist society or capitalist law; they are characteristic of a theory of law which under the cover of an objective science of law, that is to say, by pretending to describe and explain the existing law, tries to influence the formation of the law from the point of view of definite political interests.

## Criminal law as private law

That private law is a specific element of a capitalist economic

22 *Loc. cit.*, p. 119 *et seq.*

system, cannot be denied, and it is, again, a bourgeois theory, the normative or pure theory of law, which has demonstrated the connection which exists between a definite legal technique—as that of private and subjective law—and a definite economic system—as that of capitalism. But how is it possible to ignore the fact that within the legal order of capitalist society there exists not only private and subjective law but also law of a different technique, as administrative, constitutional, and especially criminal law? As far as constitutional and administrative law is concerned, Pashukanis refers to the 'bourgeois' writers who deny the legal character of these parts of the social order as typical public law. But what about criminal law, which even the most reactionary followers of the doctrine that public law is not true law do not dare to declare as non-law? Since Pashukanis cannot maintain that criminal law is not true law and since he maintains that true law is only private law, he must try to show that criminal law is private law.

According to his doctrine, the essence of private law—and hence of all law—is the antithesis of private interests which exists only in a society where the goods are possessed by private individuals. Legal relationships are market relationships, relationships constituted by the exchange of goods (commodity-exchange). In order to conceive of criminal law in this way, Pashukanis interprets the relationship between crime and punishment as exchange relationship. Just as the seller furnishes the merchandise and the buyer pays the prize, as the equivalent, the criminal furnishes the crime and the state pays with the punishment. The punishment is the equivalent of the crime; and the idea of an equivalent is at the basis of the principle of retribution, which, according to this theory, is the principle of criminal law. Pashukanis says:

> 'The idea of an equivalent—this first purely legal idea—has always the same form of goods as its source. Crime may be regarded as a special variety of turnover in which the exchange—that is to say, the contractual—relationship is established *ex post facto* : that is to say, after the wilful action of one of the parties. The ratio between the crime and the requital is nothing more than the same exchange ratio'.[23]

[23] *Loc. cit.*, p. 208.

To justify this absurd view, Pashukanis refers to Aristotle, who indeed interpreted the punishment as the adequate equalisation in exchange for the crime. On the basis of this authority—which, by the way, also justified slavery as a legal institution in complete conformity with the nature of man—Pashukanis states :

> 'Criminal law is thus integrated as a component part of the juridic superstructure in so far as it embodies one of the varieties of the basic form to which modern society is subordinate : the form of equivalent exchange with all the consequences deriving therefrom'.[24]

> 'The criminal law—in precisely the same manner as law in general—is a form of the intercourse of egoistic, isolated subjects bearing an autonomous private interest or being ideal property-owners'.[25]

If one objects that in criminal procedure it is not the injured person who seeks for an equivalent compensation of his violated private interest, but the public prosecutor, who, as organ of the state, defends a public interest, Pashukanis answers : the injured party

> 'does not disappear completely but continues to constitute the background of the criminal law action which is proceeding. The abstraction of the public interest which has been violated rests on the perfectly real figure of the injured party who takes part in the process—personally or through a representative—and gives to it living significance. Moreover, even if there is no specific person who has in fact suffered injury—even when it is only the statute which is "crying out"—this abstraction finds real embodiment in the person of the public accuser. This duality—wherein state authority itself comes out both in the character of a party (the prosecutor) and in that of judge—shows that the criminal proceeding as a legal form is indistinguishable from the figure of the injured party demanding " compensation" and is therefore indistinguishable from the more general form of agreement. The prosecutor, as befits a "party", seeks a "high price"—that is to say, stern punishment—and the accused begs for leniency—for a "discount"—and the court issues an order "in accordance with justice". Cast aside entirely this form of arrangement, and you rob the criminal process of its "juridic spirit"'.[26]

[24] *Loc. cit.*, p. 214.          [25] *Loc. cit.*, p. 224.          [26] *Loc. cit.*, p. 215.

## The ideology of retribution

This interpretation of criminal law, again, is not an objective scientific description of the legal reality which, in criminal as well as in civil law, shows nothing else but a coercive act, the sanction, as a reaction against a definite human behaviour considered as undesirable by the legal authority. That this reaction means retribution is an interpretation of this reality in accordance with a certain ideology. And this ideological interpretation is highly problematical. As a matter of fact, it was rejected even in antiquity when Protagoras taught that punishment is meaningless if it is justified as equivalent of the crime according to the principle of retribution; that the only reasonable justification of punishment is prevention by deterrence. When Aristotle, ignoring the doctrine of Protagoras, speaks of punishment as the equivalent of the crime, he only maintains the traditional justification of criminal law as an application of the principle of retribution. Pashukanis justifies the Aristotelian interpretation of criminal law by referring especially to the postulate that the degree of punishment shall correspond to the gravity of the crime, as if the crime were a substance of measurable quantity. He says :

'Punishment proportioned to fault represents in principle the same form as recompense measured by loss. First and foremost, it is characterised by numerical, mathematical expression for the "gravity" of the sentence : the number of days or months or the like during which freedom is lost, a money fine of this amount or that, the loss of such and such rights. Deprivation of freedom for a definite period indicated in advance in the sentence of the court is the specific form in which modern—that is to say, the bourgeois-capitalist—criminal law effectuates the principle of equivalent requital'.[27]

However, the idea of a certain proportion between crime and punishment ceases to be absurd as soon as the doctrine of retribution is replaced by that of prevention. It is not at all unreasonable to differentiate crimes according to the degree of harm they do to society, that is to say, to differentiate between crimes which are more harmful to society and hence should be prevented by more effective punishments, and crimes which are

[27] *Loc. cit.*, p. 218.

less harmful and hence may be punished by less effective penalties. And it is not unreasonable to assume that a punishment is the more effective the greater the evil is according to the feeling of the individual on whom it is to be inflicted as a punishment. Nobody can deny that nowadays the Aristotelian interpretation of criminal law as retribution is generally abandoned and the prevention theory generally accepted by the criminologists of capitalist society; and that, consequently, bourgeois criminologists seriously discuss the question whether the technique of punishment is the only possible or the best method to be applied for the purpose of preventing crimes.

### Criminal law and capitalist society

It may be that some crimes punishable according to the law of a capitalist society are specific of the capitalist system of economy. But this is certainly not true with respect to that crime against which this law reacts with the most severe punishment, namely, murder. For this crime is quite frequently caused by motives which have nothing to do with any economic system, as *e.g.,* the motive of sex or ambition. That in a communist society there will be no crimes, that is to say, no violations of the social order constituting that society, is a utopian view which has no basis in social experience. Anyway, there is not the slightest reason why a capitalist society should not abolish criminal law and use other methods, if such methods would prove more effective in preventing those crimes which, until now, this society has tried to prevent by punishing criminals. The ideology of retribution on which Pashukanis bases his grotesque interpretation of criminal law is no longer an obstacle to a radical reform, nay, to the complete replacement of criminal law by other institutions within the capitalist society. It is within this capitalist society, by scholars who from the Soviet point of view are bourgeois, that the most serious efforts have been made to find methods to be substituted for the technique of punishment, methods which they consider more humane and more effective than that of criminal law. That these methods have not yet been applied in capitalist society is by no means due to the fact that they are incompatible with capitalism, but only and exclusively to the fact that it has not yet been possible to elaborate the new social technique in a way which could be considered satisfactory from a scientific objective point of view. Only by misinterpreting the indisputable fact that within capitalist society, at the universities and scientific institutions of this society, supported by the governments of capitalist states, a movement for the reform and even for the abolishment of criminal law exists, can Pashukanis, referring to this movement, say that it

'cannot be conceived as if criminal law had been dominated at the beginning by false theories of requital and then the correct viewpoint of social protection had triumphed . . . the forms of bourgeois consciousness are not eliminated by a criticism of ideas alone'.[28]

His statement that the aims of the reform school can be attained only after 'the realisation of socialism' has no sufficient foundation. Besides, in the Soviet Union, which is proud to have smashed capitalism and firmly established socialism, the old technique of criminal law still prevails.

### Pashukanis' theory : a negation of the concept of law

Pashukanis' attempt, undertaken in the true spirit of Marxism, of an economic interpretation of legal phenomena does not result in a new definition but in a complete negation of the concept of law. If law is reduced to economy, the question arises why law should be identified with a specific kind of economy, namely with capitalist economy. If capitalist economy is capitalist law, why should a communist economy not be communist law? The answer—from the viewpoint of the Marx-Engels theory of state and law is that the capitalist economy, because of the exploitation of one class by another essentially connected with this method of production and distribution, can be maintained only by a coercive machinery, whereas a communist economy can be maintained without coercion. Then, law is this coercive machinery, the specific means for the maintenance of a specific economy, not this economy itself. In order to conform the legal theory to the Marx-Engels prophecy of a stateless and lawless society of perfect communism, the identification of law with capitalist economy was not necessary. This identification reduces the prophecy to the empty tautology that communism is not capitalism.

[28] *Loc. cit.*, p. 221.

**Legal rules and 'technical' rules**

Since Pashukanis defines legal relationships as relationships of capitalist production and distribution, he can subscribe unconditionally to the thesis that there will be no law in the communist society of the future. But this does not mean—according to his interpretation—that the social order of this society will have no coercive character at all. He admits that even within this society some kind of constraint will be exercised, but this constraint will have a merely technical, not a legal character. Following Engels' statement that in the communist society of the future government over persons will be replaced by the administration of things and the direction of processes of production, he makes a distinction between legal norms and technical rules. Legal regulation refers to conflicting interests; 'conversely, unity of purpose is a premise of technical regulation'. 'The treatment of a sick person', he explains,

> 'presupposes a series of rules, both for the patient himself and for the medical personnel; but inasmuch as these rules are established from the point of view of a single purpose—the restoration of the patient's health—they are of a technical character. In conjunction with their application, there may be a certain constraint as regards the patient. But so long as this constraint is regarded from the viewpoint of the same purpose (which is identical for the person exerting the constraint and for the person subjected thereto), it remains a measure which is technically expedient—and nothing more. Within these limits, the content of the rules is established by medical science and changes as that science progresses. There is nothing for the jurist to do here. His role begins where perforce we abandon this basis of unity of purpose and pass to an investigation from another viewpoint—the viewpoint of isolated subjects opposed to each other, each of whom is the bearer of his own private interest'.[29]

The assumption that there exists a 'unity of purpose' in any case whatever where constraint is exercised by one individual against another, is an obvious fiction. The very fact that one individual must be forced to comply with the will of another shows clearly that the purpose of the one, and that means his immediate purpose, is not the purpose of the other; and it is the immediate

[29] *Loc. cit.*, p. 137 *et seq.*

purpose which alone comes into consideration when 'unity' is in question. Otherwise, there would be 'unity' where there exists the greatest antagonisms. Both liberals and socialists agree with respect to the ultimate purpose of a social order : to achieve the greatest possible satisfaction of the economic needs of all. But the fact that the former try to achieve this result by free economy, and the latter by planned economy, that is to say, that they do not agree with respect to their immediate purpose, constitutes the most radical conflict of our time; and for this reason, too, a coercive order, the law—the 'jurist', as Pashukanis says—is necessary to enforce the one or the other of the two economic systems. If the relationship between the future communist society and an individual who does not comply with the social order constituting this society is supposed to be of the same kind as the relationship between a physician and his patient, and if it is assumed that there exists in this relationship a unity of purpose, then 'unity of purpose' can mean only that the communist society, when exercising restraint against a recalcitrant member, does so in the true interest of this member, although the member himself may not comprehend it and hence must be forced. An ideological school of bourgeois jurisprudence maintains just the same with respect to the punishment of a criminal by an organ of the capitalist state. It is the same fiction which Roman jurists used in order to maintain their doctrine that an individual can be bound only by his own will; a fiction that they formulated *coactus tamen volui*; the same fiction of which Rousseau took advantage when he, in order to maintain his doctrine that a man can be free even under the coercive order of the state, went so far as to say that a man may be forced to be free. It is one of the many fictions by which one tries to veil the undesirable fact that no human society is possible without coercion exercised by one man against the other. And if bourgeois writers pretend that the state is the expression of the unity of a collective will or a collective interest, they produce the same ideology as do the Marxists who assert that there will be a complete solidarity of interests within a communist society. To distinguish legal from technical regulations, that is to say, to oppose law to technique, is meaningless, because law, if not seen through the coloured glasses of a bourgeois or a proletarian, a capitalist or a socialist ideology, is by its very nature a technique, a specific social technique.

**The law of the Soviet state : bourgeois law doomed to wither away**

It follows from Pashukanis' identification of law with capitalist economy not only that there can be no law in the communist society of the future, but also that there can be no proletarian socialist law in the transition period of the proletarian dictatorship. Pashukanis expressly rejects the view that a Marxist theory of law should discover the general concepts of a 'proletarian law'. He says :

> 'In demanding for proletarian law its own new generalising concepts, this trend . . . proclaims that the form of law is deathless since it seeks to wrench that form out of the defined historical conditions which guaranteed it full flowering, and to declare it capable of constant renewal. The dying out of the categories—but not of any injunctions —of bourgeois law by no means signifies that they are replaced by new categories of proletarian law. . . . The dying out of the categories of bourgeois law will in these conditions signify the dying out of law in general : that is to say, the gradual disappearance of the juridic element in human relations'.[30]

To justify this view, Pashukanis refers to Marx' statement of the 'narrow horizon of bourgeois law' in the *Critique of the Gotha Programme.* He is convinced that he is in complete conformity with the Marx-Engels doctrine of state and law when he says :

> 'Accordingly, Marx conceived of the transition to expanded communism, not as a transition to new forms of law, but as the dying out of the juridic form in general—as liberation from this heritage of the bourgeois epoch which was destined to outlive the bourgeoisie itself'.[31]

He declares further :

> 'It must, therefore, be borne in mind that morality, law, and state are forms of bourgeois society. The fact that the proletariat may be compelled to use them by no means signifies that they can develop further in the direction of being filled with a socialist content. They have no capacity adequate to hold a socialist content and are bound to die out to the extent that it is brought into being. Nevertheless,

[30] *Loc. cit.,* p. 122.
[31] *Loc. cit.,* p. 123.

in the present transition period, the proletariat must necessarily utilise in its class interest these forms which have been
inherited from bourgeois society and thereby exhaust them
completely '.[32]

And still in his article 'The Soviet State and the Revolution in
Law' (published in 1930),[33] where he—forced by the changed
political situation—confesses to have made some mistakes in his
theory of law, he says with respect to the law in the transition
stage :

> 'How do you wish to build a final legal system when you
> start from social relationships which already comprise the
> necessity that law of every sort wither away? This is a task
> completely unthinkable. But if you reduce everything
> merely to the subjective will element—"to constraint"—
> then it is inconceivable why Marx and Engels spoke of the
> "bourgeois" form of law. It is specifically because we are
> starting from the objective relationships which the pro-
> letarian dictatorship is remaking every hour—it is speci-
> fically for this reason that we cannot be occupied with the
> creation of a system of proletarian law '.[34]

## Socialist Soviet law : law in a classless society

There can be no doubt that this was, if not the only correct
then at least a possible, interpretation of the vague statements of
Marx concerning the law in a society after the establishment of
the proletarian dictatorship. And there can be no doubt that—
at least according to Engels—there will be no state, and hence no
law identical to or in essential connection with the state, as soon
as by the nationalisation of the means of production capitalist
exploitation, and consequently the division of society into two
hostile classes, will be completely abolished. That the political
and economic development of the Soviet Union has reached this
stage, was ascertained in 1936 in the most solemn and authentic
way by its highest authority, Stalin himself, in his report on the
draft constitution. There he affirms that

> 'the complete victory of the socialist system in all spheres of
> national economy is now a fact. . . . It means that exploita-

---

[32] *Loc. cit.*, p. 201.
[33] *Loc. cit.*, p. 237 *et seq.*
[34] *Loc. cit.*, p. 278, yet in an article 'State and Law', published in 1936,
Pashukanis maintained the bourgeois character of the law of a socialist
society in the field of distribution. Cf. Schlesinger, *Soviet Legal Theory*,
p. 207.

tion of men by men has been abolished, eliminated, while the socialist ownership of the implements and means of production has been established as the unshakable founda- tion of our Soviet society. . . . Consequently, there is no longer a capitalist class which could exploit the working class. ˜Consequently, our working class . . . possesses them jointly with the whole people. And since it possesses them, and the capitalist class has been eliminated, all possibility of the working class being exploited is precluded . . . can our working class be called the proletariat? Clearly, it cannot. . . . The proletariat of the U.S.S.R. has been transformed into an entirely new class, into the working class of the U.S.S.R.'.[35]

This new 'class' is evidently no class at all, taken in the specific sense of this term as used by Marx and Engels. In this way Stalin, too, at the beginning of his literary activity, understood the concept of 'class'. In a series of articles published in 1905 and 1906, under the title 'Anarchism or Socialism', he defended the doctrine of the social-democratic party against attacks on the part of some writers belonging to a party of anarchists. In one of these articles, Stalin wrote:

'Future society will be a socialist society. This means, primarily, that there will be no classes in that society: there will be neither capitalists nor proletarians, and, con- sequently, there will be no exploitation. In that society there will be only workers engaged in a collective labour'.[36]

No classes, because no capitalists and no proletarians, no classes, because no exploitation. Hence the society of the Soviet Union is already a classless society in the sense of the Marx-Engels doctrine as interpreted by Stalin himself. Nevertheless, the Soviet state did not show the slightest symptom of withering away. On the contrary. In a new constitution it gave itself a solid legal basis. According to Article 4 of this Constitution

'The economic foundation of the U.S.S.R. is the socialist system of economy and the socialist ownership of the instruments and means of production, firmly established as a result of the liquidation of the capitalist system of economy, the abolition of private ownership of the instruments and

---

[35] Cf. my *Political Theory of Bolshevism,* p. 24.
[36] J. V. Stalin, *Works,* Vol. 1, London, 1953, p. 336.

means of production and the elimination of the exploitation of man by man'.

Hence, according to this Constitution there are no classes in the Soviet Union. In Article 1 the Constitution says : 'The Union of Soviet Socialist Republics is a socialist state of workers and peasants'. The 'workers and peasants' are not two hostile classes as the bourgeois class and the proletarian class, but form —as Article 6 of the Constitution expressly declares—'the whole people'. The Soviet state is according to its own constitution the legal organisation of its classless society. It is superfluous to say that this constitution—as any other constitution—does not anticipate any dissolution of the state it constitutes, that this constitution, as any other, claims to be valid for an unlimited period of time.

It stands to reason that an anarchistic theory such as the doctrine of Marx and Engels cannot apply to this state, or to any other state. In an address delivered in April, 1929,[37] Stalin rejected the anarchistic tendency in Bukharin's theory, his 'hostility in point of principle to every sort of state, accordingly to the state in the transition period as well', although this anarchistic tendency was in entire conformity with the spirit of the Marx-Engels doctrine.[38] In his Report to the Eighteenth

[37] 'The Right Deviation in the Communist Party of Bolsheviks', *Soviet Legal Philosophy*, p. 227 *et seq.*

[38] In the above-quoted 'Anarchism or Socialism', Stalin characterises the decisive difference between anarchism and Marxian socialism as follows : 'The cornerstone of anarchism is the individual, whose emancipation, according to its tenets, is the principal condition for the emancipation of the masses, the collective body. According to the tenets of anarchism, the emancipation of the masses is impossible until the individual is emancipated. Accordingly, its slogan is : Everything for the individual. The cornerstone of Marxism, however, is the masses, whose emancipation, according to its tenets, is the principal condition for the emancipation of the individual. That is to say, according to the tenets of Marxism, the emancipation of the individual is impossible until the masses are emancipated. Accordingly, its slogan is : Everything for the masses ' (p. 299).

In this way Stalin expresses the idea that anarchism has an individualistic, whereas Marxian socialism a collectivistic character. But this is not quite correct, for both are driving at the liberation of the masses as well as at the liberation of the individual. It is the moral idea of the freedom of the individual which is at the basis of both anarchism and Marxian socialism. Other differences are, according to Stalin, that the writers who called themselves anarchists and against whom he wrote these articles, refused the dialectical method which Marx took over from Hegel and the materialism which he borrowed from Feuerbach. None of these differences has anything to do with the decisive question : the relationship to the state, the doctrine that the state is an evil, the ideal of a stateless society, which is the essential element of anarchism and which anarchism has in common with Marxian socialism.

Party Congress,[39] where he again proclaimed 'the complete triumph of the socialist system of economy', the 'annihilation of exploitation', Stalin declared that in spite of these achievements the Soviet state will not and cannot wither away.  He went even so far as to predict :

> ' Will the state be preserved among us likewise during the
> period of communism as well?  The answer is "yes" :  it
> will be preserved unless capitalist encirclement shall have
> been liquidated and the danger of military attacks from
> without eliminated . . .'.[40]

This is indeed a radical change of the doctrine as developed by Marx and Engels, who evidently did not foresee, or did not take into consideration, the situation that would exist in case socialism should be realised only in one single state surrounded by hostile capitalist states.  They imagined the transition from the dictatorship of the proletariat to the stage of perfect communism as a relatively short period and consequently dealt with the state as a dying institution.  Since they considered the state as a specific instrument of capitalism, their hostility to capitalism was necessarily a hostility to the state as such, to every kind of state, their anti-capitalist attitude necessarily being anarchism.  But as soon as it became evident that the state was not only a coercive machinery securing a capitalist system of economy, but proved to be the necessary instrument for defending a socialist system of economy, the anarchistic tendencies of the Marxian doctrine could no longer be maintained.  Consequently, the Soviet writers who in good faith had followed that now undesirable direction were ostracised.  This was the fate of Pashukanis, whose legal theory is only the consistent application of the Marx-Engels doctrine of anarchism to the problem of law.

What Stalin said about the Soviet state is true also with respect to the Soviet law ; for the state cannot be separated from the law.  When the state and hence the law is recognised as an essential institution, then there is no political reason for denying its normative character.  It was for the political reason of developing an anti-capitalist theory of law, that the Soviet writers, at the time when the Soviet state was mainly concerned with fighting and destroying capitalism within its own society,

---

[39] *Soviet Legal Philosophy*, p. 343 *et seq.*
[40] *Loc. cit.*, p. 349.

thought it necessary to deny that the law, which they disparaged as a capitalist ideology, is a system of binding norms. But after the socialist system of economy was established and the Soviet state stabilised as its powerful guarantor, the Soviet government, again for political reasons, became vitally interested in a legal theory recognising the authority of the Soviet state, and that means the normative character, the binding force of its law as a specifically socialist legal order and not as a mere relic of bourgeois law.[41]

---

[41] Schlesinger, *loc. cit.*, p. 164 *et seq.*, writes : ' It is not difficult to understand why the Soviet dropped a theory which could only be interpreted as an apology either for capitalism or for lawlessness, in the sense of anarchy or arbitrary rule. Its temporary success can only be explained by the deep-felt dissatisfaction with the capitalist features of the N.E.P., together with the impression which the apparent revival of capitalism made on many Soviet intellectuals. Both trends worked together in furthering the acceptance of a theory open to very ambiguous interpretations, according to whether the necessarily capitalist character of any law, or the desire for its quick " withering away ", was stressed. With the downfall of the N.E.P., the latter interpretation seemed to approach its heyday '.

## CHAPTER 6

# THE REJECTION OF PASHUKANIS' THEORY

## Return to the normative theory of law

THE opposition against Pashukanis' theory of law was started by an article of P. Yudin, 'Socialism and Law',[1] pretending to present the correct, that is, the true Marxian theory of law. The only interesting contribution of this article is the definition of the law :

> 'Law is a system of norms established by the state to safeguard the existing order of social organisation. It is the actively reflected will of the dominant class, sanctifying and perpetuating the economic and political interests of that class'.[2]

This definition stands in direct opposition to the theory of Pashukanis that law is not a system of norms but an aggregate of specific relationships. There is nothing of capitalism or exploitation in Yudin's definition, so that it can be applied not only to the capitalist law but also to a coercive order the purpose of which is not to maintain capitalist exploitation (of one class by another), but just the contrary : to abolish it and to maintain a socialist economy. The definition, it is true, still contains the class element, although Yudin expressly admits that in the Soviet Union 'socialism is carried into effect' and 'under socialism there is no longer any exploitation'.[3]

The class terminology in Yudin's definition of the law is evidently preserved only to maintain the Marxian phraseology. The decisive point of this new theory of law, its main purpose is to recognise the coercive order established by the Soviet government during the so-called transition period—in opposition to the theory of Pashukanis—as true law, as Soviet law or socialist law, and the community constituted by it as a true state, as the Soviet state, to 'be rid once and for all of the hostile theories which strive to show that the state must necessarily wither away at the

[1] *Soviet Legal Philosophy*, p. 281 *et seq.*
[2] *Loc. cit.*, p. 284.
[3] *Loc. cit.*, p. 297.

present stage'.[4] These 'hostile theories' are stigmatised as 'counter-revolutionary'. The true 'revolutionary' doctrine according to Yudin is : 'The state—an instrumentality in the hands of the dominant class—creates its law, safeguarding and protecting specifically the interests of that class'.[5] The most characteristic feature of this doctrine is that exploitation is replaced by 'dominance'. That the state is—as Engels taught— an instrument in the hands of the capitalist class, used for the maintenance of the exploitation of the proletarian class, and that the state, and with the state its law, will wither away as soon as this exploitation is abolished by the nationalisation of the means of production, is no longer true. The true doctrine is now that by the abolition of exploitation by one class of another, and that means by the abolition of the capitalist state and the capitalist law, a new, a Soviet-socialist state and a Soviet-socialist law have been established, to which the doctrine of withering away does not apply.

## Soviet law : socialist public law

The spirit of this new theory of law manifests itself most clearly in the fact that the Soviet law is declared to be by its very nature 'public law', in open opposition to the doctrine of Pashukanis according to which the so-called public law is no law at all.

> 'The dictatorship of the proletariat is a state of a new type, and the law created by that state is law of a new type : Soviet, democratic law which protects the interests of each and every one of the majority of the people : the toilers. The crown was set upon this magnificent revolutionary work in the creating of an exact and strict structure of public law by the declaration and compact concerning the formation of the U.S.S.R. adopted on December 30, 1922, at the First Congress of Soviets of the U.S.S.R.'.[6]

Yudin refers to the statement of Lenin : 'We recognise nothing "private"—for us *everything* in the field of economy bears the character of *public-law* and not of private law . . .'[7]; he says further :

[4] *Loc. cit.*, p. 295 *et seq.*
[5] *Loc. cit.*, p. 286.
[6] *Loc. cit.*, p. 290 *et seq.*
[7] In a letter to Kurskii (1922), *loc. cit.*, p. 292.

8

'Only an implacable foe of socialism or a hopeless idiot
would actually fail to understand that soviet socialist law
—new in content as in the problems posed for its solution—
began to be created from the very first days of the existence
of soviet authority'.[8]

Since stress is laid on the legal character of the social order established by the Soviet government and especially on 'Soviet
authority', Yudin must reject the view of Pashukanis that the
law during the transition period is a relic of bourgeois law. He
says :

'An infinite amount of nonsense in the problem of the
form of soviet law has been talked by pseudo-specialists in
law. Their very understanding of the form of law has
nothing in common with the scientific Marxist understanding of the relationship between form and substance. Until
recently a single opinion prevailed throughout the so-called
legal front : ours is a soviet law, but in form it is bourgeois
law. . . . This reasoning has led people to think of what
is mere legal terminology—of something referable to the
external form—as the form of law, although it is not the
genuine content of law. Individual " jurists "—wresting the
form away from the content, lost in juridic terminology,
manipulating merely empty abstractions, juggled thus and
so, carrying on polemics with each other and setting in
motion concepts devoid of content—were confused to such
a degree that they were unable to distinguish where the
right side was and where the left. Thereby, they made it
easier for the foes of the socialist fatherland to perpetrate
their abominable work'.[9]

### The Soviet state : a fatherland

The new legal theory takes over from the bourgeois science
of law not only the view that the law—socialist law like capitalist
law—is a system of norms, but also one of the most characteristic
ideologies of that theory : the glorification of the state as 'fatherland'[10]; and this in conformity with the Soviet Constitution of

---

[8] *Loc. cit.*, p. 291.
[9] *Loc. cit.*, p. 293.
[10] Vladimir Gsovski, in an article 'The Soviet Concept of Law' published
in 1938 (*Fordham Law Review*, Vol. 7), wrote : 'In summarising the
evolution of soviet legal thought, it may be stated that the concepts of

1936, which in Article 133 declares defending the country as a
'sacred' duty, and 'treason to the fatherland' as 'punishable
with all the severity of the law as the most heinous of all crimes'.
Nothing is more significant of the legal theory than the statement
of Yudin that not only the writings of Lenin and the works of
Stalin but also 'the U.S.S.R. Constitution and the Election Law
are the very greatest documents. They furnish correct decisions
of the problem of the nature of the Soviet state and law'.[11]  The
scientific question of the nature of state and law is decided by the
Constitution of the Soviet Union, that is to say, the theory of
state and law laid down in the constitution is binding upon the
writers on state and law.

traditional jurisprudence which form the technique of legal reasoning are
at this time reinstated in the soviet doctrine of law. Marxism, offered
as a comprehensive single concept of life, a *Weltanschauung,* implying
its own answer in any field of social sciences, has proved to be futile for
jurisprudence. No longer desiring to create their own set of technical
legal devices, soviet jurists are content to accept the traditional' (p. 42).
[11] *Soviet Legal Philosophy,* p. 285.

## CHAPTER 7

# VYSHINSKY'S THEORY OF LAW

**Condemnation of the previous Soviet doctrine of law as an inadequate instrument of the proletariat in its struggle for socialism**

THE leading jurist in the second period is A. Y. Vyshinsky, who, in an address delivered at the First Congress on Problems of the Sciences of Soviet State and Law (Moscow, 1938),[1] outlined 'the fundamental tasks of the science of Soviet socialist law'. One of the most characteristic features of his theory of law is that it is openly and expressly presented as an effective instrument of the policy of the Soviet government, directed at the abolition of capitalism and the realisation of socialism. The essential point of his violent criticism of other legal theories developed by Soviet writers during the first period, especially by Pashukanis—and this criticism presents the greatest part of his address—is the assertion that these theories are not such an instrument but that they can be used by the enemies of the Soviet government and of socialism, that their authors, therefore, are enemies of the Soviet people, traitors, provocateurs, and the like. Vyshinsky says with reference to these theories that

> 'over a period sufficiently (and unfortunately) long, the trend of our science of law has not been in accord with the interests of the cause of socialist building. . . . Over a series of years a position almost of monopoly in legal science has been occupied by a group of persons who have turned out to be provocateurs and traitors—people who knew how actually to contrive the work of betraying our science, our state, and our fatherland under the mask of defending Marxism-Leninism and championing orthodox Marxism and the Marx-Lenin methodology'.

> 'These persons directed their energies to holding back the development of our juridic thought and to perverting the essence of our Marx-Lenin doctrine concerning law and state. These persons strove to dash from the hands of the

---

[1] *Loc. cit.*, p. 303 *et seq.*

proletariat and the toilers of our land the Marx-Lenin doctrine of law and state which proved to be so potent an
instrument in the struggle with the many bestial foes of
socialism '.[2]

'. . . the legal-science front still continues to lag behind
the demands of our epoch—behind the demands of the
party and of the government'.[3]

According to Vyshinsky, who strictly follows the line laid down
by Stalin, social science can be only Marxism.  Socialism, he
says, owes its triumph in the Soviet Union not only to the
'heroism of workers and peasants' but also to the fact that the
communist party 'which headed the worker movement as long
ago as the end of the nineteenth century'

'did so under the banner of Marxism—under the banner of
a genuinely scientific trend (the greatest and the only such
trend in the world)—under the banner of genuine science :
Marxism'.[4]

A political movement is presented as a scientific trend.  Marxism,
which is in the first place the political postulate to realise
socialism, is at the same time science, the only genuine science
that exists.  That means that Marxism is science not only in so
far as it finds out the means by which socialism, as an end, can
be realised—which may be considered as a scientific task,
although hardly as the specific task of legal science—it means
that Marxism is science also, and in the first place, in so far as it is
directed at socialism, the aim of the worker movement, as it proclaims socialism as the end which ought to be achieved by this
movement.  This, however, is not a scientific but a political function.  Quoting Stalin, Vyshinsky says : 'Marxism is the scientific
expression of the deep-rooted and inherent interests of the worker
class'.[5]  The interest of the worker class is socialism just as the
interest of the bourgeois class is capitalism.  If the movement
toward the realisation or maintenance of capitalism is, according
to Vyshinsky, not 'scientific', then the worker movement toward
socialism, the essential concern of Marxism, is not scientific
either.  Vyshinsky states that Marx and Engels—

[2] *Loc. cit.*, pp. 303, 304.
[3] *Loc. cit.*, p. 313.
[4] *Loc. cit.*, p. 305.
[5] *Loc. cit.*, p. 306.

'gave into the hands of the proletariat—struggling for its
liberation—an instrument theretofore unknown : a scientific theory.  Armed with this theory, the proletariat
acquired powers to conquer the old world and to build a
new world—a new socialist society'.[6]

But the bourgeoisie, too, conquered an old world, the world of
feudalism, and established a new, the capitalist society ; and this
society still prevails to at least the same extent as the socialist
society.  Science certainly played an important part in the victory
of the bourgeoisie over feudalism and still plays an important
part in the defence of capitalism against socialism.  But nobody
pretends that the political system of capitalism is a 'science'.
For science, as a search for means appropriate for a presupposed
end, may serve very different ends, and if it serves the realisation
of socialism it is as little 'socialist' as it is 'capitalist' if it serves
the realisation or maintenance of capitalism.  If a political
system such as socialism is presented as a science, and even as
the only genuine science, this 'science' is the typical example of
an ideology in the worst sense of this term as used by Marx.

### The 'correct and scientific' Soviet theory of law : a natural-law doctrine

If science is socialism, then it is only consistent to expect a
Soviet science of law to produce the norms of a socialist legal
order.  Stalin said that science 'knows how to create new
traditions, new norms, new purposes'.[7]  Hence Vyshinsky says :
    'A theory of law is a system of legal principles on the
    basis whereof the entire science of law—and all the branches
    of that science (irrespective of their definitive content) are
    built.  Clearly the working out of these principles cannot
    have its inception in the norms of positive law : on the con-
    trary, the norms of positive law—like all positive law as a
    whole—must be built in conformity with the principles
    established by a legal theory'.[8]

The 'theory of law' Vyshinsky has in mind is evidently not a
theory of positive law.  It is a theory which has to produce
'legal principles'.  But these legal principles are not the positive

---

[6] *Loc. cit.*, p. 307.
[7] *Bolshevik*, 1938, Nos. 10–11, p. 2, quoted by Vyshinsky, *loc. cit.*, p. 318.
[8] *Soviet Legal Philosophy*, p. 323 *et seq.*

law which is to be established on the basis of these principles. If they are to be 'legal' principles, they are legal not in the sense of positive law but in the sense of norms of an ideal law, the law that ought to be established in a socialist society. It stands to reason that these principles are the ideal norms of a socialist law. For, according to Vyshinsky, the 'legal theory' which is that 'system of legal principles' on the basis of which the positive law of the socialist state is to be established 'rests on the principles of socialism—on the principles of the socialist revolution and of the socialist state and social order'.[9] The normative principles, the ideal norms of a socialist law, cannot be deduced by the theory of law from the positive law. 'The attempt to construct a theory of law—a general theory of law so-called—through the logical adaptation of the norms of positive law' is a characteristic of bourgeois legal science.

'We encounter it in all the trends of bourgeois legal science employing the dogmatic-juridic method. All bourgeois science is occupied exclusively with the effort to construct a theory of law through a logical adaptation of the norms of positive law and making the theory piquant by seasoning it with every sort of postulate—such as the postulate of an absolute spirit, and so forth. Treatment of this sort, however, could not—and did not—afford a knowledge of law which was actually correct and scientific. To go along this beaten path of bourgeois science . . . is perfectly hopeless. To try to construct a theory of law on the basis of juridic method . . . is out of the question. The construction of a Marxist theory of law and state is impossible while holding to these propositions and asserting that the method of juridic thinking—with its specific modes of thinking—remains in force; it signifies nothing but the perpetuation of the juridic method which was the basic cause of the sterility and impotence of bourgeois legal science'.[10]

Because the task of a genuine theory of law, and that means the Soviet theory of law, is to produce a knowledge of law which is 'actually correct and scientific'—and that can only mean the knowledge of the right law—the method of this theory of law

9 *Loc. cit.,* p. 324.
10 *Loc. cit.,* p. 324.

must not be the 'juridic method', the 'method of juridic thinking'. But which could be the specific method of a 'legal' and that means 'juridic' theory if it were not a juridic method? Where can the theory of law find the normative principles on the basis of which the right socialist law can be established? Vyshinsky's answer is : in life.

'The principles of legal theory must be worked out from the beginning—and they can be worked out, not from law (even though it be positive law), but from life. From life, they take their beginning and in life lie all their sources. From life they imbibe all their life force : from the content of social relationships at whose basis lie the production relationships of the given society and from the special characteristics of the building of the given society and of the given state. A theory of law can therefore be built only upon the basis of the principles of the organisation of social relationships which are explained in the final analysis by production relationships. These last are the basis of all the social relationships in any society and in any epoch'.[11]

What is most amazing in this theory of the bolshevik Vyshinsky is that it is exactly of the same type as that bourgeois theory which the Soviet writers have derided and ridiculed more than any other theory : the natural-law doctrine, which, just as Vyshinsky, rejects a mere theory of positive law because of its 'sterility and impotence' and which, precisely in accordance with Vyshinsky's recipe, works out, or pretends to work out, principles of law 'from life,' that is, from nature in general and from the nature of society or, what amounts to the same, from the social relationships in particular; with the only difference that these principles are the ideal norms of capitalist law. If the representatives of the bourgeois natural-law doctrine work out from the social relationships of a capitalist society the ideal norms of capitalist law, their knowledge of law is as 'correct and scientific' as the knowledge of law of Soviet writers who from the social relationships of a socialist society work out the ideal norms of socialist law. But neither the one nor the other is 'correct and scientific'. For normative principles—whether socialist or capitalist—cannot be worked out from life as the actual social relationships. They can only be presupposed as

11 *Loc. cit.*, p. 324.

valid, and 'life', that is to say, the actual social relationships established in conformity with these principles may be justified by them. It is at such a justification that the bourgeois natural-law doctrine, just as the Soviet legal theory postulated by Vyshinsky, is directed. And it is because a mere theory of positive law does not furnish such a justification that it is rejected by the representatives of the bourgeois natural-law doctrine as well as by Vyshinsky, the representative of a Soviet natural-law doctrine.

Since Vyshinsky takes it for granted that a true 'science' of law can work out from life nothing else but the principles of socialist law, he comes to the conclusion :

> 'In posing the problem of the Marx-Lenin theory of law and state or, as it is called, the general theory of law and state—that is to say a theory of law and state which would provide a system of propositions based on principle and obligatory with reference to the direction and development of all legal science in its entirety and each of the specific juridic disciplines in particular—we have in view the principles which differentiate soviet law from bourgeois law. The soviet theory of law and state must afford a system of soviet socialist principles which explain and are a condition of the *socialist content* of soviet juridic disciplines and juridic institutes'.[12]

That means : a theory of law 'must' provide the principles of socialism as 'obligatory' for the development of *all* legal science, which can mean only as obligatory for all those who deal 'scientifically' with problems of law. This is quite consistent from the point of view of Marxism, which, denying the possibility of an objective, politically independent science, considers science as a mere ideological 'superstructure' and hence as an instrument of politics.

### The ideal of socialist legality

After having degraded the science of law to an instrument of Soviet policy, Vyshinsky warns this science against reducing law to policy. 'In reducing law to policy', certain Soviet writers 'have depersonalised law as the totality of statutes—undermining the stability and authoritativeness of the statutes,

---

[12] *Loc. cit.*, p. 324 *et seq.*

and suggesting the false idea that the application of the
statute is defined in the socialist state by political considera-
tions, and not by force and authority of the soviet statute.
Such an idea means bringing soviet legality and soviet law
into substantial discredit, since on this hypothesis they are
evoked to develop a "policy" and not to defend the rights
of citizens and must start from the demands of policy (and
not from the demands of the statute) in deciding any prob-
blems of court practice.   To prate of soviet law as a mere
form of policy is to intimate that in soviet statutes, in soviet
justice, and in the activity of soviet courts, the force of a
statute and the force of law are made to depend upon the
political demands of the state'.[13]

These are statements which might very well be made by a
bourgeois legal scientist, who describes the law without regarding
it as a means in the exercise of political power, but with the sole
intention of understanding it in its own authority, and hence tries
to separate the science of law from politics.   But, now, the Soviet
government—just like the government of any capitalist state—
wants to inculcate its citizens with the ideal of legality.   Consequently, Soviet legal scientists must not reduce law to politics.
The Soviet legal theory must lay the foundations of 'Soviet
legality' or 'legality in socialist society'.[14]   In order to distinguish themselves from bourgeois writers, the Soviet writers call
the legality the foundation of which they are supposed to erect
'revolutionary legality',[15] which, of course, is a contradiction in
terms.

### Soviet law as a socialist normative order will wither away only in the last phase of communism

In his fight against the legal theory of the first period as
developed by Stuchka and Pashukanis, Vyshinsky goes so far as
to reject even that part of their theories which was the result of
the most orthodox submission to Marxism, that is, the economic
interpretation of law, the reduction of law to economics.   He says
quite correctly that this is a 'distortion', the effect of which is to

---

13 *Loc. cit.*, p. 329.
14 *Loc. cit.*, p. 340.
15 For instance, Vyshinsky in his book *Revolutionary Legality on the Present
   Stage,* Moscow, 1933.   Cf. Schlesinger, *loc. cit.*, p. 200 *et seq.*

'destroy the specific character of law as the aggregate of the rules of conduct. . . . In reducing law to economics—as Stuchka did, when he asserted that law is coincident with production relationships—these gentlemen have toppled down into the morass of economic materialism'.[16]

Economic materialism, the very foundation of Marxism, a morass? It stands to reason that Vyshinsky also rejects Pashukanis' interpretation of Marx' statement about the law in a socialist society; he says:

'In asserting that law is nothing but a form of capitalist relationships, and that law can develop only in the conditions of capitalism (when law supposedly attains its highest development), the wreckers who have been busying themselves on our legal front were striving toward a single objective: to prove that law is not necessary to the soviet state—and that law is superfluous, as a survival of capitalism, in the conditions of socialism. In reducing soviet law to bourgeois law, and affirming that there is no ground for the further development of law under socialism, the wreckers aimed at liquidating soviet law and the science of soviet law. This is the basic significance of their activity as provocateurs and wreckers'.[17]

If a theory is wrong it must be anti-Marxist, and if it is anti-Marxist it is unscientific. In his work *The Law of the Soviet State*,[18] Vyshinsky writes:

'It is easy to unmask the anti-Marxian, pseudoscientific "theory" of the wreckers Pashukanis, Krylenko, and others who declared that Soviet law was simply assimilated and adapted bourgeois law. The viciousness and pseudoscience of such "theoretical" propositions lie in their perversion of the fundamental principles of the Marxist-Leninist theory of law'.

There can be not the slightest doubt that Pashukanis' interpretation of the Soviet law as an assimilated and adapted bourgeois law was in complete conformity with Marx' doctrine that the law in the transition period will still be '*mit einer buergerlichen Schranke behaftet*'; there can be not the slightest doubt that in

---

[16] *Loc. cit.*, p. 329.
[17] *Loc. cit.*, p. 328.
[18] A. Y. Vyshinsky, *The Law of the Soviet State*, pp. 57, 58.

view of the fact that in the Marx-Engels doctrine state and law
are inseparably connected with each other, the dogma of the
withering away of the state in the course of the transition period
could be applied also to the law. But since for political reasons
this view is no longer acceptable to the Soviet government,
Vyshinsky says :

> 'It is a crude perversion of Marx' doctrine of law for the
> Pashukanises, the Bermans, and others of their ilk to assert
> that the transition to developed communism was conceived
> by Marx not as a transition to new forms of law but as the
> withering away of juridical form in general—as emancipa-
> tion from this legacy of the bourgeois epoch which was
> destined to outlive the bourgeoisie itself. Such a proposition
> would be possible if—but only if—the transition from
> capitalism to communism were without a transitional
> period, which is unimaginable without descending to
> utopianism'.

Vyshinsky accuses Pashukanis of having 'perverted the Marxist
proposition that each historic epoch of class society has its own
corresponding law . . .'. This can only be a reference to the
above-quoted statement in Marx' *Einleitung zu einer Kritik der
politischen Oekonomie* 'that every form of production created
its own legal relations . . .'. Marx does not restrict the correlation of form of production and law to class society, as Vyshinsky
pretends—and must pretend—in order to avoid the otherwise
inevitable consequence which Reisner deduces from Marx' statement : that also the form of production in the communist society
of the future will create its own legal relations. For Vyshinsky
maintains the utopian idea of a lawless society of future communism. In conformity with Stalin's reinterpretation of the
Marx-Engels doctrine, he says : 'Law—like the state—will
wither away only in the highest phase of communism, with the
annihilation of the capitalist encirclement'.[19]

### The law as a normative order, not a mere ideology

Vyshinsky rejects not only the anti-normative and hence anti-
legalistic theories of Stuchka and Pashukanis but also the normative doctrine of Reisner as 'anti-Marxist'.

---

[19] *Loc. cit.,* p. 52.

'According to Reisner, law is a heap of ideological scraps of various classes. Starting from such an absolutely mistaken view of the nature and essence of law, he constructed his antiscientific, anti-Marxian statement of Soviet law as a law of compromise, as a law "of appeasement and reconciliation", going so far as to depict soviet law as the totality of proletarian law, peasant law, and—on the basis of "tolerance and compromise"—bourgeois law'.[20]

Since Vyshinsky, for political reasons, cannot accept the genuine Marxian doctrine that the law in the first period of communism has still the character of bourgeois law because it is still a law of inequality, he must declare this doctrine as anti-Marxist. It is evidently for the same political reasons that he rejects also the other, no less genuine Marxian doctrine, emphasised by Reisner, that the law is a mere ideology. That he rejects this doctrine follows from the contemptuous way in which he characterises it. Any doctrine which could impair the authority of the Soviet law —and the doctrine that the law is a mere ideology as well as the doctrine that the law is by its very nature bourgeois law, are such doctrines—must be condemned; and there is no stronger condemnation than to stigmatise it as anti-Marxist.

## Vyshinsky's doctrine of the state

Vyshinsky's contribution to the solution of the main problem of Soviet legal theory, the nature of law, consists in his effort to adapt the definition of law to the new doctrine of the state, decreed by his master, 'the mightiest genius who carried on the work of Marx, Engels, and Lenin: Stalin'.[21] A nauseous servility toward the then dictator, an intellectual prostration that surpasses the worst forms of byzantinism, is a characteristic feature of this legal science, the highest ambition of which is to be a submissive servant of the government. In the language of this science the Bolshevik party is the 'invincible communist party, the party of Lenin and Stalin'; Stalin is the 'great Stalin',[22] a 'genius in scholarship and in the Marxist theory'.[23] The constitution is 'the great Stalin Constitution'.[24] It is not

---

[20] *Loc. cit.,* p. 58.
[21] *Soviet Legal Philosophy,* p. 305.
[22] *Loc. cit.,* p. 304.
[23] *Loc. cit.,* p. 429.
[24] *Loc. cit.,* p. 305.

simply Lenin and Stalin, it is 'the genius of Lenin and Stalin' which 'continued the work of those who had set the foundations of Marxism, augmenting enormously the wealth of Marxism . . . '.[25]  Of 'the party of the bolsheviks, and the Soviet government headed by Lenin and Stalin', Vyshinsky says that they

> 'defined the direction of the policy of the Soviet state— having illuminated the lines of that direction with a genius' prevision of the future and with a genius' penetration— raising before the Soviet people the curtain of the future and illuminating the course of events in the years to come'.[26]

Lenin put into the background the prophecy of the withering away of the state and its law which Engels, for tactical rather than scientific reasons, had put into the foreground.  Stalin emphasised the importance of the Soviet state for the realisation and maintenance of socialism and declared that 'the dying out of the state will come not through weakening state authority, but through intensifying that authority to the utmost',[27] and that the state will be preserved even after the stage of perfect communism is reached, until capitalist encirclement is liquidated.  But Vyshinsky goes so far as to characterise the withering-away doctrine as presented by Pashukanis as a 'provocateur theory'.[28] He places the 'treason of Tukhachevskii' on the same level as the

> 'provocateur activity pursued by Bukharin, Pashukanis, and company, operating in the field of theory.  The attempt to preach the idea of the inevitable withering away of army and fleet here and now—an attempt, consequently, to upset the work of intensifying and making strong our capacity of defence—was aimed at handing our country over into the power of her enemies with her hands tied.  To preach the withering away of the organs of punishment and repression represented an attempt to give us over with our hands tied and our entire country as well—into the robber clutches of

---

[25] *Loc. cit.*, p. 308.

[26] *Loc. cit.*, p. 430 *et seq.*

[27] Stalin, *Questions of Leninism* (10th Russian ed.), p. 510, quoted by Vyshinsky, *loc. cit.*, p. 312.

[28] *Loc. cit.*, p. 307.  In an article published 1948, Vyshinsky declared that theoretical speculations about the eventual withering away of the law are not in the interest of the Soviet state.  Cf. Schlesinger, *loc. cit.*, p. xii.

the wreckers, terrorists, and diversionists whose traitorous undertaking—happily for us—did not succeed and who were mercilessly uprooted and destroyed by our notable Stalin intelligence service, headed by Nikolai Ivanovich Yezhov'.[29]

If science is considered to be an instrument of politics, then it is a punishable crime to advocate a wrong theory; and, then, a theory is wrong if it is a deviation from the orthodox doctrine, the orthodox doctrine being the one established by the political party in power. Vyshinsky presents the 'correct' Marxist theory of the state in a way that his readers get the impression that according to Marx and Engels the establishment of a socialist state, and not the withering away of the state, was the paramount aim of the socialist revolution. He writes:

'To the Marx-Lenin-Stalin doctrine of state and law as the moving forces of socialist triumphs and of the struggle for the communist reorganisation of our society, these gentlemen sought to contrast their own pseudo-scientific devisings as to hanging soviet law out to air, as to its bourgeois nature obstructing the realisation of the problems confronting the proletariat revolution, and as to the withering away of state and law in the conditions of the proletariat dictatorship'.[30]

And he thinks that he can discredit those who stick to the withering-away doctrine as presented by Marx and Engels by stigmatising—in complete conformity with Stalin—their view as 'anarchical',[31] as if the Marx-Engels doctrine were not a theory of anarchism, and as if Marx and Engels had not been carefully intent on distinguishing their doctrine from that of the so-called anarchists only and exclusively by their view of the way in which society can be liberated from the state, and not at all by their evaluation of the state as a fundamental evil, an instrument of exploitation. Vyshinsky's version of the Marx-Engels doctrine of the state is not a modification, it is a distortion of that doctrine.

### Vyshinsky's definition of the law

The result of Vyshinsky's theory for the definition of the positive socialist Soviet law is rather poor. It is the definition which the Institute of Law of the Academy of Sciences adopted on Vyshinsky's proposition:

[29] *Soviet Legal Philosophy*, p. 311.     [30] *Loc. cit.*, p. 309.
[31] *Loc. cit.*, p. 309.

'Law is the aggregate of the rules of conduct expressing
the will of the dominant class and established in legal order,
as well as of customs and rules of community life confirmed
by state authority, the application whereof is guaranteed by
the coercive force of the state to the end of safeguarding,
making secure and developing social relationships and
arrangements advantageous and agreeable to the dominant
class'.[32]

Judged from a purely logical point of view, this definition makes
a rather dilettantic impression. 'Law is the aggregate of the rules
. . . established in legal order' is a tautology, since an aggregate
of rules is an order, and legal order is only another term for law.
To add to 'the rules of conduct' the 'customs and rules of community life confirmed by state authority . . .' is quite superfluous, since the 'customs' are customary rules and—just as the
'rules of community life'—rules of conduct. All these rules,
whether they be 'customs' or 'rules of community life' or simply
'rules of conduct', are 'confirmed by state authority'; which
means exactly the same as that they are 'guaranteed by the
coercive force of the state'. This addition, too, is pleonastic.
It is also pleonastic to say that the law is the expression of 'the
will of the dominant class' and to add that the end of the law
is the

'safeguarding, making secure [which is the same as safe-
guarding] and developing social relationships and arrangements advantageous and agreeable [if they are advantageous they are agreeable] to the dominant class',

which means that the law serves the interests of the dominant
class. The statement that the law is the manifestation of the
'will of the dominant class' is only a figurative expression of the
idea that the law serves the interests of the dominant class.
Vyshinsky explains his definition of the law as follows:

'Law is neither a system of social relationships nor a
form of production relationships. Law is the aggregate of
rules of conduct—or norms: yet not of norms alone, but
also of customs and rules of community living confirmed by
state authority and coercively protected by that authority'.[33]

But 'customs' and 'rules of community living' are norms if they

[32] *Loc. cit.*, p. 336.
[33] *Loc. cit.*, p. 337.

are 'confirmed by state authority' and if their application is guaranteed by the coercive force of the state. For such confirmation and guarantee means that if an individual does not behave in conformity with the 'customs' or 'rules of community living', he ought to be punished, just as he ought to be punished in case his behaviour is not in conformity with the 'rules of conduct or norms'. The fact that the state attaches a sanction to a certain behaviour may be interpreted to mean that the contrary behaviour is prescribed by the state (*i.e.,* the law), that a legal norm is issued or applied by organs of the state (to speak in the usual language, differentiating between law and state). Hence, if the 'rules of conduct' are 'norms', there is no sufficient reason not to characterise the 'customs' and the 'rules of community living', too, as norms; and if by the 'customs and rules of community living' rules of actual behaviour (in contradistinction to norms) are meant, then there is no sufficient reason not to conceive of the 'rules of conduct', too, as rules of actual behaviour. But Vyshinsky has deprived himself of the possibility to describe any part of the law as rules of actual behaviour and not as norms, for he rejects the doctrine of Stuchka and Pashukanis that the law is a system of social relationships. Since social relationships manifest themselves in the actual behaviour of men, the definition of law as a system of social relationships amounts to the same as the definition of law as a system of rules of actual behaviour of men. The decisive point in the definitions of Stuchka and Pashukanis is that they deny the normative character of the law; and it is just this normative character of the law on which Vyshinsky insists. It is not possible to conceive of one part of the law—the 'rules of conduct'—as norms, and the other part of the law—the 'customs' and 'rules of community living'—as rules of actual behaviour. Such a view implies the attempt to combine two interpretations which exclude each other, and thus result in a contradiction in terms.

### The law : the will of a dominant class or of the whole people?

Purified of all its tautologies, pleonasms, and contradictions, Vyshinsky's definition of the socialist Soviet law reads as follows : Law is an aggregate of norms expressing the will of the dominant class, guaranteed by the coercive force of the State. This definition, however, applies only to the law of a society divided into

9

two classes, a dominant and a dominated class, and that means—
according to the economic interpretation of society—an exploiting and an exploited class.  But this was no longer the status of
Soviet society, where—as the 'mightiest genius Stalin' declared
—there are no longer exploiters and exploited, where the means
of production are owned by the whole people, and where, therefore, there can be no dominant class.  But Vyshinsky still speaks
of 'classes' in Soviet society.  'Our soviet people consists of the
worker class, the peasant class, and the toiling intellectuals'.  But
the 'peasant class' and the 'toiling intellectuals' are workers just
as the industrial workers are, although only the latter are called
'working class'.  Vyshinsky seems to be quite aware of these
inconsistencies.  He says his definition of the law is only 'a first
approximation' to a definition; and, finally, abandoning his
definition of the law as the expression of the will of a dominant
class only, he declares that the Soviet law is the will of the whole
people of the Soviet state.

> 'Our statutes express the will of our people which is
> ruling, and which is creating new history under the
> guidance of the worker class.  Among us, the will of the
> worker class merges with the will of the entire people.  This
> provides the basis for speaking of our soviet socialist law as
> an expression of the will of the whole people'.

> 'There has been formulated among us, a single and
> indestructible will of the soviet people—manifested in the
> unparalleled unanimity with which the people vote at the
> elections to the Supreme Soviet of the U.S.S.R. and the
> Supreme Soviets of the union and autonomous republics for
> the bloc of communist and non-party candidates'.[34]

In an article published in 1939, Vyshinsky improved his definition of socialist law by eliminating the reference to a dominant
class and to custom as an element different from the rules of
conduct.  He stated that socialist law during the transitional
period from socialism to communism is

> 'a system of norms established by the legislation by the
> State of the Toilers and expressing the will of the whole
> Soviet people, led by the working classes headed by the
> communist Party, in order to protect, to strengthen and to

[34] *Loc. cit.*, p. 339.

develop socialist relations and the building of a communist society'.[35]

In his work *The Law of the Soviet State*,[36] Vyshinsky presents two definitions : a definition of the 'law' and a definition of 'Soviet law'. Since Soviet law is a special type of law, the definition of law must be applicable to the Soviet law. This is a most fundamental requirement of logic. But Vyshinsky seems to consider himself not to be bound by it. He defines the law—the law as general category—as follows :

'Law is the totality (1) of the rules of conduct, expressing the will of the dominant class and established in legal order, and (2) of customs and rules of community life sanctioned by state authority—their application being guaranteed by the compulsive force of the state in order to guard, secure, and develop social relationships and social orders advantageous and agreeable to the dominant class'.

Then he defines Soviet law as follows :

'Soviet law is the aggregate of the rules of conduct established in the form of legislation by the authority of the toilers and expressive of their will. The effective operation of these rules is guaranteed by the entire coercive force of the socialist state in order to defend, to secure, and to develop relationships and arrangements advantageous and agreeable to the toilers, and completely and finally to annihilate capitalism and its remnants in the economic system, the way of life, and human consciousness—in order to build a communist society'.

Although the 'law' is the expression of the will of the dominant

---

[35] Published in 1939 in *Sovietskaja Justicija* (Soviet Justice), p. 10, quoted by R. Schlesinger, *Soviet Legal Theory*, p. 243 *et seq.* Schlesinger says that against the first-mentioned definition of the socialist law by Vyshinsky it has been objected ' that it neglects the all-national character of the Soviet State where no differentiation between ruling and ruled classes remains, and also that, by including Custom, it obliterates the distinction between Law and Morality : that those customs recognised by the State, and included into the system of norms established by legislation, formed itself part of the latter, while other customs were irrelevant from the legal point of view. [Goljakov, President of the Supreme Court, " Problems of Socialist Law ", *Sovietskaja Justicija*, 1939, No. 1.] Vyshinsky answered [" The XVIIIth Congress of the C.P. of the U.S.S.R. and the Tasks of the Theory of Socialist Law ", *Sovietskoje Gossudarstvo i Pravo* (Soviet State and Law), 1939, No. 3, p. 10], but himself corrected his definition by applying it concretely to the conditions of the Soviet State ', as shown above.

[36] Vyshinsky, *The Law of the Soviet State*, p. 50.

class, Soviet law is not the expression of the will of the dominant class but the expression of the will of the toilers, that is to say, of the whole people of the Soviet state.  Since the 'Soviet law' does not fall under the concept of 'law' as defined by Vyshinsky, the so-called Soviet law is neither bourgeois nor socialist law : it is no law at all.  This, of course, Vyshinsky does not mean.  What he presents as a definition of the law is, in truth—just as is his definition of the Soviet law—the definition of a special kind of law.  There is a law which is the expression only of the will of a dominant class, but there is also a law which is the expression of the will of the whole people.  Hence the law is not necessarily class law.  In order to avoid the recognition of this fact which follows from his presentation of Soviet law as law and as expression of the will of the whole people, but which is in open contradiction to the Marx-Engels doctrine as officially interpreted in the Soviet Union, Vyshinsky is forced to ignore the principles of logic.

The statement that the law is the expression of the will of the whole people, and not only of the will of a part of it which dominates over the other, means that the law guarantees the interests of all individuals whose behaviour it regulates, so that it may be assumed that the law is in the interest of all subjects, and hence in conformity with their will.  This is a well-known formula of the ideological school of bourgeois jurisprudence. Vyshinsky sees very well the ideological character of this formula —if applied to capitalist law.  He says :

> 'In capitalist society, allusions to the will of the people served as a screen which veiled the exploiting nature of the bourgeois state.  In the conditions of our country, the matter is different in principle'.[37]

But the statement that the law is the will of the entire people is an ideological fiction, whether it is used to justify the capitalist or the socialist law.  For, if the law were really in conformity with the will of all, it would not need to have a coercive character. Such a social order could be based on the voluntary obedience of its subjects, and hence would be no law at all.  This may be true of the social order of the perfect communism of the future ; but it is certainly not true of the decidedly coercive order which is the law of the Soviet state.

[37] *Soviet Legal Philosophy*, p. 339.

## CHAPTER 8

# GOLUNSKII AND STROGOVICH'S THEORY OF STATE AND LAW

### 'Classes' in a classless society

THE contradiction which exists in maintaining that there is a dominant class and that the law is the expression of its will, but at the same time, that the law is the will of the whole people, becomes evident with particular clarity in the work *Theory of State and Law,* by S. A. Golunskii and M. S. Strogovich.[1] The writers admit that as soon as the means of production have 'become social property, and so cannot be utilised for purposes of exploitation'—which is the case in the Soviet Union—'the foundation of the division of society into classes . . . disappears'.[2] But that does not mean, according to Golunskii and Strogovich, that in the Soviet Union a classless society already exists; it means only that 'the way to classless society is opened', so that the society of the Soviet Union is still a society divided into classes. In order to justify this view, the authors say with respect to the stage of socialism which is not yet perfect communism because the productivity of labour 'is still not high enough to satisfy the requirements of all the members of society', that

> 'there are still traces of class differences: the worker class is still distinct from the peasantry (although that difference is constantly being effaced, and there is no antagonistic conflict of interest between the worker class and the peasantry). There is still a difference between city and village, between intellectual and physical labour: wherefore intellectuals are preserved as a special social stratum of persons performing intellectual labour. However, they too, are not only not hostile to the worker class and the peasantry as is frequently the case under capitalism: on the contrary that stratum is itself made up of the advanced and best workers and peasants and serves their interests'.[3]

[1] Published by the Institute of Law of the U.S.S.R. Academy of Sciences, Moscow, 1940; *loc. cit.,* p. 351 *et seq.*
[2] *Soviet Legal Philosophy,* p. 351 *et seq.*
[3] *Loc. cit.,* p. 352.

From this statement follows, first, that there are only 'traces' of class differences, and, secondly, that the 'classes' which, only in traces, still exist, are : industrial workers (in the cities), peasant workers (in the country), and intellectual workers. The difference which exists between these groups is not a difference of classes, but a difference of professions, they all are workers or 'toilers'. Golunskii and Strogovich speak of the agricultural workers as of the 'toiling peasants',[4] in contradistinction to the industrial 'workers'. But there is no difference between 'working' (*rabotaiuschchii*) and 'toiling' (*trudiashchiesia*). None of these working people—the industrial, agricultural, and intellectual workers or toilers—is exploited, since there is no group which can exploit them, and hence there is no 'antagonistic conflict of interest' no 'hostility' between them, which is the essential criterion of classes in the sense of a Marxian sociology where the concept of 'classes' is inseparably connected with that of 'class struggle'. The authors expressly say that the way to reach the stage of perfect communism leads 'not through a class struggle between members of socialist society (wherein there is no exploitation of one class by another) but through friendly joint work'.[5] If there is 'friendly joint work' of the members of socialist society, then there can be no classes within this society. Opposing the socialist law to the capitalist law, Golunskii and Strogovich say :

> 'Antagonism in human relationships is always a postulate of exploiter law, whereas socialist law, on the contrary, gives expression to relationships of collaboration between persons participating in socialist building'.[6]

Expressed in genuine Marxian terminology, this means that socialist law—in contradistinction to capitalist law—is the law of a classless society, that is, a society freed from exploitation. Golunskii and Strogovich, speaking of the industrial workers as of the 'proletariat', quote the statement of Stalin that 'the dictatorship of the proletariat can be carried into effect only through a special form of alliance between the class of proletarians and the toiling masses of the petty bourgeois classes— above all, with the toiling masses of the peasantry'.[7] But this

---

[4] *Loc. cit.,* p. 358.
[5] *Loc. cit.,* p. 352.
[6] *Loc. cit.,* p. 387.
[7] Stalin, *Questions of Leninism,* p. 114 *et seq.* ; *loc. cit.,* p. 360.

statement can refer only to a stage of the Soviet state prior to the
establishment of the Constitution of 1936, when Stalin declared
that there is no longer a proletarian and hence no bourgeois class
in the socialist society of the Soviet Union. Besides, if the masses
of the petty bourgeoisie are 'toiling' and are in 'alliance' with the
'proletarians', they are not a 'class' different from and opposed to
the latter, who—just for this reason—are no longer a class in the
Marxian sense of the word. 'In the socialist state', Golunskii
and Strogovich affirm, 'all the toilers are united'[8]; and there
are only 'toilers' in this state, since to 'persons unwilling volun-
tarily to submit to socialist discipline' 'coercive measures' are
applied,[9] that is to say, they are forced to toil. And in this sense,
all the individuals belonging to the people of the Soviet state are
'united'.

## The theory of the state in the Soviet Constitution

In their work, published in 1940, Golunskii and Strogovich
still maintain that 'the socialist state is a worker-class dictatorship', a 'dictatorship of the proletariat'.[10] Such a characterisation of the Soviet state stands in open contrast to the statement
that Stalin made in his report on the Constitution and to this
constitution itself. The constitution does not call the Soviet state
a dictatorship of the proletariat. It only says in Article 2 that
'the Soviets of Toilers' Deputies', the 'political foundation of
the U.S.S.R., grew and became strong as a result of the overthrow of the power of the landlords and capitalists, and the
winning of the dictatorship of the proletariat'. That means that
the Soviet state, the socialist state of today, is the result of the
dictatorship of the proletariat, not this dictatorship itself;
although prior to the coming into force of the Constitution of
1936, the Soviet state was a dictatorship of the proletariat. This
constitution—as Golunskii and Strogovich assert—is not only
'the greatest document of our age', but 'a document of the
greatest theoretical significance, . . . a new and most valuable
contribution to the Marx-Lenin theory'.[11] The authors seem to
be aware that their theory of the Soviet state is not quite in conformity with the theory laid down in the Constitution. They

[8] *Soviet Legal Philosophy,* p. 363.
[9] *Loc. cit.,* p. 358.
[10] *Loc. cit.,* pp. 353, 354.
[11] *Loc. cit.,* p. 357.

say : ' On the one hand we speak of the dictatorship of the proletariat alone. . . . On the other hand Article 1 of the U.S.S.R.
Constitution provides that " The U.S.S.R. is a socialist state of
Workers and Peasants " '.[12]  That means that the Constitution
does not refer to the workers and peasants as two ' classes '. And
when Golunskii and Strogovich, in another connection, interpret
Article 1 of the Constitution to mean that ' state authority in the
U.S.S.R. belongs to the worker and peasant, that no other classes
exist in the U.S.S.R.' [13] (which implies that the workers and
peasants are classes), they attribute a meaning to this Article
which has no basis in its wording. Golunskii and Strogovich
refer also to Article 3 of the Constitution which provides that ' all
authority in the U.S.S.R. belongs to the toilers of city and
country as personified by Soviets of deputies of the toilers '. This
wording, likewise, does not imply that ' the toilers of city and
country ' are classes. Then Golunskii and Strogovich ask : ' Is
there not a contradiction here ? ' Of course, there is a contradiction ! But the authors try to show that it is ' only a seeming
contradiction '. And why is it only ' seeming' ? ' Because state
guidance of society (a dictatorship) is exercised only by the proletariat '.[14] By the ' proletariat ' which has ceased to exist in the
Soviet state ? They continue : ' because the guiding force in the
system of the proletarian dictatorship is the worker class and its
party—the communist party " which neither does nor can share
guidance with other parties " '.[15] That means that the Soviet
state is neither a dictatorship of the proletariat nor a dictatorship
of the worker class *and* its party, but a dictatorship of the communist party, which is certainly not a ' class ' and which only by
an obvious fiction can be identified with the worker class, falsely
presented as ' proletariat ' and ' class '.

## Golunskii and Strogovich's theory of the state

Golunskii and Strogovich's theory of the Soviet state as a
proletarian dictatorship is not only not in harmony with the
theory laid down in the Constitution, but it is also contradictory
in itself. In the just-quoted statement they say that dictatorship
is ' state guidance '. By state guidance only state government can

[12] *Loc. cit.*, p. 360.
[13] *Loc. cit.*, p. 367.
[14] *Loc. cit.*, p. 360.
[15] This is a statement of Stalin (*Questions of Leninism*), *loc. cit.*, p. 360.

be understood; but not every government is a dictatorship. On the other hand, they say: 'Persuasion is the basic method of guidance under the dictatorship of the proletariat in respect of most of the toilers'. Coercion is applied only exceptionally:

> 'In the socialist state, state coercion is applied in the form of repression (as regards the class enemies of the toilers) and of compulsory education (as regards individual, backward toilers, who are unwilling to submit voluntarily to socialist discipline), but always on the basis of persuading the majority of the toilers of the correctness and necessity of so applying it'.[16]

A 'dictatorship' that works in principle only by persuasion is certainly just the contrary of a dictatorship. Under this 'dictatorship',

> 'constraint is exerted not only with the approval, but with the active participation of a majority of the toilers. State coercion is exerted by the forces of the organised people themselves upon the initiative, and under the guidance, of state organs (soviets of deputies of the toilers, comprising representatives of the entire soviet people now that there are no longer exploiter classes in U.S.S.R.). The socialist state is genuinely an organisation of all the people, acting under the guidance of the worker class and its party'.[17]

If the socialist state is an 'organisation of all the people' and hence a perfect unity of interests, how can there be 'classes' within this state?

The only question is: Why do the Soviet writers on the one hand assert that the socialist society of the Soviet state has reached a stage where there is no exploitation of one class by another and, on the other hand, still insist on the class character of this state, thereby using the term class in a way totally different from the meaning this term has in the Marx-Engels doctrine? The only possible answer is that they want to maintain the appearance of still following the doctrine of Marx and Engels, who taught that the state is essentially the domination of one class over another and that a classless society is—by definition—a stateless society. The original view that the only purpose of this domination is the maintenance of exploitation, proved to

[16] *Loc. cit.*, p. 361.
[17] *Loc. cit.*, p. 362.

be completely incompatible with the obvious fact that the purpose of the domination during the period when the state really had the character of a dictatorship of the proletariat, was the abolition of exploitation. Hence the definition of the state changed from an instrument for the exploitation of one class by another to an instrument of the domination of one class by another. But, at this point the process of modifying the Marx-Engels doctrine stopped. To eliminate from the definition of the state not only the element of exploitation but also the class element, was too much for a theory which pretended to be orthodox Marxism. To admit that the socialist state is a state the people of which is not divided into classes would be the complete abandonment of the Marx-Engels doctrine of the state. Hence the class terminology has to be maintained. And this, of course, was possible only by a radical change of its original meaning.

The state—Golunskii and Strogovich say in another connection [18]—is an 'organisation of the dominant class'. But whereas in the capitalist state the dominant class uses the state machine 'to oppress the toiling masses', the dominant class in a socialist state—that is the proletariat—using this machine,

> 'destroys exploitation and the exploiter classes, and builds socialist society. In all its activity, the state—realising the will of the dominant class to which authority belongs— defends and guarantees the interests of that class. For this, the governing class requires that the mandates of its will be binding in society—that all citizens of the state be subject to, and observe them'.

In this respect, there is no difference between a capitalist state and the socialist state. But whereas in a capitalist state the dominant class 'forces its will upon the exploited'—the class of the proletariat—'dictates its will to the people, subordinates the people to itself', in a socialist state 'the will of the worker class, which has abolished exploitation'—and this class is here the dominant class—is 'expressing the interests of all the toilers—is binding upon all citizens'. Since in a socialist state after the nationalisation of the means of production and hence after the abolition of exploitation all citizens are 'toilers', 'expressing the interests of all the toilers' amounts to the same as expressing

[18] *Loc. cit.,* p. 365.

the will of the entire people.  Then the socialist state is not an organisation of the dominant class but of the entire people, and only because it is an organisation of the entire people, and because there is no dominant class, the will of the state is not, as in a capitalist state, enforced upon an oppressed class.  Here the contradiction in the definition of the socialist state becomes evident.

### Golunskii and Strogovich's theory of the law : the will of the entire people and at the same time the will of the dominant class

Golunskii and Strogovich's doctrine of the law is no less contradictory than their doctrine of the state.  After having defined the socialist state as an organisation of the dominant worker class which realises the will of this class, the two authors say :

> 'The law of socialist society likewise expresses the will of the dominant class, the worker class ; and—since exploiter classes have there been destroyed, and the worker class (to which the state guidance of society belongs) expresses the interests and aspirations of all the toiling people—socialist law is the will of the soviet people elevated into legislation— the will of the people who have built socialist society under the guidance of the worker class headed by the bolshevik party'.[19]

Thus, the socialist law is the will of one class only which is in some way opposed to another class, and at the same time the will of the entire people.  But, later, we read that 'all organs of authority in the U.S.S.R. express and defend the interests of workers and peasants—the overwhelming majority of the population'.[20]  Since a man's will is directed at the realisation of his interests, the statement that the law expresses the interests of the majority of the population—even if 'overwhelming'—is not consistent with the statement that it is the expression of the will of the entire people.  But it seems that it is not even the interests of the overwhelming majority which is to be expressed and defended by the will of the entire people.  For we learn also that the law of the socialist state is an aggregate of norms 'agreeable and advantageous to the dominant class'.[21]  That something is

[19] *Loc. cit.*, p. 365 *et seq.*
[20] *Loc. cit.*, p. 367.
[21] *Loc. cit.*, p. 370.

agreeable and advantageous to somebody, is—as pointed out only another expression of the idea that it is in his interest. Since the dominant class is, according to Golunskii and Strogovich, the worker class, the law cannot be in the interest of the over-whelming majority, and certainly not of the entire people, if it is only in the interest of this class. Nevertheless, Golunskii and Strogovich lay particular stress on the fact that the socialist law —in contradistinction to capitalist law—is the expression of the will and the interests of the entire people.

> 'Socialist law is a completely unique type of law, differing radically from all the species (slave-owning, feudal, and bourgeois) of exploiter law. It is unique in that it is the first law in the history of human society which is not exploiter law : it banishes exploitation, and gives expression to the interests and will of all the toiling people—of the socialist worker-peasant state. . . . Socialist law consists of the rules of conduct (norms) of socialist society. They express the will of the entire people'.[22]

To hide the contradiction that the law is the will of the entire people and at the same time only the will of a part of the people, the worker class, the authors must have recourse to a fiction, the well-known fiction of representation : the worker class represents the entire people.

> 'As the interests of the worker class in socialist society (wherein exploiter classes have been destroyed) reflect the interests of the entire people, the peasants and the intellectuals, so socialist law, too, expresses the will—and defends the interests—of all the toiling people'.[23]

---

[22] *Loc. cit.*, p. 385. In his pamphlet, *The Role of Socialist Consciousness etc.*, Konstantinov, after having emphasised that 'The victory of Socialism led to the abolition of class antagonism and to a radical change in the very nature of social development, to the abolition of everything connected with the antagonistic nature of social relationships' (p. 6), states : 'An enormously important role in the development of our society is also played by the Soviet ideas *of law*. Law always expresses the economic relationships in society. Marxism teaches that jurisprudence is but the will of the ruling class made into a law. Soviet jurisprudence is the will of the working class, and today, of the entire Soviet people, made into a law. Soviet law is the conscious expression and confirmation of the rule of the workers and peasants' (p. 83). 'Inseparably connected with Soviet law is Soviet socialist *morality,* which determines the standards of conduct of the Soviet people. Socialist morality determines the attitude of Soviet people towards each other, their attitude towards labour, society, the state, the family' (p. 84).

[23] *Soviet Legal Philosophy*, p. 385.

This fiction is quite significant of the ideological character of Golunskii and Strogovich's theory of law. And not less significant is the fact that Golunskii and Strogovich, in maintaining that the socialist law expresses the will of the entire people, use for the justification of this law the same ideological fiction as some bourgeois writers do for the justification of capitalist law.

### The law : a system of norms

The definition of law presented by Golunskii and Strogovich runs as follows :

> 'Law is the aggregate of the rules of conduct (norms) established or approved (sanctioned) by state authority, expressing the will of the dominant class, as to which the coercive force of the state guarantees their being put into operation to the end of safeguarding, making secure, and developing social relationships and arrangements agreeable and advantageous to the dominant class'.[24]

In its application to socialist Soviet law it reads :

> 'Soviet socialist law is the aggregate of rules of conduct (norms) established or approved by the state authority of the socialist state, and expressing the will of the worker class and of all the toilers ; the application of these rules of conduct is guaranteed by the coercive force of the socialist state to the end of defending, making secure and developing relationships and arrangements advantageous and agreeable to the worker class and to all the toilers, of destroying completely and finally the survivals of capitalism in the economy, mode of life and consciousness of human beings, and of building communist society'.[24a]

This definition is not very different from those proposed by Vyshinsky. Hence our criticism of the latter applies also to the former. Golunskii and Strogovich emphasise the normative character of the law. 'Law is thus composed of rules of human conduct. These are called norms in legal science—norm meaning a rule, an order, a requirement'.[25] Golunskii and Strogovich reject the view that law is a system of social relationships. They quite correctly state :

> 'Law is an aggregate of the rules of human conduct—

---

[24] *Loc. cit.*, p. 370.   [24a] *Loc. cit.*, p. 386.   [25] *Loc. cit.*, p. 368.

consequently it regulates human behaviour, human actions, the relationships of humans *inter se* and with organs of the state and with the state itself. Human relations in society are called social relations—it is these relations which are objects of regulation by law'.[26]

'There was a time when the view found expression in soviet juridic literature that the vice of the normative theory of law was its definition of law as an aggregate of norms—that is to say, of rules of conduct. Trotsky-Bukharin wreckers, who had crept into the ranks of workers in the science of soviet law, utilised this view in order to deny the significance of a legal norm. They undertook to define law as "a system of social relationships", a "form of policy", etc., asserting that this differentiates the Marx-Lenin theory of law from the bourgeois theory of law (which defines law as an aggregate of norms: that is to say, of rules of conduct). This led to a denial of the significance of soviet legislation as the dominant form of legal norms of socialist law. This view is radically unsound and extremely harmful. Law is an aggregate of norms—that is to say, of rules of conduct—among which legislation occupies the chief place. The vice of the bourgeois normative theory of law is not that it defines law as an aggregate of norms but that it distorts the very concept of a norm: isolating it from real life, and giving it idealistic character. Bourgeois theory contrasts the world of norms—concepts of what ought to be, supposedly not subject to the law of causation—with the physical world, where the law of causation is dominant. Thus the bourgeois normative theory of law does not pose the question: Why do legal norms safeguarding private property exist in bourgeois law? It simply insists that human beings must observe these norms in consequence of the eternal force inherent therein'.[27]

## Misinterpretation of the pure theory of law

The criticism of the 'bourgeois normative theory of law' is evidently directed against the pure theory of law. It is a misinterpretation of this theory which is far from giving the legal

[26] *Loc. cit.*, p. 372.
[27] *Loc. cit.*, p. 423.

norm an 'idealistic character', meaning a moral value. The pure theory of law, it is true, opposes the hypothetical judgments, called rules of law, by which the legal science describes its object, to the likewise hypothetical judgments, called laws of nature, by which the natural science describes its object. It maintains that the difference between the two judgments consists in the fact that according to the rules of law under certain conditions, among which the delict is an essential element, a certain consequence, namely, a coercive act as a sanction, ought to occur; whereas according to the laws of nature under certain conditions a certain consequence actually occurs. That means that in laws of nature the principle of causality is applied, whereas in the rules of law another principle is manifested, for which the pure theory of law has suggested the term 'imputation'. But this theory emphasises that the 'ought' in the rules of law has no moral character at all; that it only expresses the specific meaning of the connection between condition and consequence, which, established by legal norms, is described in the rules of law. This meaning is not, as that of the connection between condition and consequence in the laws of nature, that of cause and effect; the sanction is not the effect of the delict but imputed to the delict. The 'ought' in the rule of law has not a moral but only a logical significance. It is just the tendency to avoid any idealisation of the legal norms which is characteristic of the pure, that is, the normative theory of law. It is true that this theory does not pose the question as to why legal norms safeguarding private property exist in bourgeois law. But it omits this question not because it insists that human beings must observe the legal norms in consequence of 'the eternal force' inherent therein, but because this is a question that cannot be answered from the point of view of a normative theory of law. It is a question which can be answered only by a sociology of law which examines the causes and effects of the actual behaviour of the men who create the law and the men who obey or do not obey the law. That the pure theory of law does not pose the question concerned does not mean that it considers this question as inadmissible or as unimportant, but means only that it is a question which has to be answered by methods other than those of a normative theory of law. The pure theory of law does not insist that human beings must observe the legal norms, because this is a political not a scientific function; and the pure theory of law insists on a clear separation of the two functions. This theory knows nothing of an 'eternal force' inherent in the legal norms. If there is a legal theory to which such an idea is completely foreign it is the pure theory of law.

## The law : a coercive order

In maintaining that the application of the law is 'guaranteed by the coercive force of the socialist state', Golunskii and Strogovich define the law as a coercive order. This is not very consistent with their assertion that 'persuasion'—not constraint or, what amounts to the same, coercion—'is the basic method of guidance under the dictatorship of the proletariat'. The statement that the application of the legal norms is guaranteed by the coercive force of the state means only that the legal order institutes special organs competent to create and apply the law and especially to perform the coercive acts stipulated as sanctions in the legal norms. That means that what is called the law of the state is a centralised coercive order. The reference to the state is superfluous. For the state manifests its existence only in the human beings who, as organs of the legal order, create and apply this order. But Golunskii and Strogovich—following Marx and Engels—take over from the traditional bourgeois theory the dualism of law and state. They think of law and state as two different entities, and let the law emanate from the state; they say : 'law is not above the state but emanates from it'.[28] They do not see that the statement : law emanates from the state means nothing else but that the law is created by acts of human beings who are 'organs of the state' only in so far as they act in conformity with the law, that is to say, in conformity with the legal order which determines their actions. In other words : that the law emanates from the state means only that the law regulates its own creation and application. The law can be described without any reference to the state, for the state is a centralised legal order, and the so-called acts of the state are acts of human beings determined in a specific way by this order.

Marxists who believe in the future withering away of the state should have more understanding for that bourgeois doctrine which emancipates the concept of law completely from that of

[28] *Loc. cit.,* p. 393.

the state. Golunskii and Strogovich reject that theory because they identify—as do many bourgeois writers—erroneously the state with the government, which they define as 'organisation of governance and domination'.[29]  But the government is only one of the organs of the state, *i.e.*, the legal community constituted by the legal order, and the 'organisation of governance and domination' as a legal organisation is only a part of that universal organisation which is the legal order.  If the state is identical with the government and hence the Soviet state identical with the Soviet government, then, of course, a theory which defines the law without referring to the state is too dangerous to be accepted by Soviet writers.

### The relationship of state and law

One of them, I. P. Trainin, has devoted to this problem a special monograph: 'The Relationship between State and Law'.[30]  Trainin criticises quite correctly the indeed highly problematical theories advanced by traditional bourgeois jurisprudence on this subject.  But he misunderstands completely the pure theory of law of which he says :

> 'It starts from the proposition that jurisprudence may not discern inequity on the part of the state whose sole function is the effectuation of the legal order.  The state is the manifestation of law'.[31]

According to this theory the law is not a function of the state, nor is the state a manifestation of the law; the state, as a social order, is a relatively centralised legal order and in this sense identical with the law.  Trainin's positive contributions to the problem in question are very poor and do not differ from those of the traditional bourgeois jurisprudence.  They amount to the thesis that there exists an essential relationship between state and law.  He asserts that 'there is—and can be—no state (that is to say, an organisation of the dominance of a definite class) without law, precisely as there can be no law (that is to say, a system of coercive norms by means whereof that class safeguards its dominance) without a state'; that there exists 'dialectic unity of form and content of state and law' or 'correlationship and inter-

[29] *Loc. cit.*, p. 421.
[30] Izvestiya of the U.S.S.R. Academy of Sciences (*Economy and Law*, No. 5, 1945), *loc. cit.*, p. 433 *et seq.*
[31] *Soviet Legal Philosophy*, p. 435.

action of state and law'.[32] The doctrine that there is no law without a state can be maintained if by 'law' only a relatively centralised coercive order, that is, an order instituting special organs for the creation and application of the order, is understood. This, however, is not in conformity with the usual terminology, according to which the decentralised coercive orders of primitive societies as well as the likewise decentralised normative order constituting the international community are 'law', although there is no state guaranteeing this law. Behind the statements of Trainin there is the view, defended by many bourgeois writers, that the state creates and applies the law; or, as Trainin puts it, that the state 'always safeguarded and regulated law'; or that 'law was always law invested with authority by the state which made secure the corresponding legal relationships or created new ones conforming with the policy of the dominant class'[33]; or, law 'is realised through the state, which—by its authority, force, and doctrine—guarantees the effectuation of law. . . . To establish or to change the legal order is the function of the state'.[34] In all these statements the 'state' appears as an acting person. But Trainin does not make the slightest effort to analyse the phenomenon he has in mind, to describe it without the metaphor of the state as an acting person, to reduce the state as an acting person to the activity of human beings, and to answer the question why certain acts of human beings are interpreted as acts of state. If he had made such an effort, he would have seen that the law-creating and law-applying acts of human beings are acts of state only in so far as they are determined by a legal order, that their imputation to the 'state' means nothing else but that they are referred to the legal order by which they are determined, and that the state—acting through these individuals, the state as an acting person—is nothing but the personification of this legal order. But it is evident that Trainin, as many bourgeois writers, does not want, or does not dare, to dissolve this personification and thus to penetrate the veil with which this personification hides the legal reality. For this personification and its result, the dualism of state and law, especially when the state is identified with the government, has a very valuable ideological function: if the binding law is the

---

[32] *Loc. cit.*, pp. 436, 447, 449.   [33] *Loc. cit.*, p. 437.   [34] *Loc. cit.*, p. 445.

product of the state—identified with the government—then the law is justified by the authority from which it emanates, and the state, i.e., the government, is justified by its product, that is to say, its authority is sanctified by the law.

## Law and morality

In order to strengthen this mutual justification of state and law, there must be maintained not only a correlation between state and law but also between law and morality. For this ideological-political purpose many bourgeois writers maintain as an essential quality of the positive law that it is—by its very nature—at least in principle in conformity with morality. This doctrine achieves the intended justification of the law, that is to say, it succeeds in its attempt to attribute to a positive legal order, which by itself has only a relative value, the halo of absolute authority only if by morality one uniform system of norms is understood, valid everywhere and at all times. If—in view of the fact that there are many different systems of morality— morality is supposed to represent only a relative value, the state- ment that the law is in conformity with morality as an absolute valid system of moral norms, has a merely ideological character. Pashukanis, following Marx, taught that law as well as morality are specific ideologies of capitalist society. Golunskii and Strogovich reject this doctrine and assert, in complete harmony with ideological bourgeois jurisprudence, that 'the bond between law—the aggregate of the rules of human conduct—and morality is very close'.[35] They differ from the bourgeois writers only in that the latter assume that capitalism is moral, socialism immoral, whereas Golunskii and Strogovich believe that socialism is moral, capitalism immoral. Hence they state : 'Socialist law and socialist morality have a common basis and common principles; the principles of socialism',[36] whereby socialism is supposed to be an absolute value.

With this statement the Soviet legal theory of the second period attains its culmination. And just at this point it proves to be, even more than that of the first period, nothing but an off- spring of bourgeois jurisprudence, specially of that school of bourgeois jurisprudence which is characterised by its ideological tendencies, so vigorously stigmatised by Marx and Engels.

[35] *Loc. cit.*, p. 375.      [36] *Loc. cit.*, p. 379. Cf. note 22 on p. 140.

CHAPTER 9

# SOVIET THEORY OF INTERNATIONAL LAW

**International law a class law ?**

ACCORDING to the usual interpretation of the doctrine advocated by Marx and Engels in many (but not in all) of their statements, the law is essentially connected with the state, is always the law of a state. There is no law without a state and no state without a law. This means that the law is a relatively centralised coercive order, that is, an order providing for coercive acts as sanctions and instituting special organs for the creation and the application of the norms of this order, especially for the execution of the sanctions. Since, according to this view, the state has by its very nature a class character, that is to say, that the coercive machinery called state comes into existence only where society is split into a dominant class and a dominated class exploited by the former, the essential function of the law is to guarantee the exploitation of one class by another or, according to a later interpretation of the Marxian doctrine, the domination of one class, that is, of one group of subjects possessing the means of production, over another class, that is, another group of subjects, within one and the same community called the state. If so-called international law is considered to be a system of norms regulating the relationships between states independent from one another, a Marxian definition of law cannot apply to that social order. For general international law is completely decentralised; it does not institute special organs for the creation and the application of its norms, in particular, no special organs for the execution of sanctions; and, above all, within the international community constituted by international law there are no classes formed by the subjects of international law, the states; there is no domination—with or without exploitation—of one group of the subjects of international law over another group of subjects of this law. The domination of one group over another within the state is, according to the Marxian doctrine, based on the economic fact that one group is in the possession of the means of production.

No such domination exists in the relationship between the states because, according to the Marxian theory, a community is a state only if the means of production within this community are in the hands of the dominant class of this community. International law guarantees just the contrary of that which, according to the Marxian view, is the essential function of the law : it guarantees by the principle of the sovereign equality of all states —a principle on which the Soviet theory of international law lays particular stress—that no state or group of states ought to exercise a domination over another group of states. It is true that smaller states are sometimes actually more or less dependent on a so-called great power. But this is a political, not a legal phenomenon; and where exceptionally the dependence has a legal character, as in the case of a protectorate, it is based on a treaty concluded by the protecting and the protected state. That a state may be induced to conclude such a treaty is not the effect of international law but of external circumstances, which cannot be attributed to the legal order regulating the mutual relations of states. Besides, to the same extent as a state becomes legally dependent on another state it loses its quality as a state in the sense of international law. It would be in open contradiction to the facts to say that smaller powers, such as Switzerland or Sweden, Argentina or Australia, are under the domination of a great power in the same sense as the proletariat is under the domination of the bourgeoisie. The exploiting domination exercised by some states over their respective colonies is guaranteed not by international law, but by the national law of the states concerned.

The only way in which it seems possible—at least *prima facie* —to attribute to international law a class character is by referring to the fact that international law, in granting constitutional autonomy to all the states and in prohibiting all the states from intervening in the domestic affairs of any other state—a principle very much emphasised by the Soviet theory of international law—guarantees the domination which one class exercises over another class within each state. But this is true only where the internal structure of the state really has the character of the domination of one class over another, and the principles of constitutional autonomy and non-intervention in domestic affairs apply not only in case the dominant class is the bourgeoisie, as in the capitalist states, but likewise in case the dominant class is the proletariat, as in the dictatorship of the proletariat of the Soviet state during its first period. It is true also in a case where the split into a bourgeoisie and a proletariat has disappeared and state-domination is exercised not by one class over another, where the law is the expression of the will of the whole unified people, as within the Soviet state in its second period according to the doctrine of the Soviet legal scientists. That means that international law, in itself, is perfectly neutral with respect to the struggle of classes within the states subjects of this law and that, consequently, international law, guaranteeing state-domination of any kind, has in itself no class character at all. Just because international law is no class law in any sense of this term, the Soviet Government—and, following their government the Soviet legal scientists—finally recognised the existing international law as a normative order binding upon the Soviet state in its relationships to all the other states, not only to other socialist but also and in the first place to the capitalist states. Hence there exists an insoluble conflict within the Soviet theory of international law. From the point of view of the Marxian definition of the law, so-called international law is no law at all. But political interest forces the Soviet Government to recognise this law as a set of legally binding norms regulating its relationships with the other states, and the Soviet legal theorists to make the futile attempt to interpret this set of norms as law in conformity with the Marxian definition.

### The problem of international law in Stuchka's theory of law

How much the problem of international law embarrassed the Soviet theorists of law may be seen in the writings of Stuchka and Pashukanis. Stuchka maintains the Marxian doctrine that there can be no law in a society which has no classes.

'. . . wherever and in whatever form a division of mankind into classes and the dominance of one class over another are present, we find law or something analogous thereto. In our investigation, we are confining ourselves to law of the epoch of bourgeois society and of the feudal society which preceded it, as the most fully expressed model of law. But as to the sphere embraced by law, the objection on the score of international law is deemed the most dangerous.

We shall see . . . however, that international law—in so
far as it is law in general—should be in complete conformity
with this definition; and on this point the eyes of all have
been opened by contemporary imperialism—and particularly by the world war with all its consequences'.[1]
But how does Stuchka reconcile the concept of international law
with his definition of the law as 'a system (or order) of social
relationships which correspond to the interests of the dominant
class and is safeguarded by the organised force of this class'?[2]
There must be a dominant class united by the common interest
of its members in the exploitation of a dominated class. Where
is the dominant class in the international society as the
society of states? The dominant classes of the different states
are by no means united by a common interest; their interests
are evidently in conflict with one another! Stuchka writes:
'Taking our definition of law as the starting point, we assign a
relatively unimportant sphere to international law'.[3] The sphere
assigned to international law may be 'unimportant', but if it is
law at all and a law the subjects of which are states, it must be
a system of relationships of states corresponding to the interest
of a dominant class formed by some of these states, dominating
over another class formed by other states. This, of course, cannot
be shown by Stuchka. He continues:

> 'If Duguit regards the state merely as a simple fact (*un
> simple fait*), then it may be said with reference to inter-
> national law also—right down to the imperialist period—
> that all law is actually nothing more than relationships
> *de facto*'.

The statement that international law is a system of 'relationships
*de facto*' is no solution of the problem in question. For national
law, too, is according to the definition of Stuchka a system of
relationships *de facto*. Stuchka says further: 'Accordingly
plans emerged concerning leagues of nations with special coercive
authority, and phantasies of that order—possessing absolutely
*no real significance*'. That certain international organisations
had no significance is no definition of international law. Finally,
Stuchka declares: 'One thing, however, is beyond doubt: the

---

[1] *Soviet Legal Philosophy,* p. 25 *et seq.*
[2] See *supra,* p. 62.
[3] *Soviet Legal Philosophy,* p. 66.

imperialist period of capitalism creates international class
unifications and at the same time *the class struggle,* or more
accurately civil war, *on an international scale'.* The fact to
which Stuchka refers can be only the so-called international
trusts, agreements between capitalists of different states. But
these agreements are not based on international law—and hence
are not 'international' in the specifically legal sense of the term—
but on the national law of the respective states ; and imperialistic
wars—the most characteristic feature of the imperialistic period
—take place between the states ; and that means, in the Marxian
terminology, between the dominant classes of the different states.
Hence there is no 'international class unification' in the period
of imperialism, and therefore no state relationships that correspond to interests of a dominant class formed of the dominant
classes of several states. Stuchka is actually admitting this fact
when he says : 'The result of this is a certain basis even for the
bourgeois authority organised by the dominant class. Such
authority, however, is ephemeral and rapidly fades away in the
sense of a unification of the bourgeoisie, in view of the inevitable
conflict between the bourgeoisie(s) of different countries and for
capitalists of different branches'. Hence he tries to divert the
attention of his readers from the fact that he has not solved
the problem of international law by referring to the tendency of
the Soviet state to embrace all mankind :

> 'The Soviet form of state is *per se* an international
> unification of mankind (or of a portion of mankind). It is
> no less true that Soviet law has a direct tendency towards
> internationalism. And the authority organised therefor
> upon an international scale is being generated in the Com-
> munist International'.[4]

## Pashukanis' theory of international law as inter-class law

In his general theory of law Pashukanis does not deal with
the problem of international law ; he only expresses doubts concerning the stability of its basis. He says :

> 'Where the function of constraint is not organised and is
> not within the jurisdiction of a special mechanism standing
> above the parties it comes forth in the shape of "mutuality",
> so-called ; down to the present time, the principle of

[4] *Loc. cit.,* p. 66.

mutuality—where there is a condition of the equilibrium of forces—represents the sole basis of international law—a basis, be it said, which is extremely unstable'.[5]
This statement does not refer to the international law as a normative order but to the effectiveness of this order, and expresses a view widespread among bourgeois writers. In an article published in the Russian *Encyclopædia of State and Law,* 1926,[6] Pashukanis wrote: 'the international law owes its existence to the fact that the bourgeoisie exercises its domination over the proletariat and the colonies by organising itself in several trusts, separated from one another and in competition with one another'. By characterising the governments of the independent states as 'trusts' he expresses in Marxian jargon the idea that international law presupposes the existence of independent states. Then he maintains that with the coming into existence of the Soviet state international law does assume a new significance; it is now 'a form of temporary compromises between two antagonistic class-systems'. These compromises are concluded as long as the bourgeois system is no longer able to secure, and the socialist system has not yet achieved, exclusive domination. In this sense it seems to be possible to speak of an international law of the transition period (as Korovin did in a work published in 1924).[7] The significance of this transition period consists in the fact that the open struggle for destruction (intervention, blockade, non-recognition) is replaced by a struggle waged within the framework of 'norms', 'normal' diplomatic intercourse and treaties. The international law assumes the character of an inter-class law.

What Pashukanis describes by these statements is not a new significance of international law, but the methods of foreign policy which the Soviet Government applies during the transition period, that is, the period between the dominance of capitalism and that of communism, under the old and unchanged international law. He is far from defining the concept of international law in conformity with the Marxian concept of law. An 'inter-class' law is a law between classes as equal partners,

---

[5] *Loc. cit.,* p. 203.
[6] Quoted by V. E. Hrabar, ' *Das heutige Voelkerrecht vom Standpunkt eines Sowjetjuristen* '. *Zeitschrift fuer Voelkerrecht,* 14. Bd. (1927), p. 189.
[7] Cf. *infra,* p. 56.

not a law imposed by one class on another. If under international law 'compromises' between the class ruling within a capitalist state and a class ruling within a socialist state are possible, international law cannot be in the exclusive interest of the one or the other; it must be indifferent with respect to the class conflict between the bourgeoisie and the proletariat.

Also in his essay 'The Soviet State and the Revolution in Law' (1930), Pashukanis refers to the problem of international law. He says:

> '. . . if we take the proposition of Lenin, "Law is nothing without a mechanism capable of compelling the observance of legal norms", international law must then be regarded as nothing, since—as every one knows—no mechanism exists such as would compel obedience to the norms of international law'.

That means that according to the definition of law presented by Lenin international law is no law at all. However, Pashukanis does not accept this answer. Without modifying the definition of Lenin, he continues:

> 'If it be admitted that international law exists notwithstanding the absence of a single centralised mechanism of constraint in the relationships between states, and consequently that international law plays a certain part—particularly in our interrelations with capitalist encirclement—then we come up against a new problem: our definition of every sort of law as class law must somehow be brought into harmony with the fact that international law functions as mediator in the relationships between the proletariat (organised as the dominant class) and bourgeois states. Accordingly, I put forward the point of view that after the proletarian revolution international law in this sense is converted into inter-class law'.[8]

An 'inter-class' law is only by name a 'class' law; it is, as pointed out, the contrary of a class law in the sense of the Marxian doctrine. Consequently Pashukanis admits that he has not yet solved the problem of international law. He says:

> 'Nevertheless, the problem of international law remains without solution. Does international law exist? Can we regard it as a real fact in the mutual relationships between

[8] *Soviet Legal Philosophy,* p. 244 *et seq.*

the Soviet Union and the capitalist encirclement? If we can so regard it, how is our conception of class law then to be reconciled with that fact? Finally, must international law be contemplated in connection with the ideas expressed by Lenin as to the course of the struggle with this capitalist encirclement—the course of a struggle wherein temporary compromises are included? All this is subject to further consideration '.[9]

But 'further consideration' did not lead to the solution of the problem. In a textbook of international law, published in 1935, he did not demonstrate that international law is a class law in the same sense as the national law of the capitalist state; he only maintained that international law as practised between capitalist states is one of the forms with the aid of which imperialist states carry on the struggle between themselves, consolidating the division of booty, *i.e.*, territory and superprofit.[10] If this is true, if there is under the auspices of international law a struggle between the imperialist states, and that means according to the Marxian doctrine between the bourgeois classes of these states, for territory and superprofit, then international law cannot be a class law in the same sense as national law, because the struggle between two bourgeois classes is something totally different from the struggle between the bourgeois class and the class of the proletariat, *i.e.*, that class struggle in which national law is the instrument of the bourgeoisie in its attempt to suppress the proletariat. The struggle between two imperialist bourgeois classes necessarily leads to the strengthening of the one and the weakening of the other, and consequently has a highly ambivalent character with respect to the relationship of the bourgeoisie to the proletariat, which is the only relationship relevant for the class character of the law. It is just the inevitable struggle between the imperialistic bourgeoisies of the capitalist states which actually led to the establishment of the dictatorship of the proletariat in Russia and which, according to the Marxist doctrine, will ultimately lead to the mutual destruction of the capitalist states and thus to the final victory of the proletariat. If international law fosters the struggle between the bourgeoisies of the

[9] *Loc. cit.,* p. 246.
[10] According to John N. Hazard, 'Cleansing Soviet International Law of Anti-Marxist Theories', *The American Journal of International Law,* Vol. 32 (1938), p. 245.

capitalist states and hence is class law only in this sense, it is, in the last analysis, in the interest of the proletariat only, and thus —this is the paradoxical result of the Marxian interpretation of international law—a socialist rather than a bourgeois law ; hence just the contrary of that which according to the original doctrine of Pashukanis all the law by its very nature must be, in order finally to wither away.[11]

### Korovin's doctrine of an international law of the transition period: the co-existence of a socialist and a capitalist international law

Neither Stuchka nor Pashukanis were specialists in the field of international law. The first monograph on this subject written under the Soviet regime by an expert was E. A. Korovin's work *The International Law of the Transition Period,* published in 1924.[12] Whereas in the first years after the bolshevik revolution the tendency prevailed to ignore the existence of international law or to deny its legal character, Korovin declares at the very beginning of his work :

> ' It is impossible to reject international law by simply denying its existence and to dispatch the entire set of international legal norms of the present time as a bourgeois remainder by a stroke of the pen '.[13]

But this does not mean that he considers the existing international law as a legal order binding on the Soviet state in its relationships to the other states. He maintains that together with the socialist Soviet state a new international law has come into existence, regulating the relationships between this state and the capitalist states, in a way different from that of the international law regulating the relationships between the capitalist states. There is not, and never has been, a uniform general international law valid for all the states of the world. Such a world-wide general international law is nothing more but a ' myth '. In reality, there exist several systems of international law, such as a European international law regulating the

---

[11] Cf. John N. Hazard, ' The Soviet Union and International Law ', *Soviet Studies,* Vol. 1, p. 191.

[12] Quoted according to the German translation of the second Russian edition (1925): *Das Voelkerrecht in der Uebergangszeit,* published in Internationalrechtliche Abhandlungen, herausgeg. von Herbert Kraus, Berlin, 1929.

[13] Korovin, *loc. cit.,* p. 2.

relationships between the European states, especially among the great powers; an American international law; a special legal system regulating the relationships between the capitalist states and their colonies and half-colonies (protectorates, mandates); and, finally, that peculiar legal system regulating the relationships between the socialist and capitalist states.[14] Korovin does not indicate the norms which belong to this system. He says only that those norms of international law which are based on a solidarity of ideas prevailing within the capitalist states cannot apply to the relationships between the capitalist and the socialist states; but he adds that the lack of ideological solidarity does not prevent international legal relations between the two types of states. Then he specifies the spheres of interest within which such relations are possible :

(1) Humanitarian interests independent of political tendencies, such as are manifested in the fight against epidemics and the protection of historic monuments or products of art ;

(2) Material, *i.e.*, economic interests of a merely technical character, for instance concerning postal, telegraphic, rail, sea communications, and the like ; and

(3) Material interests of social, *i.e.*, political importance.[15]

In all these fields legal relations may be established by treaties between capitalist and socialist states. As to the first-mentioned relations based on humanitarian interests, it is evident that they are not—as Korovin supposes—beyond any ideological solidarity; for they are based on values or ideals common to the two types of political and economic systems. Between the second and third categories of legal relations Korovin sees an essential difference. Agreements concerning technical matters are based on a perfect harmony of interests of the contracting parties, for improvement of the technique is not only in the interest of capitalist states but also an essential condition of the realisation of socialism. Legal relations of the third category, however, are possible only on the basis of compromises between the capitalist and the socialist states. But this is not a particular characteristic of agreements between capitalist and socialist states. In view of the antagonism which normally exists between the political interests of the capitalist states, treaties regulating the political relationships among these states, too, are based on compromises.

---

[14] *Loc. cit.*, p. 7 *et seq.*          [15] *Loc. cit.*, p. 12 *et seq.*

### The pluralist doctrine and the primacy of national over international law (the dogma of sovereignty)

Korovin's doctrine that there is no general international law valid for all the states, that international law falls into different systems, each regulating only the relationships between several definite states, the 'pluralistic'[16] doctrine—as he calls it—is based on a confusion of two problems which theoretically have nothing to do with each other: the problem of the primacy of national over international law, in contradistinction to the primacy of international over national law, which refers to the reason for the validity of international law; and the problem of general, in contradistinction to particular, international, law, which refers to the spheres of validity of the norms of international law and consequently also to their material sphere of validity, *i.e.,* their content.

Korovin does not expressly raise the question as to the relationship between international and national law. But he—as all the other Soviet writers on international law—insists on the principle of unlimited sovereignty[17] of the state as essential to the relationship between the state and international law. He says—thus demonstrating the political motive of his theory—that any limitation of the sovereignty as long as the capitalist encirclement of the Soviet state exists is incompatible with the interests of the latter, since it means a victory of capitalism over socialism[18]; and he declares that the Soviet state is destined to act as the 'world master of the classical doctrine of sovereignty'.[19] As the 'classical doctrine' he considers the one advocated by some bourgeois writers, such as Jellinek and Martens, according to which sovereignty is 'self-determination', that is to say, the power of the state to determine exclusively by its own will the legal relations between itself and its subjects as well as between itself and other states; which means that the state can be legally bound only by its own will, that it is the supreme legal authority. This signifies, formulated without the aid of any personification and metaphor, that the national legal order is the highest legal order, above which there can be no other legal order. So-called international law can be considered as valid for the state only

16 *Loc. cit.,* p. 8.
17 *Loc. cit.,* pp. 34, 42 *et seq.*
18 *Loc. cit.,* p. 4.
19 *Loc. cit.,* p. 42.

if recognised as such by the state and, hence, only as part of its national law.[20] That means that the reason for the validity of international law is the basic norm of the national legal order, of which international law is considered to be a part. All this is implied in the concept of sovereignty as defined by Korovin. It means that Korovin in his interpretation of international law— just as the bourgeois writers whom he follows in his definition of sovereignty—presupposes the primacy of national over international law, in contradistinction to the hypothesis of the primacy of international law according to which the reason for the validity of the national legal orders is to be found in international law, and that means, in the last analysis, in the basic norm of this law.[21] From the hypothesis of the primacy of national law over international law it follows that there cannot be one unified international law, valid—as a unique legal order— for all the states of the world, a 'general' international law in the sense of a world law. If international law is valid only as

---

[20] Josef L. Kunz, 'Sowjet-Russland und das Voelkerrecht'. *Zeitschr. f. Voelkerrecht,* XIII (1926), p. 584, writes : 'Although bolshevism pretends to be politically progressive, the Soviet theory of international law is characterised by an outspoken reactionary tendency. This tendency manifests itself in the fact that the theory is obstinately keeping to that concept of an absolute sovereignty of the individual state which modern theory of international law is more and more rejecting. The Soviet theory—as Korovin says—identifies the cause of Soviet Russia with that of sovereignty'.

A. Patkin, 'The Soviet Union in International Law', *Proceedings of the Australian and New Zealand Society of International Law,* Melbourne (1935), Vol. 1, p. 58 *et seq.,* remarks that the Soviet theory of sovereignty is of the same type as the old monarchical doctrine of sovereignty ; its purpose is to build up hindrances to the development of international law. He says that what Korovin calls the international law of the transition period is 'neither "international" nor "law"', it is simply 'a chapter of Soviet municipal law built on the basis of party dictatorship'.

[21] According to Rudolf Schlesinger, 'Soviet Theories of International Law', *Soviet Studies,* Vol. 4, No. 3 (1953), p. 334 *et seq.,* Korovin, in a later publication, rejected expressly the hypothesis of the primacy of international over national law. He accepted Vyshinsky's thesis that the internal policies and tendencies of a state necessarily conditioned its behaviour on the international stage, but he added that this implied that the conduct of a state was conditioned 'in other words, first and foremost, by its public law'. Schlesinger reports that some soviet critics of Korovin agreed with his rejection of the primacy of international over national law, but objected that his statement : the conduct of the state on the international stage is conditioned by its public law, was a revival of the Hegelian interpretation of international law as external public law. But this interpretation of international law is the inevitable consequence of the hypothesis of the primacy of national over international law, accepted by Korovin as well as by his critics.

part of a national law, there are as many international laws as there are national laws; and then the Soviet state has—as any other state—its own international law regulating its relationships with the other states. This is the pluralistic construction of international law that follows from the sovereignty doctrine accepted by Korovin as by many bourgeois theorists. It answers only and exclusively the question as to the reason for the validity of international law, which—according to this view—is the 'will' of the state for which this law claims to be valid.

## The political doctrine of sovereignty

In so far as the doctrine of sovereignty expresses only the view that the state—or, what amounts to the same, the legal order constituting the state—is presupposed as the supreme legal authority, it has a theoretical, and not a political character. But Korovin uses the sovereignty doctrine also as a purely political principle, that is to say, as the postulate that the legal power of the state should not be restricted. He is against the establishment of a world state as an enterprise 'quite removed from reality',[22] because it would imply the abolition of the sovereignty of the states. But he adds: sovereignty should not be identified with nationalism or imperialism, at least as far as the sovereignty of the Soviet Union is concerned, which by its very nature is neither nationalistic nor imperialistic; its 'social nature completely precludes even the possibility of such a transformation'.[23] Professor Korovin cannot be so naïve as to believe that any one who is not under the discipline of the communist party will consider the effective control which the Soviet government has established over Czechoslovakia, Hungary, Poland, and other 'sovereign' states to be the result of a policy which has nothing to do with imperialism or nationalism. Although Korovin insists upon the maintenance of the sovereignty of the states, he admits that under certain circumstances restrictions upon sovereignty are justifiable. He says: 'in the interests of the preservation and consolidation of sovereignty, as a factor of universal progress, it becomes necessary temporarily to limit to a considerable degree the sovereignty . . .'[24]—of Czechoslovakia,

[22] Eugene A. Korovin, 'The Second World War and International Law', *The American Journal of International Law*, Vol. 40 (1946), p. 747.
[23] *Loc. cit.*, p. 747.
[24] *Loc. cit.*, p. 744.

Hungary, and the other satellites of the U.S.S.R.? Not at all!
That the sovereignty of these states is limited, no Soviet writer
would admit. It is the sovereignty of Germany and Japan, the
states defeated in the Second World War, to which Korovin
refers as to 'the most aggressive nations'. Only 'peace-loving'
states should have the privilege of unlimited sovereignty: a
highly problematical principle as long as there is no impartial
authority competent to decide the question, which state is peace-
loving and which is aggressive. And no such authority can be
established as long as the Soviet doctrine of sovereignty is maintained.

### Korovin's theory of the sources of international law

As pointed out, the view that national law has primacy over
international law, based on the presupposition that national law
is the supreme legal authority, refers only to the reason for the
validity of international law. Nothing follows from it with
respect to the content of the international law, even if this law
is considered to be valid only as part of a national law. In
particular, it is not possible to conclude from the primacy of
national over international law that the content of the international law of one state may be different from that of another
state. For, according to this hypothesis, the validity of international law is based on its recognition by the state concerned;
and the recognition of international law necessarily implies the
recognition of those rules of international law which determine
the sources of international law, that is to say, the procedures
by which international law is created: custom and treaties.
That means that by recognising international law a state recognises it as it exists as created by custom and treaties, and as it
will be modified only by custom and treaties. Korovin expressly
admits that custom and treaties are the sources of international
law.[25] But he maintains that the relationship which exists
according to the socialist international law between the two
sources is different from that existing according to the bourgeois
international law. He thinks that according to the latter, custom
is the primary, treaties only a secondary source. Customary

[25] Cf. H. N. Makarov, 'Die Voelkerrechtswissenschaft in Sowjetrussland',
*Zeitschrift fuer auslaendisches oeffentliches Recht und Voelkerrecht*,
Bd. VI (1936), p. 489.

international law can only be 'fixed', *i.e.*, codified, by treaties (as, *e.g.*, the law of war or the law concerning diplomatic intercourse), whereas according to the socialist international law, treaties are the primary, custom is a secondary—or, as he puts it, a 'subsidiary' or 'auxiliary' source. The first of the two statements is certainly not correct. General international law created by custom cannot be codified only but also complemented and even modified by treaties, provided it has not the character of *jus cogens;* and there can be no doubt that many norms of general international law created by custom have only the character of *jus dispositivum.* The statement that according to socialist international law custom is only a secondary source, is not clear, and Korovin does not explain it at all. Besides, his doctrine of the relationship between custom and treaties has not been accepted by the other Soviet writers, especially not by Pashukanis who recognised without any reservation both sources as equally important.

Korovin's attempt to minimise the importance of custom as a source of international law may be explained by the fact that custom as a law-creating fact is not necessarily constituted by the habitual behaviour or practice of all the state members of the international community, so that a state may be bound by a norm of international law created by a custom in the establishment of which this state did not participate. Hence the binding force of customary law may run into conflict with the sovereignty of the state as conceived by the Soviet theory. Korovin's treatment of customary international law may be explained also by the fact that existing general international law is in its entirety customary law, and that he considered this so-called general international law as identical with the international law of the 'bourgeois West',[26] and different as far as its content is concerned, not only from the socialist, *i.e.*, the international law of the Soviet state, but also from the American

[26] Korovin, *The International Law of the Transition Period*, p. 7.    N. N. Alexeiew und Leo Zaitzeff, 'Sowjetstaat und Voelkerrecht', *Zeitschrift f. Voelkerrecht*, XVI (1932), p. 211, remark with respect to this doctrine of Korovin: 'It is the tendency of the revolutionary period [of the Soviet state] to emancipate the international law as far as possible from the traditional notions of the bourgeois theory and to build it up on new principles established by treaties. We have examined the international relations of the Soviet state and we think that we can ascertain that the Soviet international law has remained within the sway of the traditional notions'.

international law and the international law regulating the relationships between the capitalist states and their colonies and half-colonial territories. But if there are differences between a European and an American international law, they are differences between the particular international law constituted by the treaties concluded or the custom established by the European states in their mutual intercourse, on the one hand, and the particular international law created in the same way by the American states in their mutual relationships. Both particular international laws, the European as well as the American—if they exist at all—are based on a general international law which, as far as its content is concerned, is common to the European and American states. It is on the basis of the norms of this general international law, instituting custom and treaties as the procedures of creating international law, that the European and the American law—each as a particular international law—have come into existence, provided that they exist at all; that is to say, if it is possible to distinguish a certain type of international legal norms valid only for the European states from another type of international legal norms valid only for the American states. The fact—if it is a fact—that there exist different systems of international law, valid only for a certain region or a certain group of states, is not only compatible with but even based on the existence of a general international law, valid for all the states, whether the reason for the validity of this international law is considered to be the basic norm of a national or the basic norm of the international legal order.

As to the law regulating the relationships between the capitalist states and their colonial and half-colonial territories, it is to a great extent not international but national law; and in so far as it is international law—in the case of protectorates and mandates—it is established by treaties and has only a particular character. The fact that the Soviet state will not conclude such treaties does not constitute a difference between a bourgeois and a socialist international law, but only a difference between the international policy of the capitalist states and the international policy of the Soviet state. Besides, the legal basis of the mandate system was the Covenant of the League of Nations, to which the Soviet state adhered; and the trusteeship system, which is not very different from the mandate system, is part of the Charter of the United Nations, to which the Soviet state is one of the original contracting parties.

### Korovin's theory of the subjects of international law

It is easy to show that the differences which according to the theory of Korovin exist between the capitalist and the socialist international law are by no means differences between two international legal orders. Korovin mentions in the first place a difference with respect to the subjects of international law. He does not deny that states are the subjects of the socialist as well as of the capitalist international law; but he rejects the traditional view that states are the only subjects of international law. He maintains—in conformity with the doctrine prevailing among bourgeois writers—that not only the states but also international organisations of states are subjects of international law. He asserts too, that certain philanthropic associations, especially the so-called 'international' associations of workers, and above all the so-called Communist International, are to be considered as subjects of international law. But there can be hardly any doubt that only associations of states constituted by international agreements can be subjects of international law, in so far as positive international law and not a product of wishful thinking is in question.

### Alleged differences between capitalist and socialist international law

As to the state as subject of international law, Korovin emphasises that according to the Marxian doctrine the state is nothing but the domination of one class over another, and not, as the bourgeois theorists pretend, a personality, implying the fiction of a unity which, in reality, does not exist. Hence he defines international law as an aggregate of legal norms determining the rights and duties of the ruling classes as the collective bodies participating in the international intercourse.[27]

27 This definition is in the first Russian edition (cf. Makarov, *loc. cit.,* p. 483). In the German translation of the second Russian edition the definition of the state as domination of one class over another is maintained and the doctrine of the personality of the state rejected; but the chapter on the subjects of international law concludes with the statement: 'within the international law of the first quarter of the twentieth century the relatively widest sphere of legal activity belongs—until further notice—to the sovereign state' (p. 33).

Different doctrines concerning the nature of the state are completely irrelevant from the point of view of international law. If there are subjects of the rights and duties stipulated by international law, these subjects are 'persons', since 'person' means nothing but subject of rights and duties; and the concept of person is always the result of a personification. Whether the rights and duties of the state stipulated by international law are interpreted to be the rights and duties of the ruling class or· the rights and duties of the whole people conceived of as a unit, has no consequences as far as the content of these rights and duties are concerned. These rights are to be exercised and these duties are to be fulfilled by the organs of the state; and whether these organs are considered to be organs of the ruling class or organs of the whole people makes no difference from the point of view of international law. Since Korovin does not deny that the states are subjects of international law he deals with the states as with juristic persons, whatever his doctrine concerning the nature of the state may be. It is true, he tries to deduce from the Marxian doctrine of the state certain consequences with respect to the content of the socialist international law, in contradistinction to that of the bourgeois international law. He argues : if the state is to be identified with the ruling class, Soviet Russia, identical with its proletarian class, is not bound to pay the debts contracted by Russia under the rule of its bourgeoisie.[28] However, the answer to the question whether Soviet Russia has to pay the debts contracted by Czarist Russia depends only on the answer to the question as to whether Soviet Russia is from the point of view of international law the same state as Czarist Russia, or, more exactly formulated, whether a change of the ruling class brought about by a revolutionary change of government has, according to international law, the legal effect of annulling the international obligations established by the state under the government overthrown by the revolution. There can be no doubt that the answer to the second question is according to existing international law in the negative ; and this answer holds even if it is assumed that the state is identical with its ruling class. If this view implies that in case of such a change a new state has come into existence, then, according to international law, the new state is obliged to pay the debts contracted by the old state. But

[28] Korovin, *loc. cit.*, p. 28.

neither Korovin nor any other Soviet writer denies that it is Russia, the same Russia which was under the rule of the Russian bourgeoisie before the bolshevik revolution and afterwards has been under the rule of the Russian proletariat, within which the change of the ruling class has taken place. The Marxian doctrine of the class character of the state cannot be used to justify the annulment of the debts of Czarist Russia by the government of Soviet Russia. Korovin himself tries to justify this annulment also in another way, namely, by the *clausula rebus sic stantibus*.[29] He says that according to the socialist international law the clause is applicable only and exclusively in case a legal order is replaced by another, which in principle is totally different from the former. A revolutionary change in the entire economic and political structure of a state constitutes that change of circumstances, which, according to international law, allows the state concerned to annul by a unilateral act obligations accepted by it prior to this change. Consequently the Soviet state is not obliged to pay the interest on loans raised by the Czarist government for the purpose of suppressing the revolution.[30] That means that the *clausula rebus sic stantibus* is part of socialist international law, just as it is part of bourgeois international law according to a doctrine advocated by many bourgeois writers; if there is a difference, it is only its interpretation by Soviet theorists, which differs from that by bourgeois writers. But there are differences in interpretation of the *clausula* also among bourgeois writers, and there are even bourgeois writers who deny that the *clausula* is part of positive international law.

Other differences which allegedly exist between the socialist and the bourgeois international law concern the principle of the legal equality of the states. Korovin admits that this principle was originally the unshakable dogma[31] of the theory of international law, but he maintains that the 'international reality'—which can only mean the practice of the states—has more and more deviated from it. He refers to certain treaties by which the political preponderance of the great powers over the small powers has been secured, and asserts that Soviet Russia in its international practice is—in opposition to the capitalist states—

29 *Loc. cit.,* p. 111.
30 *Loc. cit.,* p. 111.
31 *Loc. cit.,* p. 43.

the protagonist of that principle of equality.[32]   Consequently the Soviet government rejects the solution of international problems by a majority vote of the states concerned[33]; it insists on the principle of unanimity, thus refusing to allow the settlement of disputes by a majority decision of an international tribunal.[34] That means that the Soviet government will not conclude treaties the purpose of which is to make smaller states politically dependent on the Soviet Union, or treaties conferring upon an international agency the power to adopt by a majority vote decisions binding upon all the contracting parties.   But all this does not constitute a difference between a socialist and a bourgeois international law, but only a difference between two policies, both based on one and the same international law.   And that there is no essential difference between the policy of the Soviet government and that of the governments of the capitalist states can hardly be denied in view of the treaties the Soviet Union has recently concluded with Czechoslovakia, Bulgaria, Hungary, and other smaller states; and, last but not least, in view of the Charter of the United Nations, which confers on the five great Powers the veto right, the typical example of a treaty establishing legal inequality in the relations between the great and the small powers.

As to the question of intervention, very much disputed in the bourgeois theory of international law, Korovin—as many bourgeois writers—does not exclude it without reservations. He rejects only intervention of one state for the purpose of suppressing a socialist revolution within another state[35]; which may be rejected also by a bourgeois interpretation of international law.

As to the law of war in the sense of a *jus ad bellum*, Korovin declares that the only war a socialist state will wage is a war for the purpose of defending itself in its existence as a ruling class ('class self-defence').   Since according to his theory the state is by its very nature a class state, Korovin's statement means nothing else but that according to the socialist international law the only justifiable war is a war of self-defence, which is a doctrine advo-

[32] *Loc. cit.*, p. 44.
[33] *Loc. cit.*, p. 46.
[34] *Loc. cit.*, p. 46 *et seq.*
[35] *Loc. cit.*, p. 52.

cated by many bourgeois writers interpreting bourgeois international law.

The result of an objective analysis of Korovin's theory of a socialist international law valid together with a capitalist international law (or several capitalist international laws), of the assumption of two (or several) legal systems of different content, shows that what Korovin presents as different legal systems is either a difference of international policy, carried out by treaties having the character of particular international law, based on one and the same general international law; or a difference in the interpretation of this law. Differences in the interpretation of one and the same legal order are inevitable, and must be distinguished from the difference which is the effect of two different legal orders; although it may be admitted that this distinction constitutes only a relative, not an absolute separation of the two cases.

**The new doctrine of Korovin : the imperialistic international law of the past and the democratic international law of the coming period**

Korovin's theory of a special socialist international law, valid beside a bourgeois international law, and particularly his doctrine concerning the subjects of international law have been rejected by other Soviet theorists [36]; of course, not for scientific, but for political reasons. As soon as the Soviet government was aware that it could use the existing international law in its own interest and that it was of great importance to be recognised by the other governments as the government of a state in its capacity as a subject of an international law, it could not allow a doctrine which denied the existence of such a law as common to all the states. The fact was too evident that international law, by imposing upon all states the obligation to respect mutually their territorial integrity and political independence and prohibiting them from intervening in the domestic affairs of other states, protects its subjects and consequently also the Soviet state. In a

---

[36] Especially by Pashukanis in his above-mentioned *Textbook of International Law* (1935). An excellent critical analysis of this work is given by Joseph Florin, ' La Théorie bolchéviste du Droit international public ' in *Revue Internationale de la Théorie du Droit, XII* (1938), pp. 97–115. Cf. also Jean-Ives Calvez, *Droit international et Souveraineté en U.R.S.S., Cahiers de la Fondation Nationale des Sciences Politiques*, 48, Paris, 1953, p. 98 *et seq.*

letter to the review *Sovetskoe gosudarstvo* of May 5, 1935,[37] Korovin condemned as 'ultra leftist' his 'attempt to construe a special socialist international law of the transition period' and confessed that he had 'underestimated the importance of the juridical forms and especially of the state as the only subject of international law by substituting the class and the party for the state'.

In the above-quoted article, 'The Second World War and International Law', published in 1946, Korovin defines international law—referring to a legal order binding upon all the states of the world (*i.e.*, to one general international law)—'as the sum-total of legal norms guaranteeing international protection of the democratic minimum'.[38] But he restricts this definition to the international law 'in the coming period of history'. It seems that the international law valid in the past period is, according to this view, essentially different, since it did not guarantee international protection of the democratic minimum. Thus Korovin advocates again a doctrine of two different international laws, but now they are not valid at the same time but the one follows the other. He admits that the difference between the two international laws, the democratic and the non-democratic one, is not absolute but relative. For he asserts: 'This, of course, does not preclude the existence in contemporary international law'—as a transition period?—'of anti-democratic trends, survivals and forms, beginning with the imperialistic and ending with the feudal. It is no less indisputable, however, that the process of overcoming them, the struggle for their abolition and the affirmation of the principles of democracy in international relations, constitutes an immediate objective which unites the progressive elements of contemporary mankind'. According to this view of Korovin, there exists an evolution of general international law from a non-democratic, *i.e.*, imperialistic and feudal stage, to a democratic stage. But what does he mean by democracy guaranteed within the international community of states by general international law? Since democracy is a form of government and the international community of states has no government, there is hardly any possibility of a democratic or anti-democratic international law. Besides, as far as the form of

[37] A German translation of this letter is published by Makarov, *loc. cit.*, p. 486.
[38] *The American Journal of International Law,* Vol. 40 (1946), p. 743.

government of the states, members of the international community, is concerned, general international law of the past as well as of the present time is strictly indifferent. It leaves the determination of the form of government to the national law and makes no difference as far as the obligations, responsibilities and rights of the states are concerned between democratic and non-democratic states. Korovin does not say what he means by democracy. He says only what he does not mean by this term:

> ' Thus the principles of a new and broader democracy going farther than parliamentary forms and election ballots yet directly expressing the will and heroic ardour of the popular masses are entering the international arena as well '.[39]

The ' democracy ' referred to in this statement is indeed the form of state government. How the principles of such a democracy expressing the will of the popular masses can enter the international arena where governments, and not popular masses, are the acting agents, is difficult to understand. That the new international law protects only democratic states and withdraws its protection from non-democratic states, is evidently not true; and there is not the slightest tendency of such a development within general international law. Later Korovin says:

> ' Genuine democracy and juridical levelling have nothing in common, and the organisation of international relations on formal and levelling principles would be a crying violation of the most elementary equality . . . '.[40]

Here it seems that Korovin understands by democracy the principle of equality and by democracy in international law the principle of the equality of the states. If so, then there is no difference between the international law of the past and that of the present and coming periods, since this principle is and always has been a principle of general international law. It is especially with respect to the United Nations that Korovin defines the international law of the coming period as a law guaranteeing a democratic minimum. Referring to the Teheran Declaration, he says:

> ' The United Nations have resolved not only to wipe off the face of the earth Nazism and Fascism together with their

[39] *Loc. cit.*, p. 745.
[40] *Loc. cit.*, p. 746.

brigand theory and practice, but also to establish a "world family of democratic countries" based on democratic principles of foreign policy . . . .'.[41]
Now it is clear that the democracy Korovin has in mind is not—as he maintains—a principle of international law but a principle of the foreign policy of certain states, which has nothing to do with the principle of equality. Here, again, we face the confusion of law and politics so characteristic of the Soviet legal theory. But Korovin refers also to the Charter of the United Nations [42] as an example of democratic international law. The Charter, however, is only particular, not general international law, since it is a treaty to which not all the states are parties. Its claim to be binding upon non-member states is highly problematical and will hardly be recognised by Soviet writers, who insist upon sovereignty as an essential characteristic of the state. The Charter does not—as the Teheran Declaration promised—constitute a world family of democratic states. Among its principles is none which gives preference to a definite form of government, and no definite form of government, especially not a democratic form of government, is a condition of admission to the United Nations. As a matter of fact, there are among the members of this organisation states which cannot be considered as democratic from any point of view. In addition the Charter recognises the principle of sovereign equality of all states, that is, just that 'formal and levelling' principle to which Korovin opposes 'genuine' democracy. It is on this principle of formal equality according to which norms binding upon a state can be created only with its consent—and that means by treaty—that the Charter, as a treaty, confers, with the consent of all the contracting parties, upon the five great Powers certain privileges and thus establishes a material inequality among the members of the community constituted by it. But—strange as it may seem—it is just this inequality which Korovin praises as the true equality. He says :

'to recognise that the latter [the five great Powers] have special international rights not only does not undermine the principle of equality in international relations but for the first time in history provides this principle with a stable legal foundation '.[43]

[41] *Loc. cit.*, p. 743.    [42] *Loc. cit.*, p. 746.    [43] *Loc. cit.*, p. 747.

But just a few lines before, he has asserted : ' It is nothing new in history for Great Powers to occupy a privileged position '.[44] Where, then, is the fundamental change in the development of general international law from a non-democratic, nay, anti-democratic to a democratic law ? If general international law, binding upon the capitalist as well as the socialist states, is a democratic law in the sense democracy is understood in Soviet theory, how can this international law be something similar to a class law ? Korovin's new theory of modern international law as a democratic law in contradistinction to a previous anti-democratic international law is as untenable as is the old theory of international law as a socialist law in contradistinction to a capitalist international law.[45]

[44] *Loc. cit.*, p. 746.

[45] Korovin's distinction between an imperialistic and a democratic international law is more or less in conformity with a doctrine which—in opposition to his original theory of a capitalist and a socialist international law—recognises only one international law valid for all the states, socialist and capitalist, but insists upon the existence of two different lines within this law : a democratic-pacifistic, progressive line, followed by the socialist Soviet state, and an imperialistic, reactionary line, followed by the capitalist states. Cf. R. Schlesinger, *loc. cit.*, p. 281 *et seq.* If these two lines really exist—which is more than doubtful—they are not two lines of international law but two different types of foreign policy.

　　There are especially two problems which might give rise to the view of two lines within international law, a democratic-socialist and an imperialist-capitalist one : the recognition of a community as a state or of a body of individuals as the government of a state, and the compensation of aliens in case of a general expropriation or confiscation of private property within a socialist state. As to the first problem, the question of the constitutive or merely declaratory character of recognition is of great importance. In view of the fact that the capitalist states were very reluctant to recognise the Soviet government, it is quite understandable that Soviet jurists insisted upon a merely declaratory character of recognition, and denounced the doctrine according to which recognition has a constitutive character as an imperialistic ideology used by the capitalist states for the purpose of justifying intervention in the domestic affairs of foreign people. (Cf. Makarov, *loc. cit.*, p. 491.) That recognition is constitutive can hardly be considered as a specifically capitalist imperialistic doctrine, since the opposite view is advocated by many bourgeois theorists, and probably for the same political reason which determined the attitude of the Soviet writers : the idea of the sovereignty of the state the legal existence of which, or the legal existence of the government of which, is in question. If the state is sovereign, its legal existence or the legal existence of its government cannot depend on the act of another state. But how fallacious this political argument is becomes evident by the fact that if one starts not from the sovereignty of the recognised state but from the sovereignty of the recognising state, the constitutive character of the recognition follows.

　　The question as to whether a state which on the basis of national law nationalises the private property—or a certain kind of private property, the property in the means of production—situated within its territory is

**Korovin's return to the concept of the state as a juristic person ; his distinction between a social-historical and a legal concept of the state** •

One of the most decidedly rejected doctrines of Korovin was his denial of the juristic personality of the state, which concept he declared to be incompatible with the essence of the state as a domination of one class over another.[46] It is quite understandable that the Soviet government, in the interest of its political prestige in international affairs, was not satisfied with a theory according to which it did not represent the Soviet state as a unit, but did represent only one of the two classes existing within this state or the political party as the leader of this class. Hence Korovin was forced to abandon his doctrine. In a review of Teracouzio's *The Soviet Union and International Law*,[47] he asserts that it is erroneous to present as a Soviet doctrine the view that the state, because it is by its very nature the domination of one class over another, cannot be conceived of as a juristic person—the very view he advocated in his earlier work.[48] Now,

obliged by international law to compensate citizens of another state, is a question of the interpretation of international law. There is a generally recognised principle of this law according to which each state has the right to form its political and economic organisation without any interference on the part of other states. It is the principle of constitutional autonomy, guaranteed by international law. Whether and to what extent this principle is restricted by the norms of general international law concerning the treatment of aliens, is a question which may be answered in different ways and actually is disputed among the writers on international law, even among those considered as ' bourgeois '. There is, it is true, a certain tendency towards the establishment of a rule of international law imposing upon a socialist state the obligation to compensate citizens of another state for losses suffered through nationalisation laws. But it is hardly possible to maintain that such a rule has already been firmly established ; and in view of the fact that the existing socialist states are opposed to such a rule, it is not very likely that it ever will be. Hence, if there is a difference in this respect between the capitalist and the socialist view, it is a difference of interpretation of one and the same general international law, and not a difference between two international laws or two lines of the international law.

46 As to Pashukanis' criticism, cf. Florin, *loc. cit.*, p. 106 *et seq.*

47 *Harvard Law Review*, Vol. 49, 1935–1936 (1936), p. 1392 *et seq.*

48 This view was rejected by Pashukanis in his *Textbook of International Law* as ' pseudo-revolutionary '. Pashukanis tries to show that Korovin's doctrine according to which the concept of the state as a juristic person is incompatible with the class character of the state, makes any differentiation between the Soviet state and other organisations impossible and leads to the ' ultra-leftist ' identification of the proletarian state with the communist party. Cf. Florin, *loc. cit.*, p. 102 *et seq.* Pashukanis, of course, does not deny the class character of the state. As a Marxist he must assert that the state is by its very nature the domination of one class over another. But he tries to show that the class character of the

Korovin maintains that the rejection of the concept of the state as a juristic person is the result of the inadmissible confusion of the social-historical and the legal conception of the state. The social-historical conception of the state, he says, is indeed the domination of one class over another.

> ' But the class which has taken possession of the state apparatus is the class which has already overcome the resistance of some classes and succeeded in leading the other classes of its country : it acts not in the name of the proletariat or the bourgeoisie, but in the name of the state. Therefore . . . the Soviet state as a juridical conception, as a sovereign, as a subject of law is in no way to be distinguished from the conception generally accepted in international law '.

It is quite significant that the distinction between a social-historical and a legal (juristic) concept of the state has been made long before Korovin by a bourgeois writer, Georg Jellinek, in his *Allgemeine Staatslehre,* published in 1900. It has been proved logically untenable for the simple reason that two different concepts cannot define the same object. If the state is conceived of as a juristic person it is supposed to constitute a unit ; and if this unit is a juristic unit it consists in the fact that one and the same legal order is valid for all the individuals who are supposed to belong to the ' state ', in spite of the conflicts of interests which actually exist among these individuals. From this legal point of view, the state is this legal order, the unity of which is metaphorically presented as a juristic person. If by the social-historical concept of the state something different from the legal order is meant, this concept refers to an object different from that of the legal concept ; and if the object of this concept is the state, the social-historical concept cannot be a definition of the state but of something else, even if it is assumed that the individuals who form the state as a juristic unit, in so far as they are subjected to the same legal order, form also a unit regardless of their subjection to one and the same legal order. But it has been

---

state does not preclude its presentation as a juristic person. In its international relations the state appears as a unit which allows personification. The proletariat as the ruling class within the Soviet state does not only represent itself as a class, but in the sphere of international relations it monopolises the legal representation of the entire nation. Cf. Florin, *loc. cit.,* p. 106 *et seq.*

proved that it is not possible to demonstrate other than a juristic criterion of that unit which we call state, that the 'sociological' unity of the state, the state as sociological, that is, real, not merely juristic unit, is a fiction maintained to justify the fact that one and the same legal order is imposed upon individuals who, in reality, are divided into groups of conflicting interests.[49]

That the two concepts of the state offered by Korovin refer to two different objects, is obvious. The 'social-historical' conception refers to the domination, and that means the suppression of one class by another, to the struggle of the two classes in which the one uses coercive measures for the suppression of the other. In the Marxian doctrine this suppression by coercive measures of one class by another is called 'state'. It is something totally different from the 'leading' of one class by another after the resistance of the latter is overcome and thence a class struggle no longer exists. For, if such a situation really existed—as Korovin maintains—a real unity would be established in the relationships between the two groups, whereas no such unity exists as long as the struggle between the classes takes place; and according to the Marxian doctrine only as long as such struggle exists that phenomenon exists which this doctrine calls a 'state'. There can be little doubt that the characterisation of the relationship between the proletarian class and the bourgeois class in the dictatorship of the proletariat as mere leadership, instead of suppressive domination in a situation of class struggle, is in open contradiction to the facts admitted by the Soviet writers. Just like the bourgeois writers, Korovin uses a fiction, the fiction of a real unity, in order to justify the merely legal or juristic unity expressed in the concept of the state as a juristic person. He does not—as he pretends to do—distinguish a social-historical and a legal conception of the state; he substitutes for the Marxian 'social-historical' conception another, likewise social-historical conception as a fictitious basis of the legal conception of the state prevailing in the bourgeois theory of international law.

---

[49] Cf. my *Der soziologische und der juristische Staatsbegriff*, 2nd ed. 1928, and *General Theory of Law and State*, 1945, p. 181 *et seq.*

**Korovin's return to the doctrine that the state is the sole subject of international law**

Together with the denial of the juristic personality of the state, Korovin abandoned also his view concerning subjects of international law other than the states. He declared that the doctrine according to which the state is not the sole subject of international law is not a Soviet doctrine, but was 'the personal opinion of Professor Korovin which he himself later renounced'.[50] However, in his article, 'The Second World War and International Law',[51] he says:

> 'The war has shaken the traditional conception of the state as the sole subject of international law. The tremendous activity, heroism and self-sacrifice of the working class and its decisive influence on the outcome of the war have received further consolidation in the establishment of such powerful international associations of the working people as the World Trade Union Federation, which numbers 65,000,000 members. Can it now be stated, without giving offence either to tact or to common sense, that while any state, even a tiny one which plays no role whatsoever in international relations, is a subject of international law, an international organisation of 65,000,000 members is a *quantité négligeable* for international law? If international law is to deal with realities and not with fictions, it must admit that the conception of subject is not an absolute category existing out of space and time'.

The organisations of the working people to which Korovin here refers are 'international' not in a legal but only in a political sense, since they are not established on the basis of international law, and that means, not by an international agreement to which only states could be contracting parties, but on the basis of some national law. The fact that individuals belonging to different states are members of such organisations does not suffice to confer upon the latter an international character in a legal sense. The obligations, rights and responsibilities of these organisations are only those stipulated by the national law under which the respective associations are established. The statement of Korovin may be the expression of a wish or postulate: it is not the description of positive international law.

[50] *Harvard Law Review*, Vol. 49, 1935–1936 (1936), p. 1393.
[51] *The American Journal of International Law*, Vol. 40 (1946), p. 745.

**The Soviet theory concerning the status of individuals in international law; the interpretation of the London Agreement for the prosecution of war criminals**

The doctrine that states are the only subjects of international law implies the view—prevailing until recently also among bourgeois writers—that individuals cannot be subjects of international law, that only national law may impose obligations and responsibilities and confer rights upon them; and that, consequently, international law may become valid for them only through the national law. But when at the end of the Second World War by an international agreement individuals were made responsible for violations of international law, it became evident that—as had been maintained long before by a few writers—individuals can directly be subjects of obligations and responsibilities as well as subjects of rights established by norms of international law. However, although the Soviet Union was a contracting party to the London Agreement of August 8, 1945, by which individual criminal responsibility for violations of international law was established, Soviet writers refuse to recognise the fact that individuals can be, and actually are, not only indirectly, that is to say, in their capacity as organs of a state, but also directly, that is to say, as private persons, subjects of international obligations and rights, and that by international law responsibility of individuals and not only of states can be established. In order to maintain this position they interpret the international agreement in question as an act of national legislation performed by the governments of the four Powers occupying Germany. At the twenty-ninth meeting of the first session of the International Law Commission of the United Nations General Assembly, on May 27, 1949, the representative of the Soviet Union, Mr. Koretsky, declared with respect to the London Agreement and the judgment of the Military Tribunal established by this agreement that

> 'it could not be affirmed that "the individual is subject to international law, including international penal law". That conclusion could not be drawn automatically from the fact that certain criminals had been judged and condemned by an international tribunal created, not on the basis of international law, but because the four Powers represented on it had assumed sovereignty over the territory of the state

of which the criminals were nationals.   The idea that the
individual was subject to international law was not generally
accepted;  there could not therefore be any question of
proclaiming it as a principle.   According to the large
majority of legal theories, the State alone was subject to
international law.   It did not seem possible to say that
"international law, including international penal law, has
precedence over municipal law ".   It was true that the idea
was expressed in the provisions of article 14 of the draft
declaration on the rights and duties of states which the
commission had just adopted, but Mr. Koretsky maintained
that the precedence of international law over national law
had never been recognised and the Charter of the Nürnberg
Tribunal was no argument in favour of that concept.   It
was the precedence of national law—in other words,
national sovereignty—which enabled nations to govern
themselves as they wished . . . '.[52]

It is true that the governments of the four Powers which occupied
the territory of Germany had established themselves as the
Government over this territory and its population.   But the
London Agreement was concluded by them not in their capacity
as the government of Germany.   The contracting parties
expressly declared in the Preamble of the Agreement that they
were acting 'in the interest of all the United Nations'.   And,
above all :  the Agreement has been—in conformity with the
express provision of Article 5—adhered to by many other states.
In addition, the Agreement provided not only for the prosecution
of German war criminals but for the prosecution of the European
Axis War Criminals, a purpose which certainly could not be
pursued by an act of the national legislation of Germany.   Hence
the international-law character of the London Agreement cannot
be denied.

The fact that the London Agreement has the character of
international law is quite independent of the question as to
whether international law has 'precedence over municipal law',
or municipal law precedence over international law.   If 'precedence' means the same as 'primacy' both views—correctly
interpreted—refer only to the reason for the validity of the two
legal orders, not to their content.   Hence the international-law

52 United Nations General Assembly, Doc. A/CN.4/SR. 29, p. 8.

character of the London Agreement can be recognised even if one rejects the hypothesis of the primacy or precedence of international law over national (municipal) law and accepts the primacy or precedence of national (municipal) law over international law, as does the Soviet theory of international law by insisting on the sovereignty of the state. The above-quoted declaration of the Soviet delegate presupposes that only if international law had precedence over national law could an international agreement establish individual criminal responsibility; which implies the—unfortunately widespread—fallacy of inferring from the one or the other of the two hypotheses concerning the relation of international and national law a possible or actual content of the two legal orders.

## Soviet theory concerning human rights under international law

As to the status of individuals under international law, the Soviet theory is most contradictory. On the one hand it lays stress on the protection of the individual and a legal guarantee of his rights. Against the statement that Marxism preaches 'depersonification', Korovin declared: 'The whole force of Marxism is in the aspiration to guarantee to the individual the full-valued worthwhile existence of man'.[53] But, on the other hand, the dogma of the sovereignty of the state leads to the view that the individual cannot be a subject of international law, which implies that there can be no effective protection of the rights of individuals against violations of these rights by their own state. At the ninth meeting of the first session of the International Law Commission, April 25, 1949, the representative of the Soviet Union, Mr. Koretsky, said that he

'did not believe that man was a subject of international law. He did not agree with the concept of the individual subject of international law. Nevertheless, human rights must be mentioned particularly in view of the crimes which had been committed by Fascism'.[54]

If individuals cannot be subjects of international law, they can have rights or duties only through the state. This view is clearly expressed in a statement made by Vyshinsky in his capacity as the representative of the Soviet Union at the 183rd meeting of the

[53] Korovin, in *Harvard Law Review*, Vol. 49, p. 1392.
[54] United Nations General Assembly, Doc. A/CN.4/SR 9, p. 11.

General Assembly of the United Nations on December 10, 1948, with regard to the Declaration of Human Rights[55] :

'The draft declaration of human rights appeared to endorse that reactionary view directed against national sovereignty and was therefore entirely inconsistent with the principles of the United Nations. It was sometimes argued that the declaration of human rights should not touch on matters of national significance because it was devoted to the rights of individual human beings. It was impossible to agree to such a view, if only because human rights could not be conceived outside the state; the very concept of right and law was connected with that of the state. Human rights meant nothing unless they were guaranteed and protected by the state; otherwise they became a mere abstraction, an empty illusion easily created but just as easily dispelled'.

A statement made by the U.S.S.R. delegation in the Commission on Human Rights, on May 18, 1948, with Regard to Drafts and Proposals on Implementation contains the following passage :

'The implementation plan entails the establishment of various international instances in which communications and complaints with regard to the violation of human rights, from both states and governments and private individuals or associations of such individuals, would be considered. It thus conflicts with the whole system of international public law regulating the relations between states. In addition, the plan, if it is adopted, will have the effect of transforming a dispute between a private individual or group of individuals and their state or government into an international dispute, thereby substantially enlarging the area of international differences, frictions and incidents, unnecessarily burdening and aggravating international relations and undermining the foundations of peace. Furthermore, the transference to a special committee, special international court or even, as contemplated in some implementation plans, to the Commission on Human Rights of the prerogative conferred upon the General Assembly and the Economic and Social Council of making recommendations

55 United Nations *Official Records*, General Assembly, 3rd session, Part 1, 1948, Plenary Meetings, p. 923 *et seq.*

to States on questions of human rights would upset the powers as established by the Charter and the distribution of those powers as between the main and the auxiliary organs of the United Nations, and would, further, encourage interference in the internal affairs of members of the United Nations which is contrary to the Charter'.[56]

The view that individuals cannot be subjects of international law is incorrect even under the presupposition that international law is conceived of as part of national law. For there can be no doubt that by an international agreement, and hence by international law—even if conceived of as part of national law—such rights can be established, and the states parties to the agreement may be obliged to respect these rights. There can be no doubt that these rights may be guaranteed by the establishment of an international tribunal to which the individuals have direct access and which is competent to decide whether a right established by the agreement has been violated by an act of state, and to annul this act or to order the government concerned to annul it; and there is no sufficient reason to deny the possibility of providing, in the constituent agreement, for measures to enforce the decisions of the international tribunal. This is certainly the most effective way to guarantee the so-called fundamental human rights which, in so far as they constitute restrictions of the state's freedom of action, can be violated only by the state. Hence it is contrary to positive law—or, at least, to the possibilities offered by positive law—to maintain that rights of individuals can be established only by the state and can be protected only by the state, and not by an international organisation, and to reject on this basis the establishment of international tribunals which may be invoked directly by individuals. The view that there exists an inseparable connection between the rights of the individual and his state cannot be based on positive law; it can only erroneously be deduced from an alleged nature of the law or the state, by the argument that the establishment of a tribunal competent to protect internationally established rights of individuals is incompatible with the nature of international law or with the nature of the state. In this respect the Soviet theory is quite in conformity with the theory advocated by many

---

[56] United Nations Economic and Social Council, E/CN.4/SR 154. Cf. also E/CN.4/SR 115.

bourgeois writers who try to justify a policy directed against any
restriction of the authority of the state by arguments pretending
to be legal.

In the above-quoted statement of the Soviet delegation to
the United Nations—just as in the writings of many non-
communist authors—the theoretical aspect of the problem is not
clearly separated from the political one. The question as to
whether it is legally possible that individuals may be direct
subjects of international law and the question as to whether it is—
from some point of view or another—desirable to make
individuals direct subjects of international law, are two different
questions. The Soviet argument that a treaty conferring rights
directly upon individuals and offering them access to an international court would aggravate international relations and undermine the foundations of peace, may be to a certain extent correct.
But the attempt to guarantee and protect certain interests of
individuals by international law originates in the fact that real
or alleged violations of these interests by the government of the
individuals concerned are the cause of disturbances which
endanger international peace, as, for instance, the treatment of
the German minorities in Czechoslovakia or Poland. Hence
the political argument set forth by the Soviet delegation may be
outweighed by this counter-argument.[57]

## Krylov's attempt to apply the Marxian definition of law to international law

In 1946, Sergey Krylov, Soviet member of the International
Court of Justice, delivered a series of lectures on 'The Fundamental Concepts of International Law' at the Academy of
International Law at The Hague.[58] If a representative Soviet
jurist, as Krylov, presents at this academy—which from the Soviet
point of view must be considered as an institute of bourgeois
science—a theory of international law, we may expect to get
from him the genuine Marxian interpretation of the phenomenon

[57] The Soviet writer Sergey Krylov says in his work quoted *infra,* p. 447
*et seq.*: 'the United Nations is competent to study the legal situation of
the individual in the international life in order to eliminate any threat
to international peace and security which might be caused by a violation
of the rights and freedoms of the said individual'.

[58] Sergey Krylov, 'Les Notions principales du Droit des Gens'. *Recueil des
Cours de l'Académie de Droit International* (1947), I, tome 70, pp. 411–
476.

concerned and to learn why international law, too, is to be conceived of as an ideological superstructure set up on relationships of production, and an instrument of the exploiting domination of one class over another. Krylov seems to be aware of this task. For he begins his lectures with the statement that the law—the law in general—is 'one of the superstructures set upon the economic basis'[59]; and, applying this formula to international law, he says :

> 'The international or interstate law must therefore be defined as a juridic superstructure set up on the world economy, representing the results of the competition and co-operation of the dominant classes of the various states in their external international relations'.[60]

The deviation from the original Marxian view is obvious. International law is not an 'ideological' but a 'juridic' superstructure; it is set up not on relationships of production but on the 'world economy'. Krylov does not explain what he means by 'world economy' and does not make the slightest effort to show the relationships which exist between the norms of international law and the 'world economy'. Whatever may be understood by this term, there can be no doubt that the relation between international law and so-called world economy is totally different from the relation which, according to Marx, exists between the law of the state and the relationships of production. The essential function of this law is to maintain a definite system of production—a capitalist system or, if the existence of a specific socialist law is admitted, a socialist system of production. 'World economy' cannot be identified with a definite system of production, especially if the co-existence of different systems of production within the so-called world economy cannot be denied. Besides, the norms of general international law regulating the mutual relations of the states leave the establishment of the political as well as the economic system of the individual states completely to these states, without interfering in this sphere of interests, considered as the domestic affairs of the states. International law—in contradistinction to national law—is completely indifferent in this respect. Since Krylov does not demonstrate the contrary, his definition of international law has no foundation.

[59] *Loc. cit.*, p. 415.
[60] *Loc. cit.*, p. 417.

As to the class character of international law, Krylov states : 'the class character is, without any doubt, proper to international law in all its formations'[61]; and he says, referring to the period of imperialism :

> 'The international law, which is an instrument for expressing the will of the dominant classes of the states, reflects, during this period, in the first place the will of the dominant classes of the great powers of the universe, which exercise a particular influence on the development of the international relations and thereby on the international law'.[62]

Since according to the Marxian view, the state is the domination of one class over another, the will of the dominant class is the will of the state. Hence the statement that international law expresses the will of the dominant classes means nothing else but that international law expresses the will of the states, which is the consequence of the doctrine that the reason for the validity of international law is its recognition by the state for which it claims to be binding; a doctrine shared by the majority of the bourgeois writers. The question, however, to which a Marxist has to give an answer is, how the dominant classes of the capitalist states, in spite of their antagonistic interests, could recognise a legal order binding upon all of them, and, especially, how the great powers could do so, although this legal order did not at all guarantee in their mutual relations the domination of one of these classes over another; and, last but not least, how a socialist state, that is, the proletarian class dominating in this state, could recognise as binding upon itself a law established as the expression of the will of the bourgeois classes of the capitalist states. That Krylov's statement gives no answer to these questions may be justified by the fact that it refers only to the international law of the period of imperialism. But the answer could be expected in his definition of the international law which applies to the relations between the socialist state and the capitalist states. This definition runs as follows :

> 'International law is an aggregate of norms regulating the relationships between states in the process of their competition, their struggle and their co-operation, expressing the

[61] *Loc. cit.,* p. 418.
[62] *Loc. cit.,* p. 419 *et seq.*

will of the dominant classes within these states and guaranteeing the coercion exercised by the states individually or collectively'.[63]

Let us notice that according to this definition, international law is a set of norms, not of social relationships *de facto*, and that there is only one international law, and not a socialist international law besides several capitalist international laws. The anti-normative as well as the pluralistic view, abandoned by Krylov, had been accepted by previous Soviet writers only in order to comply with the Marxian doctrine. According to Krylov's definition, international law expresses the will of the dominant classes of the states on which it is binding. It is evident that this is the formula by which Krylov tries to comply with the request to define international law as class law. That the law is the expression of the will of a dominant class means— as pointed out—that the law is established in the interest of one class as the dominant class, and against the interests of another, as the dominated class. This is the essential characteristic of a 'class' law. But, according to Krylov's definition, international law is the expression of the will of the dominant classes of all states, hence not only the will of the bourgeois classes of the capitalist states but also of the will of the dominant class of the socialist Soviet state, which originally was the proletarian class and is now—if a class at all—certainly not a bourgeois class. If international law is in the interest of the bourgeois classes of the capitalist states and at the same time in the interest of the proletarian class of a socialist state, or of the people of a socialist state which is not split into a bourgeois and a proletarian class, then international law cannot be a class law in the sense of the Marxian doctrine. But Krylov asserts that his definition

'corresponds to the general definition of the law which has been given by the academician A. Y. Vyshinsky, and which is now prevailing in the Soviet theory of law'.[64]

According to this definition, the law—as pointed out[65]—is the will of a dominant class, guaranteed by the coercive force of the state. If there is a dominant class, there must be also a dominated class, and if the application of the law is to be guaranteed

---

[63] *Loc. cit.,* p. 420.
[64] *Loc. cit.,* p. 420.
[65] Cf. *supra,* p. 128.

by coercion, this coercion is to be directed against the dominated class. Vyshinsky's definition, to which Krylov refers, is a definition of a coercive order imposed by one class upon another, within one and the same state, *i.e.,* the definition of national law as a normative order regulating the relationships between individuals in their capacity as organs and members of one and the same state, not a definition of international law as a normative order regulating the relationships between states, *i.e.,* the relationships between individuals in their capacity as organs and members of different states. In so far as Krylov's definition is to be understood as corresponding to Vyshinsky's definition, the 'coercion exercised by the states' to which the former refers, must be the coercion which the dominant class of one state exercises against the dominated class of the same state; that means that it could be only a definition of national, not international law. However, Krylov intends to define a legal order 'regulating the relationships between states', hence the coercion to which he refers must be exercised by states 'individually or collectively' against other states; and this means, by the ruling class of one state against the ruling class of another state. It is highly characteristic that his definition does not indicate against whom the coercion is directed the exercise of which is guaranteed by international law. It is by this ambiguity that he maintains the appearance of a correspondence of his definition of international law with Vyshinsky's definition of law. But a normative order which guarantees the exercise of coercion by the dominant class of one state against the dominant class of another is not the law defined by Vyshinsky, and is no law in the sense of the Marxian doctrine, because no class law at all. This is especially manifest in case the coercion guaranteed by this normative order is exercised by the dominant class of a socialist state against the dominant class of a capitalist state. Hence Krylov's definition, too, is no solution of the problem of international law from the point of view of the Marxian doctrine. It only confirms the complete failure of this doctrine in its application to the legal relations among states.

According to Krylov's definition there exists an international law common to all the states—capitalist or socialist—so that any differentiation between a capitalist and a socialist international law is excluded. This, of course, may be considered as an outspoken anti-Marxian view. Hence Krylov has to modify it somehow. He does so by presenting the above-mentioned doctrine of the two lines in international law: the imperialist-reactionary and the democratic-progressive line. Krylov speaks of layers or strata of international law. It is possible, he says, 'to distinguish various layers of international law of more or less democratic shade'.[66] And he asserts that the coming into existence of the socialist Soviet state and its participation in the international relations 'have changed the character of international law by increasing the democratic tendencies which existed in the bud in this law and by introducing new socialist principles'.[67] In reality, no such change in the character of international law has taken place. Krylov's statement is only a typical form of Soviet ideology to assert that the foreign policy of the Soviet Union is democratic and socialistic.

## Dualism or monism in the Soviet theory of international law

Although Krylov pretends to deal with the fundamental concepts of international law he does not even raise the question as to the reason for the validity of international law. He is evidently not aware of the fact that on the answer to this question depends the determination of the relationship between international and national law, one of the most important problems of a theory of international law. He speaks, it is true, of 'the foundation of international law',[68] but under this heading he has nothing else to reveal than the truism that the international relations are determined—or, as he says, 'composed' (*composé*)—by two elements: 'the competition or even the struggle among the states, and their co-operation for the purpose of securing the peace and the satisfaction of other political and economic interests'.[69] That does not mean that Krylov has no use for the one or for the other answer to the question concerned. Many of his statements presuppose a definite opinion concerning the reason for the validity of international law. But he is not conscious of this presupposition and hence gets involved in contradictions.

Krylov admits that most of the norms of contemporary inter-

---

[66] *Loc. cit.,* p. 420.
[67] *Loc. cit.,* p. 422.
[68] *Loc. cit.,* p. 415 *et seq.*
[69] *Loc. cit.,* p. 416.

national law originate in relationships among bourgeois states. In spite of the fact that these norms are, according to his definition of this law, binding upon all the states, the socialist Soviet state included, he speaks of these norms—in contradistinction to the 'new norms' called forth by the new socialist state—as of the 'bourgeois international law' and raises the question as to whether the U.S.S.R. 'can accept without reservation' the institutions of this bourgeois international law. The answer, he asserts, must be in the negative. 'It stands to reason that the U.S.S.R. must reject some of the institutions of the bourgeois international law'.[70] Whether this statement is compatible with his definition of international law is—in this connection—of no importance. The essence is only that it presupposes the view that the norms of international law are binding upon the U.S.S.R. only if they are accepted, and that means recognised by this state.

As to the sources of international law, Krylov still maintains the original doctrine of Korovin that 'international custom has not the same importance as international treaties to the U.S.S.R., although the latter, without any doubt, recognises custom with respect to certain questions of general importance'; this means that the U.S.S.R. recognises certain norms of international law based on international custom. 'It stands to reason that the Soviet Union accepts only those customs [meaning norms of customary law] which correspond to democratic principles . . .'.[71] Since treaties are, as a rule, binding only upon the contracting states, there seems to be no difficulty in considering the consent of the state as the reason for the validity of conventional international law. The situation is different with respect to general customary international law in case of norms created by a custom in which a definite state has not participated. Krylov asserts repeatedly that the Soviet Union is a new state which did not participate in the customs by which the norms of 'bourgeois' international law have been created. His statement that the Soviet Union does not recognise all of these norms but only some of them is most important because it implies the view that only those norms of general customary international law are binding upon the Soviet Union which are recognised by this state.

Discussing the problem of the sources of international law

70 *Loc. cit.,* p. 433.
71 *Loc. cit.,* p. 441.

Krylov maintains that the legislative and judicial acts of a state, too, may be sources of international law, under the condition that the national statute in question or the practice of the national courts

> 'is recognised beyond the territory of the state within which it originates. . . . Thus all the sources of the national law may become sources of international law from the moment they refer to international relations and are recognised by other states'.[72]

Even a norm created by the act of one state may become binding upon other states if it is recognised by these states. This doctrine, too, presupposes the view that the reason for the validity of the norms of international law is their recognition by the state for which they claim to be valid. Recognition is an act of the state which can be performed only on the basis of the law of this state, the national law. Hence the doctrine that the reason for the validity of international law is its recognition on the part of the states concerned amounts to the view that the validity of international law is based on the validity of the national law of the state for which international law claims to be valid. It is only another formulation of this view when international law is declared to be valid only as part of, or incorporated into, national law. This is the essence of what is called the primacy of national over international law. It is—as pointed out—the consequence of the assumption of the sovereignty of the state. Krylov, as all the Soviet writers, emphatically insists on this point. He declares that 'the concept of sovereignty is the basis of the contemporary international law'. Consequently he rejects the idea of a 'world state' as a 'reactionary utopia' 'incompatible with the concept of sovereignty'[73]; and it is obviously for the same reason that he also rejects the view according to which individuals may be subjects of international law.[74] He asserts:

> 'the Soviet science highly appreciates the doctrine of sovereignty as the expression of the right of national self-determination (*auto-détermination*). It defends that doctrine as a weapon in the struggle for the independence and liberty of the state, for its national autonomy (*auto-détermination*)'.[75]

---

[72] *Loc. cit.*, p. 444.
[73] *Loc. cit.*, p. 435.
[74] *Loc. cit.*, p. 446 *et seq.*
[75] *Loc. cit.*, p. 452.

All this can mean nothing else but that the state—and with the state the national law which constitutes the state as a legal community—is to be considered as the supreme legal authority; and that consequently international law can be considered as being legally binding upon the state only when recognised by the state, that the reason for the validity which international law claims to have for a state is—as expressed in a frequently used figure of speech—only and exclusively the 'will' of this state. The will of the state is a figure of speech for the validity of national law.

In spite of the fact that many of his essential statements presuppose the hypothesis of the primacy of national over international law, Krylov expressly rejects this view. He says:

'In Anglo-American literature, in some constitutions and in the judicial practice it is usual to say that international law is a "part of national law". However, this statement is correct only in case a state has included in its legislation the text of an international treaty signed by it or if it has accepted within its domestic jurisdiction (*plan interne*) some other sources of international law, for instance, some customs or usages. The statement, on the contrary, is not correct in the numerous cases where a state only confirms, *i.e.*, recognises the sources of international law. In these cases the norms of international law and those of national law coexist without being united'.[76]

That means that Krylov considers international law as part of national law only in case a norm of international law has been transformed into national law, especially if the text of a treaty has been inserted into a statute adopted by the legislative organ of the state which has concluded that treaty. His error consists in ignoring the fact that the act by which a state 'recognises' a norm created by international custom or an international treaty is a law-creating act, just as the act of the legislative organ by which a statute is issued. He evidently attributes to the act by which a state recognises international law only a declaratory character although he asserts in the above-quoted statements that if a norm of international law is not recognised by the Soviet state it is not binding upon it; from which it follows that it is by the recognition of the norm that it becomes binding upon the

[76] *Loc. cit.*, p. 445.

recognising state.   Hence recognition has not a merely declaratory but a constitutive character, just as has a legislative act.
Krylov does not expressly reject the other monistic construction,
that of the primacy of international over national law.   But
this construction is inacceptable from the point of view of
his sovereignty dogma.   In declaring that international and
national law ' coexist' without being united, he accepts the
dualistic construction of the relationship between international
and national law, which is in open contradiction to his doctrine
of recognition.[77]   For if international law is valid for a state only
if and to the extent as it is recognised by this state—as Krylov
again and again maintains—a definite relationship between the
two normative systems, constituting the unity of one universal
system, is established, which comprises both of them.   Krylov's
doctrine of recognition inevitably presupposes a monistic construction.

It must, however, be admitted that the same confusion of an
allegedly dualistic construction with the decidedly monistic view
of the primacy of national over international law as the consequence of the sovereignty dogma is not at all restricted to the
Soviet theory of international law.   It is widespread among
bourgeois writers.   For it was from the very beginning inherent
in the dualistic construction of the relationship between international and national law.[78]   And it must further be admitted that

[77] The same contradiction exists in Pashukanis' theory of international law.
In his analysis, Florin (*loc. cit.*, pp. 104 *et seq.*, 110), points out that a
dualistic interpretation of the relationship between international and
national law seems to be the most compatible with Pashukanis' theory.
Pashukanis expressly rejected the view that international law is a legal
order superior to national law, *i.e.*, the hypothesis of the primacy of
international law.   He characterised this view as a political ideology of
bourgeois pacifism.   (Cf. Florin, p. 109.)   In so far as he included in his
criticism also the pure theory of law, he misunderstood this theory which
shows that the hypothesis of the primacy of international law, as well as
the opposite hypothesis of the primacy of national law, are both, from
the point of view of legal science, equally possible as the two versions of
legal monism.   It was the pure theory of law which first has shown that
the choice between the two views is determined not by scientific but by
political reasons and that the primacy of international law is, consciously
or unconsciously, connected with a pacifistic view, whereas the primacy
of national law corresponds to an imperialistic and nationalistic view.   It
is only legal monism—as a postulate of the science of law—on which the
pure theory of law insists.   Pashukanis' attitude toward the primacy of
national over international law is not clear.   He did not reject this view,
which follows from his assumption of the sovereignty of the state and of
international law as valid for the state.
[78] Cf. my *Das Problem der Souveraenitaet und die Theorie des Voelker-
rechts*, 2nd ed. 1928.

some Soviet writers, as *e.g.*, Vyshinsky, avoid this confusion by advocating a monistic view on the basis of the primacy of national over international law, as a consequence of the doctrine of sovereignty as an essential quality of the state. Vyshinsky rejects only the primacy of international over national law, because, as he quite correctly assumes, this view is incompatible with the assumption of the sovereignty of the state.[79]

---

[79] Vyshinsky, *Voprosy mezdunarodnovo prava i mezdunarodnoj politiki,* Moscow, 1949, p. 472 *et seq.*, quoted by Calvez, *loc. cit.*, p. 163 *et seq.*

# CONCLUSION

1. The attempt to develop a theory of law on the basis of Marx' economic interpretation of society has completely failed; and the reason for this failure is in the first place the tendency to substitute for—instead of adding to—a normative interpretation of the law, that is, a structural analysis of a specific system of norms, a sociological inquiry of the conditions under which such a normative system comes into existence and is effective. That the Marxian sociology takes into consideration only economic conditions is in this respect a shortcoming of secondary importance. The Marxian theory of law, abandoned in the Soviet Union because of its incapacity to grasp the normative meaning of the law, is only a variation of sociological jurisprudence, widespread in non-communist countries.

2. In spite of the Marxian postulate of an anti-ideological science, the Soviet theory of law has an outspoken ideological character. That means that its presentation of the positive law, especially of the law of the non-communist states and international law, is not objective in a scientific sense but essentially determined by the political interests of the Soviet government. In this respect the Soviet theory employs certain conceptual devices which, although produced by bourgeois jurisprudence, are denounced as ideological and radically rejected by a science of law freely developed in non-communist states.

3. The ideological character of the Soviet theory of law is the inevitable consequence of the Marxian principle—contrary to the anti-ideological postulate—that social science in general and the science of state and law in particular has to be political, that is to say, that it has to result in formulas which can be used as instruments in the political struggle of one group against another. The deplorable status of Soviet legal theory, degraded to a handmaid of the Soviet government, should be a grim warning to social scientists that true social science is possible only under the condition that it is independent of politics.

13

# INDEX

Alexeiew, 162.

anarchism,
 Marx-Engels social theory as, 40 f.
 political, and economic authoritarianism, contradiction between, 48 f.
 rejected by Stalin, 109 f., 127

antagonism (conflict) in reality as logical contradiction, 4, 18, 23 f., 25, 49, 98

anti-anarchistic tendency of Soviet theory of state and law, 109 f., 127

anti-ideological tendency
 of bourgeois science, 57, 75
 of bourgeois theory of law, 14, 95

anti-normative theory (doctrine) of law, 64 ff., 89 ff., 124 f., 185

*a priori* principles, the law as expression of, 13 f.

Aristotle's interpretation of criminal law, 100 ff.

autonomy, constitutional, 149, 170, 173

Babb, viii
Bachofen, 38 f.
Bakunin, 40
Barth, 10, 22
Berman, 124
Bober, 10
Boukharin, 53, 109, 126, 142

bourgeois (capitalist)
 law. *See* Law, bourgeois
 jurisprudence. *See* Jurisprudence, bourgeois
 science. *See* Science, bourgeois
 state and proletarian (socialist) state, 27, 52, 138
 theory of law. *See* Theory of law, bourgeois

Bracke, 33

Calvez, 168, 192

capitalism,
 imperialistic period of, 152
 and private law, 99
 and subjective law, 99

capitalist
 encirclement, 124, 154 f.
 *See also* Bourgeois

causality and imputation, 143

class justice, 66 f.

class law, 62 ff., 65, 67 ff., 71 ff., 112, 128, 129 ff., 132, 185
 international law as, 148 ff., 184

class struggle
 and concept of classes, 67, 69, 134
 and international law, 150, 154

classes,
 concept of, 1, 27 f., 53 f., 67, 69, 108, 112, 134, 138
 and concept of state, 2, 26 f., 53 f., 138
 conflict between, as logical contradiction, 25
 exploitation as element of concept of, 1, 28 f., 53, 108, 112, 134
 without exploitation, 108, 112 f., 134
 gradual disappearance of, 53 f.
 Soviet constitution on, 108 f., 135 f.
 in Soviet state, 108, 130, 133 ff., 137
 Stalin on, 107 f., 130

classless society, communistic society of the future as, 27, 54 f., 66 ff.

coercion
 as element of concept of law, 67, 70 f., 128 f., 132, 144, 154, 186
 not an element of international law, 154, 186

coercive character of proletarian (socialist) state, 53 f.

cognition, Marx' and Engels' theory of, 4 ff.

colonies, 149, 153, 163

communist idea of justice, 34, 35, 83, 87
 as distinguished from socialist principles of justice, 61

communist party, Soviet state as dictatorship of, 136

communist society of the future, 6, 24 f., 27, 28, 32, 33 ff., 36 f., 54 f., 60 f., 66, 79 ff., 86 ff., 88, 102, 105
 a classless society, 27 f., 54 f., 66 f.
 complete solidarity of interests in, 105
 no crimes in, 102
 freedom in, 28, 61